Temperature
Control

Temperature Control

Myer Kutz

*Senior Mechanical Engineer, American Science and
Engineering Co., Cambridge, Mass.*

John Wiley & Sons, Inc.

NEW YORK   LONDON   SYDNEY

Library of Congress Catalog Card Number: 67-29939

GB 471 51123X

Printed in the United States of America

To the Memory of My Father

Preface

Temperature Control is an introduction to a large but particular class of problems: control of temperatures of masses contained within environments that may vary widely not only in temperature and pressure but also in their capabilities for accepting or providing heat. The book is a compendium of information relevant to a tremendous range of physical situations, including, for example, those in which an entire temperature control system, both the mass being controlled and the control equipment, is in a highly dense volume; those in which a controlled mass is remote from the control equipment; those in which temperatures of several masses are being controlled simultaneously by a single system; and those in which the temperature of the environment is higher than that of the controlled mass.

The book is arranged as follows: The first three chapters are devoted to descriptions of the mechanisms of conduction, radiation, and convection heat transmission. The fourth chapter is a transition from the basic equations of heat transfer to some methods of fixing rates of heat flow and heat exchange. Chapter 5 introduces methods of controlling temperatures and analytical and practical techniques for achieving control. Components of temperature control systems are discussed in Chapters 6 through 9. Chapter 10 concerns the control of spacecraft temperatures.

The book is intended to relate the basic empirical and mathematical principles of the science of heat transfer to a specific engineering task, namely, control of the temperature of a mass, to enable the reader to recognize the essential nature of a variety of problems, and to put in order the factors important to the approaches to their solutions. Although it is assumed that the reader will have a basic knowledge of the science of thermodynamics, the mechanisms of conduction, radiation, and convection heat transmission are discussed in the first three chapters. Theoretical and empirical bases of temperature control designs are furnished and methods of their implementation are described in detailed commentaries on useful devices.

I have directed the book (a) to engineers working in various fields who need to solve temperature control problems and who want a reference of useful basic theoretical and practical information and (b) to students who have completed formal courses in thermodynamics and heat transfer and would like to supplement their reading with a practical work. Further, the book should be especially valuable to engineers whose past approach to solving temperature control problems has consisted mainly of purchasing and adjusting expensive electronic equipment. Application of proper analytical and practical techniques of thermal design, preceding temperature control systems analysis and implementation, sets the stage, as it were, for the introduction of a temperature control system that will operate with maximum efficiency and will be of minimum complexity and cost. The book bridges a rather large gap, therefore, between the principles of heat transfer and the fundamentals and impedimenta of automatic feedback control. Finally, this book will be an aid to temperature control and heat transfer specialists as a source of information about the operation and characteristics of equipment used in temperature control work.

My purpose in this preface is to pick out of the text related topics or discussions, which may or may not be grouped together there, and thus provide an outline that departs from the formal arrangement of chapters. Such an outline will give the reader insight into the materials covered which he would not necessarily gain by scanning the table of contents or index. To that purpose, then, the book may be divided into the following topics:

1. The mechanisms of three basic modes of heat transfer.
2. Equations for computing the rates of heat transfer in common physical situations.
3. Thermal properties of materials and surfaces.
4. Employment of materials and surfaces with certain thermal properties.
5. Methods for fixing rates of heat transfer.
6. Fundamentals of heat exchangers.
7. Introduction to methods of controlling temperatures and analytical and practical techniques for achieving control.
8. Elements used to sense temperatures and to excite other elements of temperature control systems.
9. Elements of electronic temperature control systems.
10. Control of satellite temperatures.

The mechanisms of heat conduction in metallic and nonmetallic solids are treated with particular emphasis in Chapter 1. The nature of radiation heat transfer between solid surfaces is described in Chapter 2, and in the opening sections of Chapter 3 there is a discussion of convection heat transfer—that between a solid surface and a fluid in contact.

The fundamental relation for the steady-state rate of heat conduction in a homogeneous body, or through a nonhomogeneous body, is illustrated in Chapter 1. Included is the derivation of an equation that expresses the statement of conservation of heat energy about a mass whose temperature may be changing with time. The basic equation for radiation heat transfer between surfaces with various properties and in any orientation to one another is developed in Chapter 2. In Chapter 3 various empirical formulas are provided for determining the rates of convection heat transfer between fluids in several flow conditions and a number of different surfaces.

The thermal properties of substances and surfaces are discussed in several portions of the book. In some instances important representative values of these properties are listed. The reader will need these values in order to perform heat transfer computations. Furthermore, these discussions and lists will enable him to decide which substance, surface, or surface quality will satisfy a particular design goal. The reader must evaluate his capabilities for altering the magnitude of a property of a given medium and the manner in which certain circumstances can affect it.

Discussions of thermal properties and their uses are located in the text as follows. Values of *thermal conductivity* of certain gases, liquids, and solids are described in Chapter 1. Variations of these values with temperature are given, as are also variations with pressure for gases and liquids, and the nonconductive qualities of insulating materials are examined.

Values of *specific heat* of solids are discussed in Chapter 1. Radiation heat transfer properties of selected solid surfaces and coatings are listed in Chapter 2, and properties of materials and coatings used for the external surfaces of satellites appear in Chapter 10. The thermal properties of fluids important to determining rates of convection heat transfer are discussed in Chapter 3. Equations for comparing the performances of fluids in several convection situations are provided in Chapter 4.

The characteristic variations of electrical resistance with temperature of conductors and semiconductors are examined in Chapter 6. Such variations are employed in a variety of resistance elements which measure temperature and excite temperature control components. The Joule heating effect in conductors is employed in the resistance heaters mentioned in Chapter 7. Thermal expansion properties of solid and liquid metals and the use of those properties in mechanical thermostats are covered extensively in Chapter 8.

Chapter 9 commences with an account of the discovery of thermoelectric phenomena shown by a couple of two conductors in contact. Such phenomena in conductive and semiconductive couples give rise to the construction of heat pumps and temperature-measuring devices. Materials with high heats of transformation are discussed in Chapter 10. These substances may be employed in certain temperature control situations.

Several methods or devices for fixing rates of heat transfer are discussed in a number of places in the text. The employment of extended surfaces and the substitution of one fluid for another, in both instances to improve a rate of convection heat transfer, are covered in Chapter 4; also treated there is the question of thermal contact resistance between solid surfaces in contact. By passing currents through the thermoelectric couples described in Chapter 9 heat can be caused to flow from lower to higher temperatures. The use of bimetallic elements to regulate heat transfer rates is mentioned in Chapter 8, and control of the effective radiation properties of surfaces is discussed in a section of Chapter 10.

Chapter 4 also emphasizes heat exchanger (and cold plate) effectiveness and constructions for improving the performance of compact core exchangers. The optimum arrangement of a cooled electronics package and a cold plate can be inferred from the discussion.

The temperature control problem and the analytical approaches to its solution are introduced and defined in Chapter 5. The analysis leading to the implementation of a temperature control system proceeds first from considerations of thermal design, which are presented in Chapter 5. Included therein are discussions of the following items: positioning of the elements (heaters, sensing elements, controlling elements) of temperature control systems, methods for developing mathematical models of thermal situations, techniques of analysis of mathematical thermal models, equations describing the responses of controlled and uncontrolled masses to changes in their thermal situations, and basic thermal design equations. An introduction to the fundamentals of temperature control systems analysis is also provided in Chapter 5.

Devices used to measure temperature and to excite control equipment are covered in the text as follows. Resistance elements constructed of conductors (often referred to as resistance thermometers) and semiconductors (called thermistors) are treated mathematically and for their practical applications in Chapter 6. The characteristics of the two principal types of element and of particular versions of each type are examined there; the categories are compared for their accuracy of performance, convenience of employment, and cost, among other criteria.

The functioning and use of mechanical thermostats, both those with bimetallic elements and those of the mercury-in-glass variety, are explained in Chapter 8. The operation of several versions of these instruments is compared with regard to their capabilities for precision control work. Thermal design techniques for improving the performance of a thermostat-commanded control system are discussed also.

Thermocouples are treated in Chapter 9.

Various electronic devices used in temperature control systems are described in Chapters 6 and 7. The Wheatstone bridge, an arrangement of fixed and variable resistances in which indicated and desired signals may be compared, is presented in Chapter 6. The devices described in the beginning of Chapter 7 (silicon controlled rectifiers, unijunction transistors, magnetic amplifiers) are those that may be used to time-proportion the operation of such temperature control components as electric heaters and fans; several features of these components are also discussed in Chapter 7. The emphasis in the descriptions is generally on the functioning of the components; furthermore, for the Wheatstone bridge, electrical resistance heaters, and fans and blowers provisions for ensuring proper operation of the components are stressed.

In Chapter 10 on temperature control of satellites particular attention is paid to the actual methods. The chapter opens with information useful in the performance of preliminary calculations on the rates of heat transfer from the solar system to a satellite and from the satellite to space, thus enabling the reader to estimate temperatures on the surfaces of the satellite and the temperature distribution within it. These design guidelines are valuable in the selection of the particular passive or active temperature control instrument that will maintain a certain temperature range at a given point in the satellite. For more exact solutions of satellite temperatures as the vehicle traverses its orbit the references should be consulted.

I should like to acknowledge the contributions of Mr. Kenneth Britting and Mr. Paul Payne and to thank the following colleagues and friends who reviewed portions of the manuscript: Mr. Archie Arpiarian, Dr. Jacques Bonneville, Mr. Charles Kalina, Mr. Ronald Stone, Mr. Melvin Tracey, Mr. James Waldron, and Dr. Joseph Wiza. I am grateful also to my wife Cynthia who not only endured the project but also did editorial work on the manuscript.

Myer Kutz

Cambridge, Massachusetts
1967

Contents

*Temperature
Control*

1

The Mechanics of Heat Conduction

1.1 FOURIER'S LAW OF HEAT CONDUCTION

Fourier's* law of heat conduction, published in 1822, states that in a substance under the influence of a unidirectional temperature gradient heat will flow from hotter to colder points at a rate described by the equation

$$q = -kA \frac{dT}{dx},\qquad(1.1)$$

where q is the rate of heat flow, k is a property of the substance (its thermal conductivity), A is the cross-sectional area of the substance perpendicular to the direction of heat flow, and dT/dx is the temperature gradient at a point.

In the English system of British thermal units degrees Fahrenheit, feet, hours, and pounds the units of the terms of Fourier's equation are

$$[\text{Btu/hr}] = \left[\frac{\text{Btu/hr}}{\text{ft}^2 \, {}^\circ\text{F/ft}}\right][\text{ft}^2][{}^\circ\text{F/ft}].$$

* Baron Jean Baptiste Joseph Fourier (1768–1830) was a contemporary of Napoleon Bonaparte. The son of a poor tailor of Auxerre, he was orphaned at the age of eight. With a bishop's influence he was admitted to a military school at Auxerre conducted by the Benedictines, and there he exhibited literary and mathematical abilities. At twelve years of age he wrote sermons used in Paris; at twenty-one, he delivered his first mathematical Memoir before the Academy of Sciences. Fourier wished to enter the artillery where he could employ his mathematical talents, but he was refused entry because of his low birth. He taught mathematics at the military school (1784) but left his position to promote the Revolution. Later (1795) he taught at Ecole Normale in Paris and was offered a chair of analysis at Ecole Polytechnique. Fourier became known to Napoleon and accompanied him to Egypt in 1798 to help construct an educational program. Fourier was made governor of low Egypt; he returned to France in 1801 and became provincial governor of Isere.

The negative sign in (1.1) occurs because, although the distance dx is taken positive in the direction of heat flow, that flow is from a higher to a lower temperature potential.

1.2   DERIVATION OF BASIC EQUATION OF HEAT CONDUCTION

The derivation of the general equation of heat conduction proceeds from a consideration of the conservation of heat energy, which may be described by the following equation: the difference between the rates of heat flowing into and away from a system plus the amount of heat generated per unit time

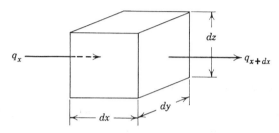

Figure 1.1   Parallelepipedon of differential size.

within that system equals the amount of heat stored per unit time within the system.

Consider the system of Figure 1.1, a parallelepipedon of differential size. The rate of heat flowing into the parallelepipedon in the x direction, for example, is given by

$$q_x = -(dy\ dz)\frac{\delta}{\delta x}(k_x T).* \tag{1.2}$$

The rate of heat flow away from the right side of the parallelepipedon is

---

At that time (1807), Fourier, encouraged by the Academy of Sciences, developed the mathematical theory of the laws of propagation of heat. In the *Theorie Analytique de la Chaleur* he expounded the Fourier series (in which almost any function of a real variable can be represented by a series including the sines and cosines of integral multiples of the variable) and applied it to the solution of boundary value problems in partial differential equations. The work, published in 1822, inspired Ohm's thoughts on electricity. In 1808 Fourier was made a baron. In 1815 he rejoined Napoleon during the Hundred Days; upon the latter's return from Elba Fourier lost his governorship. He settled in Paris in 1816 and was made a member of the Academy of Sciences in 1817 and joint secretary of that organization in 1822. It is told that he believed desert heat to be ideal for health and that he lived swathed like a mummy in overheated rooms.

* k_x may be a function of temperature and direction.

given by

$$q_x = -(dy\ dz)\frac{\delta}{\delta x}(k_x)\left(T + \frac{\delta T}{\delta x}\ dx\right)$$

$$= -(dy\ dz)\left[\frac{\delta}{\delta x}(k_x T) + \frac{\delta}{\delta x}\left(k_x \frac{\delta T}{\delta x}\right)\ dx\right]. \qquad (1.3)$$

The total rate of heat flow into the differential parallelepipedon in the three orthogonal directions x, y, and z is $q_x + q_y + q_z$; the last two quantities are similar in form to q_x. The total rate of heat outflow in the x, y, and z directions is $q_{x+dx} + q_{y+dy} + q_{z+dz}$; again, the last two quantities are similar in form to $q_x + d_x$.

The amount of heat stored per unit time in the differential volume $dx\ dy\ dz$ is given by

$$q \text{ stored} = \rho C_p (dx\ dy\ dz)\frac{\delta T}{\delta \theta}, \qquad (1.4)$$

where ρ = the density of the material in the parallelepipedon $dx\ dy\ dz$,
C_p = the specific heat of that material,
θ = time.

The values (on a comparison basis) of the specific heat of various materials are given in Table 1.1.

Any heat developed within $dx\ dy\ dz$ is expressed by

$$q \text{ developed} = q'(dx\ dy\ dz), \qquad (1.5)$$

where q' is the heat energy developed in unit volume and time.

From energy balance considerations,

$$q_x + q_y + q_z - (q_{x+dx} + q_{y+dy} + q_{z+dz}) + q \text{ developed} = q \text{ stored}. \quad (1.6)$$

Thus,

$$\frac{\delta}{\delta x}\left(k_x \frac{\delta T}{\delta x}\right) + \frac{\delta}{\delta y}\left(k_y \frac{\delta T}{\delta y}\right) + \frac{\delta}{\delta z}\left(k_z \frac{\delta T}{\delta z}\right) + q' = \rho C_p \frac{\delta T}{\delta \theta}. \qquad (1.7)$$

If thermal conductivity k is independent of temperature and direction, (1.7) becomes,

$$k\left(\frac{\delta^2 T}{\delta x^2} + \frac{\delta^2 T}{\delta y^2} + \frac{\delta^2 T}{\delta z^2}\right) + q' = \rho C_p \frac{\delta T}{\delta \theta}. \qquad (1.8)$$

The *steady-state* condition is defined as one in which temperature is not changing with time. The right-hand side of (1.8) vanishes in this case. The *transient* condition is defined as one in which temperature *is* changing with time.

Table 1.1[a]   Comparison of Materials: Specific Heat[b] (Btu/lb °F)

Material	High	Low	Material	High	Low
Nylon 6 and 11	0.6	0.4	Low-expansion nickel alloys	0.123	0.120
Allyl (cast)	0.46	0.26	Austenitic stainless steels	0.12	...
Polyester, rigid	0.56	0.30	Cobalt-base superalloys	0.12	0.09
Polyethylenes	0.55	0.46	Ferritic stainless steels	0.12	0.11
Nylon 66 and 610	0.5	0.3	Alloy steels	0.12	0.10
Polypropylene	0.46	...	Nitriding steels	0.12	0.11
Beryllium	0.45	...	Vanadium	0.12	...
Cellulose acetate	0.42	0.3	Carbon steels	0.11	0.10
Cellulose acetate butyrate	0.4	0.3	Cr–Ni–Fe superalloys	0.11	0.10
Cellulose propionate	0.4	0.3	Free-cutting steels	0.11	0.10
Phenolics, GP	0.40	0.36	Alloy steels (cast)	0.11	0.10
Polyvinyl butyral	0.4	...	Martensitic stainless steels	0.11	...
ABS resins	0.38	0.35	Nickel-base superalloys	0.11	0.09
Acetal	0.35	...	Wrought irons	0.11	...
Acrylics	0.35	0.34	Inconel	0.109	...
Modified polystyrenes	0.35	0.30	Cr–Ni–Co–Fe Superalloys	0.108	0.10
Nylon, glass-filled	0.35	0.30	Beryllium copper	0.10	...
Phenolics, high shock	0.35	0.31	Copper alloys	0.10	0.09
Polystyrene, GP	0.35	0.33	Nickel and its alloys	0.10	0.13
Rubber phenolics	0.33	...	Zinc and its alloys	0.10	0.95
Silicon carbide	0.33	0.29	Cupro–nickels	0.09	...
Phenolics, very high shock	0.32	0.28	Leaded brasses	0.09	...
Vinylidene chloride	0.32	...	Nickel silvers	0.09	...
Polyvinyl alcohol	0.3	...	Phosphor bronzes	0.09	...
Polystyrenes, glass-filled	0.27	0.24	Plain brasses	0.09	...
Prefoamed polystyrene, rigid	0.27	...	Silicon bronzes	0.09	...
Micas	0.25	0.13	Tin and aluminum brasses	0.09	...
TFE fluorocarbons	0.25	...	Columbium and its alloys	0.074	0.065
Magnesium alloys	0.245	...	Zircon and its alloys	0.07	...
Aluminum and its alloys	0.23	0.22	Molybdenum and its alloys	0.065	0.061
CFE fluorocarbons	0.22	...	Tin–lead–antimony alloys	0.065	...
Borosilicate glass	0.2	...	Rhodium	0.059	...
Soda-lime glass	0.2	...	Palladium	0.058	...
Fused silica glass	0.19	...	Ruthenium	0.057	...
Polycrystalline glass	0.19	0.18	Silver	0.056	...
Aluminum silicate glass	0.18	...	Tin and its alloys	0.05	...
Carbon	0.18	...	Tantalum	0.036	...
Graphite	0.18	...	Hafnium	0.035	...
96% Silica glass	0.18	...	Tungsten	0.034	...
Lead silicate glass	0.17	0.16	Lead and its alloys	0.032	0.031
Alumina cermets	0.16	0.14	Gold	0.031	...
Heat-resistant alloys (cast)	0.14	0.11	Iridium	0.031	...
Stainless steels (cast)	0.14	0.11	Osmium	0.031	...
Malleable irons	0.13	...	Platinum	0.031	...
Titanium and its alloys	0.13	0.12	Thorium	0.03	...
Monel	0.127	...	Uranium	0.03	...

[a] Reference 10; by permission of the Reinhold Publishing Company.
[b] Values represent high and low sides of a range of *typical* values.

Values of specific heat of substances increase with increasing temperature; cf. References 5 and 12.

1.3   STEADY-STATE UNIDIRECTIONAL CONDUCTION

Consider an infinitely wide slab (Figure 1.2) of homogeneous material whose thermal conductivity is independent of temperature. The left-hand edge X_1 of the slab is at temperature T_1, and its right-hand edge X_2 is at temperature T_2. It is desired to find the steady-state heat flow rate q/A in the x direction.

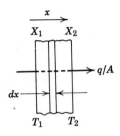

The unidirectional steady-state heat flow rate per unit area over any differential distance dx is expressed by Fourier's equation,

$$\frac{q}{A} = -k\frac{dT}{dx}.$$

Figure 1.2   Slab of infinite width.

Rearranging the above equation and integrating it between the edges of the slab, we have

$$\int_{X_1}^{X_2} dx = -\frac{kA}{q} \int_{T_1}^{T_2} dT, \tag{1.9}$$

$$X_2 - X_1 = \frac{kA}{q}(T_1 - T_2). \tag{1.10}$$

Thus

$$q = \frac{kA}{\Delta X}\Delta T, \tag{1.11}$$

where $\Delta T = T_1 - T_2$ and $\Delta X = X_2 - X$.

This equation may be written in the form

$$q = \frac{\Delta T}{R}, \tag{1.12}$$

where $R = kA/\Delta X$ is the thermal resistance of the substance through which the temperature potential ΔT is driving the heat flow q. Relation 1.12 is analogous to Ohm's law, $i = \Delta E/R_e$, where q is analogous to current flow i, ΔT is analogous to voltage potential ΔE, and R is analogous to electrical resistance R_e.

1.4   THERMAL RESISTANCE OF COMPOSITE BODIES

Consider next several slabs joined together as in Figure 1.3. The steady-state heat flow rate in the x direction is computed.

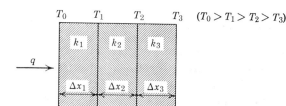

Figure 1.3   Heat flow through composite wall of three materials.

At steady state, the rate of heat flow through each of the slabs is the same. Thus

$$q = \frac{T_0 - T_1}{R_1} = \frac{T_1 - T_2}{R_2} = \frac{T_2 - T_3}{R_3}, \tag{1.13}$$

where R_n is the thermal resistance of the nth slab.

From combinations of (1.13),

$$q = \frac{T_0 - T_3}{R_1 + R_2 + R_3} \tag{1.14}$$

or

$$q = \frac{\Delta T_1 + \Delta T_2 + \Delta T_3}{R_1 + R_2 + R_3} = \frac{\Delta T}{\Sigma R}. \tag{1.15}$$

Thus thermal resistances acting in series may be combined in the manner of electrical resistances acting in series. Furthermore, if heat is transferred across a temperature potential by several heat transmission modes acting simultaneously, the effects of those various modes may be superimposed on one another and their thermal resistances may be combined in parallel.

The vagaries of contact at the intersurfaces of the slabs of the preceding discussion produce thermal resistances at those intersurfaces. (The thermal resistance R_{ab} across the intersurface between the surfaces a and b of two slabs in contact is defined by

$$R_{ab} = \frac{T_a - T_b}{q}, \tag{1.16}$$

where T_a and T_b are the temperatures of the surfaces denoted by the subscripts.) Those contact thermal resistances, neglected here, are dealt with in Section 4.4.

1.5   VALUES OF THERMAL CONDUCTIVITY

Orders of magnitude of thermal conductivities of various classes of materials at ordinary temperatures are given in Table 1.2. The values of

Table 1.2   Orders of Magnitude of Thermal Conductivity

Material	Thermal Conductivity (Btu/hr ft^2 °F/ft)
Gases at atmospheric pressure	0.004–0.10
Insulations	0.02–0.12
Nonmetallic liquids	0.05–0.40
Nonmetallic solids (brick, stone, concrete)	0.02–1.5
Liquid metals	5.0–45
Alloys	8.0–70
Pure metals	30–240

thermal conductivity of most materials vary with temperature, those of pure metal crystals being exceptions over some temperature ranges, and those of some materials vary with pressure. These variations and constancies will now be discussed.

1.6 VALUES OF THERMAL CONDUCTIVITY OF GASES

The values of thermal conductivity of gases increase with rising temperature. The progressions of the values of k for air and helium are listed in Table 1.3. The relative magnitudes of these values of the two gases are noteworthy also.

Thermal conductivity of gases is virtually independent of pressure under near-atmospheric conditions. Gaseous heat conduction is a process of diffusion in which molecules wander from warmer to cooler zones, and vice versa, and in which kinetic energy is exchanged when molecules collide. According to the kinetic theory of gases, the mean free path* of a gas molecule is inversely proportional to absolute pressure. The numerical density of molecules is directly proportional to absolute pressure. Therefore gaseous thermal conductivity should be independent of pressure, and it is, except at low pressures, where the mean free path exceeds the dimension of the gas space and thermal conductivity is then proportional to absolute pressure.

Table 1.3   Values of Thermal Conductivity of Air and Helium

Temperature (°F)	0	200	400	600	800
k_{air} (Btu/hr ft °F)	0.0133	0.0174	0.0212	0.0250	0.0286
k_{helium}	0.078	0.097	0.115	0.129	0.138

* The distance a molecule travels before colliding with another.

1.7 VALUES OF THERMAL CONDUCTIVITY OF LIQUIDS

At 1 atm pressure, the values of thermal conductivity of water, certain aqueous solutions, and a few organic liquids (glycerine and ethylene glycol) increase with rising temperature up to a certain temperature, but values of k for most nonmetallic liquids (all alcohols, for example) decrease with rising temperatures. McAdams [11] recommends Smith's [13] equation for estimating the thermal conductivity of nonmetallic liquids at 86°F and 1 atm:

$$k = 0.00266 + 1.56(C_p - 0.45)^3 + 0.3\left(\frac{\rho'}{M}\right)^{1/3} + 0.0242\left(\frac{\mu'}{\rho'}\right)^{1/9}, \quad (1.17)$$

Table 1.4 Data of Bridgeman [1] on the Effect of Pressure on Thermal Conductivity of a Number of Liquids

Liquid	Temperature (°C)	Conductivity at 0 kg/cm²	Relative Conductivity as a Function of Pressure in kg/cm²						
			0	1000	2000	4000	6000	9000	12,000
Methyl	30	0.000505	1.000	1.201	1.342	1.557	1.724	1.927	2.097
alcohol	75	493a	1.000	1.212	1.365	1.601	1.785	2.007	2.191
Ethyl	30	0.000430	1.000	1.221	1.363	1.574	1.744	1.954	2.122
alcohol	75	416a	1.000	1.233	1.400	1.650	1.845	2.083	2.278
Isopropyl	30	0.000367	1.000	1.205	1.352	1.570	1.743	1.963	2.150
alcohol	75	363	1.000	1.230	1.399	1.638	1.812	2.030	2.211
Normal butyl	30	0.000400	1.000	1.181	1.307	1.495	1.648	1.842	2.008
alcohol	75	391	1.000	1.218	1.358	1.559	1.720	1.923	2.099
Isoamyl	30	0.000354	1.000	1.184	1.320	1.524	1.686	1.893	2.069
alcohol	75	348	1.000	1.207	1.348	1.557	1.724	1.934	2.126
Ether	30	0.000329	1.000	1.305	1.509	1.800	2.009	2.251	2.451
	75	322a	1.000	1.313	1.518	1.814	2.043	2.316	2.537
Acetone	30	0.000429	1.000	1.184	1.315	1.511	1.659	1.864	Freezes
	75	403a	1.000	1.181	1.325	1.554	1.738	1.960	2.137
Carbon	30	0.000382	1.000	1.174	1.310	1.512	1.663	1.834	1.962
bisulphide	75	362a	1.000	1.208	1.366	1.607	1.789	1.998	2.154
Ethyl	30	0.000286	1.000	1.193	1.327	1.517	1.657	1.815	1.928
bromide	75	273a	1.000	1.230	1.390	1.609	1.772	1.944	2.121
Ethyl	30	0.000265	1.000	1.125	1.232	1.394	1.509	1.628	1.724
iodide	75	261	1.000	1.148	1.265	1.442	1.570	1.715	1.837
Water	30	0.00144	1.000	1.058	1.113	1.210	1.293	1.398	Freezes
	75	154	1.000	1.065	1.123	1.225	1.308	1.412	1.506
Toluol	30	0.000364	1.000	1.159	1.286	1.470	1.604	1.768	(2.394b)
	75	339	1.000	1.210	1.355	1.573	1.738	1.932	2.089
Normal	30	0.000322	1.000	1.281	1.483	1.777	1.987	2.245	2.481
pentane	75	307a	1.000	1.319	1.534	1.855	2.122	2.440	2.740
Petroleum	30	0.000312	1.000	1.266	1.460	1.752	1.970	2.215	2.379
ether	75	302a	1.000	1.268	1.466	1.780	2.026	2.324	2.561
Kerosene	30	0.000357							
	75	333	1.000	1.185	1.314	1.502	1.654	1.839	2.054

a Extrapolated.
b Toluol freezes at 9900 kg/cm² at 30°. The figure is for the solid at 11,000.

Table 1.5 Thermal Conductivity of Water

Temperature (°F)	32	50	70	90	100	150	
k_{water} (Btu/hr ft² °F/ft)	0.319	0.332	0.347	0.359	0.364	0.384	
Temperature	200	250	300	350	400	450	500
k_{water}	0.394	0.396	0.395	0.391	0.381	0.367	0.349

where the units of k are Btu/hr ft² °F/ft,

$\quad C_p$ is specific heat,

$\quad \rho'$ is specific gravity relative to water,

$\quad M$ is average molecular weight,

and $\quad \mu'$ is viscosity in centipoises.

The equation has been checked by Smith for 46 liquids. The maximum error is 25% for glycerine; the errors for remaining liquids are within 15%, and the average error is 6.7%.

Bridgeman [1] studied the variation of the thermal conductivity values of liquids with increasing pressure and found increases of these values with increases in pressure, as shown in Table 1.4.

Water is the best conductor of heat among the nonmetallic liquids. The values of thermal conductivity of aqueous solutions decrease with increasing concentration. The progression of the thermal conductivity values of water with rising temperature is listed in Table 1.5. Values of k for several other liquids, both nonmetallic and metallic, are presented in Table 1.6.

1.8 THERMAL CONDUCTION IN SOLIDS

Solid crystalline substances are composed of crystals which are aggregates of atoms bound to one another in regular geometric patterns called lattices.

Table 1.6 Thermal Conductivity of Liquids

Liquid	Approximate Thermal Conductivity (Btu/hr ft² °F/ft)	
Glycerine ($C_3H_8O_3$)	0.165	(at 68°F)
Aniline (C_6H_7N)	0.104	(at 32°F)
Olive oil	0.101	(at 39°F)
Toluene	0.086	(at 86°F)
Mercury	4.7	(at 50°F)
Freon 12 (CCL_2F_2)		
(saturated liquid)	0.04	(at 32°F)
n-Butyl alcohol	0.10	(at 60°F)
Ammonia	0.29	(at 45°F)
Kerosene	0.086	(at 68°F)
Vaseline	0.106	(at 59°F)
Acetone	0.103	(at 68°F)

The atoms are themselves in motion continuously, and that motion is limited to oscillations about equilibrium positions. The higher the temperature of a solid is, the more violent are the oscillations of its atoms. Temperature is thus a manifestation of kinetic energy.

Thermal conduction in metals is accomplished mainly by the abundant free electrons, the carriers of electricity, which are so loosely bound to the atoms that they can move readily through the crystal lattice. If a temperature gradient is imposed on a metal specimen, the electrons in the hotter portion of the specimen acquire faster speeds than do those in the colder portion. The electrons in a metal belong not to the individual atoms but to the solid as a whole. The more energetic electrons can flow from the hotter to the colder part of the metal specimen and the less energetic portion can flow to the hotter part, thus transferring kinetic energy between the parts at different temperatures.

Theory and experimental evidence show that heat flow is greater the farther each electron can travel before it is diverted. Imperfections in a crystal in a particular specimen are created by substitutions of atoms of foreign material for atoms of the pure metal or by the restless thermal motion of the atoms around their equilibrium positions in the perfect crystal lattice. The imperfections scatter electrons and impede heat flow.

Thermal and electrical conductivities of metals are related by the Wiedemann-Franz-Lorenz equation,

$$L = \frac{k}{k_e} \frac{1}{T} = \text{constant}, \tag{1.18}$$

where k = thermal conductivity,
  k_e = electrical conductivity,
  T = absolute temperature,
  L = Lorenz number.

Thermal conductivity of a pure metal crystal is independent of temperature except at the smallest temperatures. The average length of the electron paths decreases with increasing temperature, but the amount of heat carried by each electron is proportional to the temperature.

Heat is transported in nonmetallic solids by atomic vibrations. A heated atom moves back and forth with enough vigor to transmit motion to its neighbors, and atomic kinetic energy is thus transferred from the hotter to the colder portions of a solid. This flow of kinetic energy shows up as heat flow on a macroscopic scale.

This heat transfer mechanism is identical with that by which sound waves are transported in a solid, and thus the process may be described as waves of disturbances radiating through a crystal lattice at the appropriate velocity of sound. These waves are transient lattice imperfections called phonons. They have wavelengths, directions, frequencies, and polarizations, and interact in the manner of any series of waves with the exception that, because of the nonharmonic nature of atomic bonding forces, the phonons can affect one another or be scattered. This interaction of phonons is one of the mechanisms by which heat energy is transported through a solid.

The value of thermal conductivity in a nonmetallic crystalline solid is proportional to the number of phonons present, which increases rapidly with temperature; to the speed of the phonons, which is equal to the speed of sound waves in a solid and varies only slightly with temperature; and to the free path that each phonon travels before it collides with some imperfection in the crystal. Such a collision reflects a phonon back toward a relatively warm portion of a solid. The variation of the free path with temperature and from one nonmetallic solid to another controls, more than any other factor, the thermal conductivity of all nonmetallic solids. At ordinary temperatures solids are supplied generously with phonons, for there are pulses of atomic vibrations moving in all directions. As the temperature of a solid rises, the number of phonons increases. Thermal conductivity by phonons decreases, however, for the phonons impede each other's movement so that their path lengths diminish faster than their population expands.

1.9 VALUES OF THERMAL CONDUCTIVITY OF SOLIDS

For most homogeneous solids (including commercially available metals) the value of k varies linearly with temperature:

$$k = k_0(1 + at),$$

with k_0 the value of thermal conductivity at $0°F$. For most good conductors, with aluminum and brass being exceptions, a is negative.

Values of thermal conductivity of crystalline materials decrease with rising temperature, while those for amorphous or glassy substances increase with rising temperature. Values of k for some nonmetallic solids, such as carborundum bricks, or metals with impurities, pass through maxima (for the former materials) or minima (for the latter) as accounted for by the equation

$$k = \frac{1}{a_1 T + a_2 + (a_3/T)}. \qquad (1.19)$$

A maximum value of k is possible if a_2 and a_3 are positive; a minimum value if a_1 and a_3 are negative.

Values (on a comparison basis) of the thermal conductivities of materials are given in Table 1.7.

In the case of unidirectional heat flow in a plane slab, for example, the temperature distribution in the direction of heat flow is shaped by the manner

Table 1.7[a] Thermal Conductivity[b] of Materials (Btu/hr/ft²/°F/ft)

Material	High	Low	Material	High	Low
Silver[c]	242	...	Beryllia[e]	9.52	...
Copper	226	196	Austenitic stainless steels[c]	9.4	9
Chromium copper	187	...	Columbium carbide	8.2	...
Gold[c]	172	...	Carbon[c]	5	3
Aluminum and its alloys	135	67.4	Calcia[e]	4.1	...
Plain brasses	135	67	Zircon	3.6	2.9
Graphite[c]	120	70	Cordierite and Forsterite	2.4	0.9
Phosphor bronzes	120	29	Polycrystalline glass	2.1	1.1
Beryllium copper	110	100	Steatite	1.94	1.45
Leaded brasses	104	67	Electrical ceramics	1.6	0.9
Tungsten[c]	96.6	...	Magnesia[e]	1.5	...
Aluminum and its alloys (cast)	92.5	51.0	Wood comp. board	1.5	0.08
Beryllium[c]	87	...	Wool felts (1 in.), sheet	0.91	0.30
Molybdenum and its alloys	84.5	67.1	Silicon nitride[e]	0.9	...
Magnesium alloys	80	24	Epoxies (cast)	0.8	0.1
Tin and aluminum brasses	67	58	Silica glasses[c]	0.8	...
Zinc and its alloys	65.3	60.5	Silica, vitreous[e]	0.8	...
Tungsten carbide cermet	50.1	25.7	Borosilicate glasses[c]	0.7	...
Rhodium[c]	50	...	Alkyds	0.60	0.30
Columbium and its alloys	42	31.5	Wood comp board, soft board	0.6	0.3
Platinum[c]	42	...	Lead silicate and soda-lime glasses[c]	0.5	...
Palladium[c]	41	...	Zirconia[e]	0.5	...
Alloy steels[c]	38.5	21.7	Polyvinyl alcohol	0.46	...
Tin and its alloys	37	34	Melamines	0.41	0.17
Nickel and its alloys[e]	36	8.7	Micas	0.4	0.2
Wrought irons[c]	34.5	...	Phenolics (molded)	0.39	0.10
Iridium[e]	34	...	Wool felts (1 in.), roll	0.39	0.24
Aluminum bronzes (cast)	33	22	Plastics laminates, high pressure	0.29	0.17
Tungsten-titanium carbide cermet	32.9	16.5	Ureas	0.24	0.17
Tantalum	31.5	...	Cellulose adetate and propionate	0.19	0.10
Silicon bronzes	31	20	Polyethylenes	0.19	...
Gray irons (cast)[c]	30	28	Ethyl cellulose	0.17	0.09
Nitriding steels[c]	30	...	CFE fluorocarbons	0.145	...
Malleable irons	29.5	...	Nylons 6, 11, 66, and 610	0.14	0.10
Alumina cermets[d]	29	...	Styrene-butadiene and nitrile rubber	0.14	...
Silicon carbide[e]	29	9	TFE fluorocarbons	0.14	...
Tin bronzes (cast), leaded	28	...	Acetal	0.13	...
Carbon and free-cutting steels[c]	27	...	Cellulose nitrate	0.13	...
Alloy steels (cast)[c]	27	...	ABS resins	0.12	0.08
Tin bronzes (cast), high leaded	27	...	Acrylics	0.12	0.10
Cupro-nickels and nickel silvers	26	17	Nylon, glass-filled	0.12	...
Thorium	21.4	...	Polyesters (cast)	0.12	0.10
Martensitic stainless steels[c]	21.2	11.7	Silicone rubber	0.12	0.11
Nodular or ductile irons[c]	20	18	Polypropylene	0.11	0.10
Lead and its alloys[c]	19.6	16.0	Neoprene rubber	0.11	...
Cobalt-base superalloys[d]	18.0	11.9	Polycarbonate	0.11	0.05
High-temperature steels[d]	17.3	15.8	Polyvinyl chloride	0.10	0.07
Boron nitride[d]	16.6	...	Silicones (molded)	0.097	0.089
Ultra-high-strength steels[d]	16.6	...	Polyvinyl formal	0.09	...
Boron carbide[e]	16	...	Natural rubber	0.08	...
Heat-resistant alloys (cast)[c]	15.2	7.7	Polystyrenes, GP	0.08	0.06
Ferritic stainless steels[c]	15.1	12.1	Modified polystyrenes	0.07	0.02
Cr-Ni-Fe superalloys[d]	15	12.2	Butyl rubber	0.05	...
Nickel-base superalloys[d]	15	9.5	Vinylidene chloride	0.05	...
Stainless steels (cast)[e]	14.5	8.2	Urethane foamed-in-place, rigid	0.03	0.01
Uranium	14.5	...	Neoprene foams	0.029	0.021
Tin-lead-antimony alloys[c]	14	...	Prefoamed cellulose acetate, rigid	0.027	0.025
Tantalum carbide	12.8	...	Butadiene-acrylonitrile foams	0.025	0.021
Age-hardenable stainless steels[c]	12.1	8.87	Natural rubber form	0.025	0.021
Zirconium carbide	11.9	...	Silicone foams, rigid	0.025	...
Alumina ceramics[c]	10.7	6.2	Phenolic foamed-in-place, rigid	0.02	...
Low-expansion nickel alloys[c]	10.3	7.8	Polystyrene foamed-in-place, rigid	0.02	...
Titanium carbide	9.9	...	Prefoamed epoxy, polystyrene, rigid	0.02	...
Titanium and its alloys[c]	9.8	4.3	Butadiene-styrene foams	0.018	...
Zirconium and its alloys[c]	9.6	8.1	Thoria[e]	0	...

[a] Reference 10; by permission of the Reinhold Publishing Company.
[b] Values represent high and low sides of a range of *typical* values at room temperature except where noted.
[c] At temperatures between 20 and 212°F.
[d] At temperatures between 212 and 1800°F.
[e] At temperatures above 1800°F

in which the thermal conductivity values of the slab material vary with temperature. Thus, if the slab's thermal conductivity is invariant with temperature, the temperature gradient across the slab is linear, as in Figure 1.4*a*; if, however, the slab's thermal conductivity decreases in value with decreasing temperature, the temperature gradient across the slab bends downward with temperature change, as in Figure 1.4*b*; if, finally, the slab's thermal conductivity increases in value with decreasing temperature, the

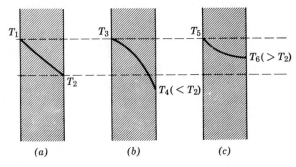

(*a*)   (*b*)   (*c*)

Figure 1.4 Temperature distributions with (*a*) *k* constant, (*b*) *k* decreasing with decreasing temperature, and (*c*) *k* increasing with decreasing temperature.

temperature gradient across the slab bends upward with temperature change, as in Figure 1.4*c*. In most engineering calculations, however, the value of thermal conductivity at the average slab temperature would be employed exclusively.

1.10 INSULATION

In a porous nonhomogeneous solid (such solids are used as insulation), the value of thermal conductivity at a given temperature is a function of the apparent density of the material.

Consider the porosity P of a nonhomogeneous material, given by the following equations:

$$P = 100\,\frac{V - V_s}{V} = 100\,\frac{(W_s + W_a)/\rho_a - W_s/\rho_s}{(W_s + W_g)/\rho_a}, \tag{1.20}$$

where V_s = volume of the solid substance of the material,
  V_g = volume of gas in the pores of the material,
  W_s = weight of solid substance,
  W_g = weight of gas,
  ρ_s = density of solid substance,
  ρ_a = apparent density of material.

Thus, because $W_s \gg W_g$, from the preceding equation,

$$P = 100\,\frac{\rho_s - \rho_a}{\rho_s}. \tag{1.21}$$

For a constant value of ρ_s, an increase of porosity P (or gas content in the insulating material) decreases the apparent density ρ_a. Decreasing ρ_a produces a reduction in the over-all thermal conductivity of the material since the value of thermal conductivity of gases is less than that of solids.

The apparent thermal conductivity of porous insulating materials increases with rising temperature. For maximum capability for insulation, the direction of heat flow in a given nonhomogeneous material should be such that it is perpendicular to fissures in the material.

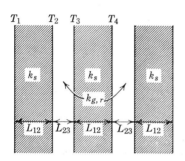

Figure 1.5 Portion of porous insulation.

Consider the portion of insulation shown in Figure 1.5. The thermal resistance over a typical combination of solid material and gas-filled, or evacuated, pore is the sum of the resistances of the two substances:

$$R_{13} = R_{12} + R_{23}. \tag{1.22}$$

The over-all thermal resistance R_{13} may be expressed by the ratio L_{13}/k_a, where k_a is the apparent thermal conductivity of the insulating material. Similarly, R_{12} is given by L_{12}/k_s, where k_s is the thermal conductivity of the material's solid substance.

R_{13} is the combination of two thermal resistances acting in parallel: the conduction resistance of the gas in the fissure, L_{23}/k_g, where k_g is the thermal conductivity of that gas, and the resistance to radiative heat exchange between the wall of the fissure.

The rate of heat flow per unit area by radiation between the walls of a fissure at temperatures T_2 and T_3 is given by

$$q_r = \sigma\epsilon(T_2{}^4 - T_3{}^4),^* \tag{1.23}$$

which is equivalent to

$$q_r = \sigma\epsilon(T_2{}^2 + T_3{}^2)(T_2 + T_3)(T_2 - T_3). \tag{1.24}$$

If T_2 and T_3 are approximately equal, as is the case here,

$$q_r = 4\sigma\epsilon T_{23}{}^3(T_2 - T_3). \tag{1.25}$$

* Cf. Chapter 2.

Equation 1.25 is in a form analogous to Ohm's law with radiation thermal resistance R_R given by

$$R_R = \frac{1}{4\sigma\epsilon T_{23}^3}.$$ (1.26)

Thus,

$$\frac{1}{R_{13}} = \frac{k_g}{L_{23}} + 4\sigma\epsilon T_{23}^3.$$ (1.27)

Furthermore, substitution into (1.27) yields

$$\frac{L_{13}}{k_a} = \frac{L_{12}}{k_s} + \frac{1}{(k_g/L_{23}) + 4\sigma\epsilon T_{23}^3}.$$ (1.28)

and

$$k_a = \frac{L_{13}}{L_{12}/k_s + [(k_g/L_{23}) + 4\sigma\epsilon T_{23}^3]^{-1}}.$$ (1.29)

As the temperature of the insulation increases, the second term of the denominator of the right-hand side of (1.29) decreases, and k_a thereupon increases. At high temperatures, this term becomes zero, and

$$k_a = \frac{L_{13}}{L_{12}} k_s.$$ (1.30)

With the value of ϵ low enough to prevent radiation, and $k_g \ll k_s$,

$$k_a = \frac{L_{13}}{L_{23}} k_g.$$ (1.31)

Finally, it is noted that bridges of solid substance across the fissures decrease the resistance to heat flow and thus increase the value of k_a.

REFERENCES

[1] Bridgeman, P. W., *The Physics of High Pressure*, Bell, London, 1949.
[2] Encyclopaedia Britannica, 9.
[3] Heilman, R. H., *Ind. Eng. Chem.*, **28**, 782 (1936).
[4] Hutchison, T. S., and D. C. Baird, *The Physics of Engineering Solids*, Wiley, New York, 1963.
[5] *International Critical Tables*, McGraw-Hill, New York, 1929.
[6] Jakob, M., *Heat Transfer*, Vol. I, Wiley, New York, 1949.
[7] Kowalczyk, L. S., "Thermal Conductivity and Its Variability with Temperature and Pressure," *Trans. ASME*, **77**, 1021 (1955).
[8] Kreith, F., *Principles of Heat Transfer*, International Textbook, Scranton, Pa., 1958.
[9] Marks, L. S., *Mechanical Engineer's Handbook*, (6th ed.), McGraw-Hill, New York, 1958.

[10] *Materials in Design Engineering*, Materials Selector, Mid-October, 1966.

[11] McAdams, W. H., *Heat Transmission* (3rd. ed.), McGraw-Hill, New York, 1954.

[12] Sinnott, M. J., *The Solid State for Engineers*, Wiley, New York, 1963.

[13] Smith, J. F. D., "Thermal Conductivity of Liquids," *Trans. ASME*, **58** 1.719 (1936).

[14] Sproull, R. L., "The Conduction of Heat in Solids," *Scientific American* (November, 1963).

[15] Wulff, J., H. F. Taylor, and A. J. Shaln, *Metallurgy for Engineers*, Wiley, New York, 1952.

2

Radiant Heat
Transfer Between Solids

2.1 RADIATION EMITTED BY AN IDEAL RADIATOR

A heated body emits electromagnetic waves at all frequencies v, or wavelengths λ ($\lambda = c/v$, where c is the speed of light), but predominantly at a particular wavelength corresponding to the body's absolute temperature. Figure 2.1 contains several wavelength-distributed radiant emission curves. The amount of radiation emitted per unit area, unit time, and unit wavelength at each wavelength by an ideal radiator at a particular temperature is plotted against wavelength. Thus, the area under each curve is the total amount of radiation emitted per unit area and unit time by an ideal radiator at a particular temperature. Furthermore, as the absolute temperature of a heated body rises, the length of the predominant wavelength of the body's radiant emission decreases. The total amount of radiant energy emitted per unit area and unit time, the total emission power E_b, increases with rising temperature. Also, most of the emission occurs at wavelengths of a relatively narrow band around the predominant wavelength.

The emissive power of a body is a function of the radiative characteristics of the surface of that body; an ideal radiator is one which emits the maximum possible total amount of radiation at a given temperature.

2.2 ABSORPTION, REFLECTION, AND TRANSMISSION OF ARRIVING RADIATION

Of the radiant energy striking the surface of a body, part is absorbed, part is reflected, and the remainder is transmitted through the body. This

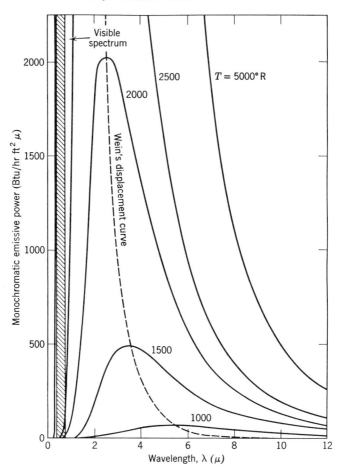

Figure 2.1 Spectral distribution of monochromatic emissive power for an ideal radiator at various temperatures.

statement is described by the equation

$$\alpha + \rho + \tau = 1, \tag{2.1}$$

where α = the absorbitivity of the surface of the body, or the fraction of the total radiant energy absorbed by the body,

ρ = the reflectivity of the surface of the body, or the fraction of the total radiant energy reflected by the body,

τ = the transmissivity of the body, or the fraction of the total radiant energy transmitted through the body.

In engineering calculations, no energy is transmitted through solid opaque materials. Therefore $\tau = 0$, and

$$\alpha + \rho = 1. \tag{2.2}$$

Reflection of radiation may be either specular or diffuse. The specular type arises from surfaces which have mirrorlike finishes; the angle of reflection of radiation equals its angle of incidence in that case. Most surfaces, however, are of sufficient roughness* to produce diffuse reflection of radiation, in which there is equal distribution of radiant flux density to all directions of space.

The relative magnitudes of the quantities α, ρ, and τ of a heated body depend on the wavelength of the radiation absorbed by the body, on the temperature of the body, on its material and thickness, and on its surface characteristics.

2.3 KIRCHHOFF'S LAW: THE BLACK BODY

A surface or body which absorbs the total amount of radiant energy incident upon it, reflecting and transmitting none ($\alpha = 1$; ρ, $\tau = 0$), is called a black surface or black body.

Kirchhoff, in 1860, suggested that a perfectly black surface can be produced with a hollow enclosure having only one small opening. Radiation entering the opening undergoes multiple reflections and absorptions inside the enclosure and is weakened at each reflection so that virtually no portion of it can leave the enclosure. The area of the opening is considered a black surface.

The black surface is considered to be the surface having characteristics against which those of other surfaces are compared.

Kirchhoff's law, also proposed in 1859–1860, asserts that, if two surfaces of equal area are at the same temperature and if one absorbs n times more of an arriving radiant energy than the other, then at the same temperature the former surface emits n times more of the identical radiation than does the latter surface.

Consider Jakob's proof of the foregoing statement: an opaque ($\tau = 0$) and diffusely reflecting surface is in thermal equilibrium with radiation arriving from all sides of the hemispherical space above the surface. (The source of the radiation, therefore, is at the same temperature as the surface under consideration.)

The considered surface and thermal situation are defined further by the

---

* The asperities of these surfaces are large compared with one wavelength.

following:

W_b = arriving radiant energy per unit time and unit area,

W = emitted radiant energy per unit time and unit area; W_b and W are called radiation flux densities,

ρ = reflectivity of considered surface,

α = absorptivity of considered surface.

Considerations of energy conservation give the equation

$$W_b = \rho W_b + W \tag{2.3}$$

(the rates of arriving and leaving energy are equal)

or

$$W_b = \rho W_b + \alpha W_b \tag{2.4}$$

(the arriving energy is partly reflected and partly absorbed).

Combining (2.3) and (2.4),

$$
\begin{aligned}
W &= (1 - \rho)W_b, \\
\frac{W}{W_b} &= \alpha.
\end{aligned}
\tag{2.5}
$$

If $\alpha = 1$, $W = W_b$; in that case, the flux density of radiation in equilibrium with that of a diffusely radiating surface is equal to that of a black body at the same temperature. Since the value of α is generally less than 1, the flux density of emission, W, is smaller than that of a black body, W_b. The ratio W/W_b is called emissivity and is denoted by ϵ. Thus, by definition, the emissivity and the absorptivity of a surface are equal at any particular temperature. Hence, for two surfaces, the first of which has the absorptivity α, and the second the absorptivity $\alpha_2 = \alpha_1/W$,

$$\frac{W_1}{W_2} = \frac{\alpha_1}{\alpha_2} = n \tag{2.6}$$

is the ratio of absorbed or emitted radiation flux densities at any particular temperature or wavelength, and thus also for total radiation at all wavelengths.

2.4 BLACK-BODY RADIATION

In 1879 Stefan, the Austrian physicist, deduced from Tyndall's experimental data that the energy radiated by a black body depends on its temperature only and is proportional to the fourth power of the absolute value of that temperature. In 1879, Ludwig Boltzmann derived this fourth-power law from thermodynamical considerations. The Stefan-Boltzmann law is

$$E_{bb} = \sigma T^4, \tag{2.7}$$

where, if E_{bb} is in Btu/hr ft^2 and T is in degrees Rankine (degrees Fahrenheit plus 459.7), $\sigma = 0.1714 \times 10^{-8}$.

The emissive power given by the Stefan-Boltzmann law represents the total energy radiated by a black body in all directions of a half space.

Max Planck (1858–1947) dealt with the question of the wavelength distribution of the energy radiated from hot dark bodies at various temperatures. He derived a single formula which fitted experimental data in both the infrared and ultraviolet spectra of the radiated emission from various heated substances. Planck made the assumption that a body does not radiate continuously throughout the spectrum; electromagnetic waves can exist only in the form of certain discrete packages, or quanta. The energy content of each package, Planck lectured to the Berlin Physical Society on December 14, 1900, is related to the corresponding frequency by a constant, h, 6.55×10^{-27} erg-secs, deduced from the radiation data.

Planck at that time derived from the quantum theory an equation illustrating the distribution of emissive power among the various wavelengths,

$$E_{b\lambda} = \frac{C_1 \lambda^{-5}}{_eC_2/\lambda T_{-1}},\tag{2.8}$$

where $E_{b\lambda}$ = monochromatic emissive power of a black body, in Btu/hr ft^2 μ,
   λ = wavelength, in microns,
   T = temperature of the black body, in degrees Rankine ($^\circ$F + 459.7),
   $C_1 = 1.1870 \times 10^8$ Btu μ^4/ft^2 hr,
   $C_2 = 2.5896 \times 10^4$ $^\circ$R μ.

At a given temperature, the monochromatic emissive power radiating from a black body varies from a value of 0 at $\lambda = 0$ through a maximum and back to zero at $\lambda = \infty$. At a particular wavelength, the monochromatic emissive power increases with temperature; at shorter wavelengths, values of this power increase faster than do power values at longer wavelengths, so that the maximum value of power shifts to shorter wavelengths as the temperature rises.

Wien's displacement law expresses the relationship between the wavelength λ_{max} at which $E_{b\lambda}$ is a maximum and absolute temperature:

$$\lambda_{max} T = 5215.6 ^\circ\text{R } \mu.\tag{2.9}$$

The area under a curve of monochromatic emissive power versus wavelength at a particular temperature is related to that temperature by the Stefan-Boltzmann equation:

$$\int_0^\infty E_{b\lambda}\, d\lambda = \sigma T^4.\tag{2.10}$$

2.5   RADIATION CHARACTERISTICS OF REAL SURFACES

Real bodies emit radiant energy at rates lower than those of black bodies. If a body at the same temperature as that of a black body emits a constant fraction of the energies emitted by the black body at different wavelengths (if, in other words, the shape of the energy-wavelength curve of the considered body is the same as that of the black body but is displaced on the energy scale) the body is called gray. Therefore, the emissivity of a gray surface is the ratio of radiant emission from that surface to the emission from a black surface, or ideal radiator, at the same temperature:

$$\epsilon_{\text{gray}} = \frac{E_{\text{gray}}}{\sigma T^4},\tag{2.11}$$

where the units of both numerator and denominator are Btu/hr ft^2. Also, the emissivity of a gray body is independent of wavelength.

Kirchhoff's law asserts that at thermal equilibrium emissivity and absorptivity are equal. Since the emissivity of a gray body is independent of wavelength, the absorptivity of the body is also invariant with temperature.

The characteristics of most real surfaces deviate from those of gray surfaces in that their values of emissivity and absorptivity vary with wavelength or temperature. For good electrical conductors, emissivities are rather low and are substantially proportional to absolute temperature, thus decreasing in value with increasing wavelength. The value of emissivity of a metallic surface increases with oxidation and roughening, however. Electrical nonconductors generally experience an opposite change in emissivity with temperature variation: their emissivities, which are much higher than those of conductors, usually increase (irregularly) with increasing wavelength (decreasing temperature). The emissivities of most nonmetals are above 0.8 at low temperatures. Table 2.1 provides representative values of normal total emissivity of various surfaces. The references indicated are secondary sources; these authors selected values from several references. Deviations from the values given in Table 2.1 are to be expected in practice. A more complete commentary is available in Reference 1.

Normal emissivity is that measured at normal incidence of radiant energy; hemispherical emissivity is that averaged over all angles between normal and grazing with the cosine of the angle made with the surface used as a weighting factor. The difference between the two types of emissivity can be greatest for metals (at most, 30%), where $\epsilon \ll 1$. Measurements show that for nonconductors, such as wood, paper, and oxide films, values of emissivity decrease at large values of emission angle; for polished metals an opposite trend is observed. Thus for polished metallic surfaces $\epsilon_{\text{mean}}/\epsilon_{\text{normal}} = 1.2$; for nonmetallic surfaces $\epsilon_{\text{mean}}/\epsilon_{\text{normal}} = 0.96$.

Table 2.1   Representative Values[a] of Normal Total Emissivity of Various Surfaces

Material	Temperature[b] (°F)	Emissivity
Metals		
Aluminum		
Polished	100–2500	0.04–0.19
Oxidized	100–1110	0.11–0.19
Brass		
Polished	100–600	0.10
Oxidized	110–1110	0.61–0.59
Chromium, polished	100–2500	0.08–0.04
Copper, polished	100–1000	0.04–0.18
Gold, pure, highly polished	440–1160	0.018–0.035
Magnesium	100–2500	0.07–0.24
Electroplated, polished	74	0.045
Electroplated, not polished	68	0.11
Platinum, pure, polished plate	440–1160	0.054–0.104
Silver, polished	100–700	0.022–0.031
Stainless steel		
18-8, polished	100–1000	0.15–0.22
18-8, weathered	100–1000	0.85
Bricks, red, rough, but no gross irregularities	70	0.93
Enamel, white fused on iron	66	0.90
Glass, smooth	72	0.90
Paints		
Aluminized lacquer	100–500	0.65
Black or white lacquer	100–200	0.80–0.95
Flat black lacquer	100–200	0.96–0.98
Oil paints, all colors	212	0.92–0.96
Radiator paint, white,		
cream, bleach	212	0.79, 0.77, 0.84
Water	32–212	0.95–0.963

[a] Compiled from tables in References 6 and 7.
[b] Temperatures and emissivities appearing in pairs and separated by dashes correspond; linear interpolation is allowed.

The wavelength band in which the bulk of radiation is emitted or absorbed defines average values of emissivity and absorptivity for heat-transfer calculations. The temperature of the body from which the radiation originates determines the wavelength band of interest for that energy, and if the monochromatic emissivity $\epsilon_{\lambda T}$ is known the emissive power of a body can be found by plotting the product $\epsilon_{\lambda T} E_{b\lambda T}$ over that wavelength band and measuring the area under that curve. Furthermore, the average emissivity value of a real body at a given temperature can be found from the ratio of the area yielding the emissive power of a real body at that temperature to the emissive power of a black body at the same temperature. Total average emissivity ϵ_T is thus the integral over-all wavelengths of the spectral emissivity weighted according to the black-body energy-wavelength distribution at the same temperature. Therefore

$$
\epsilon_T = \frac{\displaystyle\int_0^\infty \epsilon_{\lambda T} E_{b\lambda T}\,d\lambda}{\displaystyle\int_0^\infty E_{b\lambda T}\,d\lambda} ;
$$

$$
\alpha_T = \frac{\displaystyle\int_0^\infty \alpha_{\lambda T} G_{\lambda T_s}\,d\lambda}{\displaystyle\int_0^\infty G_{\lambda T_s}\,d\lambda} .
$$

(2.12)

where T = temperature of the surface,

$E_{b\lambda T}$ = Planck's black-body function for a surface at temperature T,

$G_{\lambda T_s}$ = radiation approaching the surface coming from the surroundings at a temperature T_s,

$\alpha_{\lambda T}$ = monochromatic absorptivity of a surface at temperature T,

$\epsilon_{\lambda T}$ = monochromatic emissivity of a surface at temperature T.

If a body receives radiation whose bulk is at wavelengths different from those at which it emits most of its radiation, the average values of ϵ and α pertaining to the surface of this body are not necessarily the same; α corresponds both to the temperature of the body considered (T) and that at which the arriving radiation was emitted (T_s) and ϵ corresponds to the temperature of the body considered.

2.6 INTENSITY OF RADIATION

Consider a diffuse surface, dA_1. Its radiant flux density is invariant with direction in space; it emits all its radiation to a hemispherical surface placed directly over it, as in Figure 2.2.

The amount of heat radiated from surface dA_1 to an element of hemispherical surface dA_2 is found from the definition of the intensity of radiation from dA_1 in space, i. The intensity i is defined as the radiant energy propagated in a given direction per unit solid angle and per unit of surface dA_1 projected on a plane perpendicular to the direction of propagation. Thus,

$$
dq_{1-2} = i\,dA_1 \cos \frac{dA_2}{R^2} .
$$

(2.13)

A surface radiating in this fashion is said to obey Lambert's cosine law; dA_2/R^2 is the element of solid angle dW subtended by dA_2 at dA_1, and $dA_1 \cos dW$ is the effective area of dA_1 seen by dA_2. The intensity i is thus

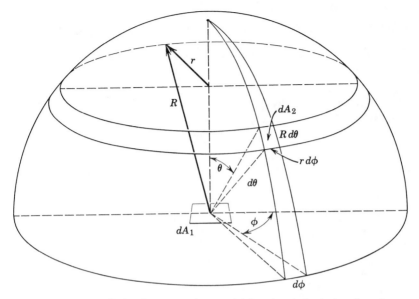

Figure 2.2 Radiation from area element dA_1 into hemispherical surface A_2.

given by

$$i = \frac{dq_{1-2}}{dA_1 \cos dW} \frac{\text{Btu}}{\text{ft}^2\text{-hr-steradian}}. \qquad (2.14)$$

For a diffuse surface, i is constant in all directions. The emissive power of surface dA_1 is the intensity of emitted radiation integrated over the intercepting hemisphere A_2. The area dA_2 is given by $R\,d\theta r\,d\phi = R^2 \sin\theta\,d\theta\,d\phi$. The area of the ring including dA_2 is $2\pi R^2 \sin\theta\,d\theta$. The rate at which energy emitted from dA_1 is intercepted by that ring is given by

$$dq_{1-\text{ring}} = \frac{i\,dA_1 \cos\theta(2\pi R^2)\sin\theta\,d\theta}{R^2}; \qquad (2.15)$$

$$dq_{1-\text{ring}} = 2\pi i\,dA_1 \cos\theta \sin\theta\,d\theta. \qquad (2.16)$$

Integration of (2.16) from $\theta = 0$ to $\theta = \pi/2$ yields the total radiation from dA_1 intercepted by the hemispherical surface A_2:

$$q = E\,dA_1 = 2\pi i\,dA_1 \int_0^{\pi/2} \cos\theta \sin\theta\,d\theta = dA_1 \pi i \sin^2\theta \Big|_0^{\pi/2}; \qquad (2.17)$$

$$E\,dA_1 = \pi i\,dA_1;$$

$$E = \pi i. \qquad (2.18)$$

Similarly,

$$E_\lambda = \pi i_\lambda. \qquad (2.19)$$

2.7 RADIATION INTERCHANGE BETWEEN BLACK SURFACES

The rate of heat transferred between two black surfaces depends on the temperatures of those surfaces and on the geometrical relationship between them.

Consider the two surfaces, A_1 and A_2, of Figure 2.3, which are separated by a nonabsorbing substance. The elemental areas dA_1 and dA_2 are a distance

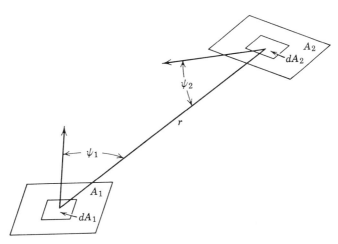

Figure 2.3   Geometry of black surfaces A_1 and A_2.

r apart. The rate of radiant energy emitted by dA_1 and received by dA_2 is

$$dq_{1-2} = i_1 \cos \psi_1 \, dA_1 \, dW_{1-2}, \tag{2.20}$$

where $i_1 =$ intensity of radiation from dA_1,
$dA_1 \cos \psi_1 =$ projection of dA_1 seen by dA_2,
and $dW_{1-2} =$ the solid angle subtended by dA_2 as seen from the center of dA_1.

The solid angle dW_{1-2} is given by the area of the receiving surface perpendicular to the direction of propagation of radiation divided by the distance separating the emitting and receiving surfaces. Thus,

$$dW_{1-2} = \frac{dA_2 \cos \psi_2}{r^2}, \tag{2.21}$$

and

$$dq_{1-2} = \frac{i_1 \cos \psi_1 \cos \psi_2 \, dA_1 \, dA_2}{r^2}. \tag{2.22}$$

Also, since $i_1 = E_1/\pi$,

$$dq_{1-2} = E_1 \, dA_1 \left(\frac{\cos \psi_1 \cos \psi_2 \, dA_2}{\pi r^2}\right), \tag{2.23}$$

where the term in the parentheses is the fraction of total radiation emitted by dA_1 that arrives at dA_2.

Similarly, the energy radiated by the element of surface dA_1 that is received by dA_2 is given by

$$dq_{2-1} = E_2 \, dA_2 \frac{\cos \psi_2 \cos \psi_1 \, dA_1}{\pi r^2}. \tag{2.24}$$

Thus, the net rate of radiant energy exchanged, dq, between the two elements is given by

$$dq = (E_{b1} - E_{b2}) \frac{\cos \psi_1 \cos \psi_2 \, dA_1 \, dA_2}{r^2}, \tag{2.25}$$

and the rate of radiant energy exchange, q, between the black surfaces A_1 and A_2 is

$$q = (E_{b1} - E_{b2}) \int_{A1} \int_{A2} \frac{\cos \psi_1 \cos \psi_2 \, dA_1 \, dA_2}{r^2}. \tag{2.26}$$

The double integral of (2.26) may be written in either of the shorthand notations $A_1 F_{1-2}$ or $A_2 F_{2-1}$, where F_{1-2}, a shape factor evaluated on the basis of area A_1, is the fraction of total radiant energy leaving A_1 that is intercepted by A_2, and F_{2-1} is a shape factor evaluated on the basis of area A_2 and is the fraction of total radiant energy emitted by A_2 that is received by A_1. Since in a two-body system the heat gained by one body is that lost by the other, $A_1 F_{1-2} = A_2 F_{2-1}$.

Therefore

$$q = (E_{b1} - E_{b2}) A_1 F_{1-2} = (E_{b1} - E_{b2}) A_2 F_{2-1}, \tag{2.27}$$

and the value of q is independent of the choice of emitting surface. The shape factor for infinite parallel plates is 1; that for the situation where one body is completely enclosed by another (and neither body can see any part of itself) is also 1. Shape factors for other geometrical situations are given in References 4, 8, and 9.

Recalling, furthermore, the Stefan-Boltzmann law, $E = \sigma T^4$,

$$q = \sigma A_1 F_{1-2}(T_1^4 - T_2^4) = \sigma A_2 F_{2-1}(T_1^4 - T_2^4). \tag{2.28}$$

The form of (2.27) is analogous to Ohm's law, $I = \Delta V/R$, where the heat flow q is analogous to current flow I, the difference between total radiant emissions ΔE is analogous to voltage potential ΔV, and the area-weighted shape factors $A_1 F_{1-2}$ and $A_2 F_{2-1}$ are analogous to the reciprocal of electrical

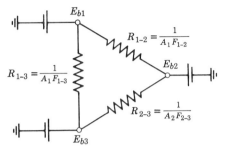

Figure 2.4 Analogous network representing typical black-body radiant heat transfer problem.

resistance $1/R$. The radiant heat exchange between a number of black surfaces may be represented by an analogous electrical network, such as the one shown in Figure 2.4.

2.8 RADIATION INTERCHANGE BETWEEN GRAY SURFACES

The reflection of radiant energy arriving at a surface can be neglected if the value of emissivity of that surface is greater than 0.9.

The rate of radiant energy exchange between gray surfaces which obey Lambert's cosine law and reflect diffusely is computed as follows.

Consider a diffuse gray surface of an opaque body. A radiosity term, J, defined as the rate per unit area at which radiant energy leaves the surface, is introduced. Since no energy is transmitted through the opaque body,

$$J = \rho G + \epsilon E_b, \tag{2.29}$$

where J = radiosity, in Btu/hr ft²,

G = radiant energy arriving at a unit area of the considered surface per unit time, in Btu/hr ft²,

E_b = black-body emissive power of the surface, in Btu/hr ft²,

ρ = reflectivity of the gray surface,

ϵ = emissivity of the gray surface.

A heat balance for the reflecting surface yields the equation

$$\left(\frac{dq}{dA}\right)_{net} = J - G. \tag{2.30}$$

Since the gray body in question is opaque, $\tau = 0$, $\rho + \epsilon = 1$, and, employing (2.29),

$$\left(\frac{dq}{dA}\right)_{net} = \frac{\epsilon}{\rho}(E_b - J). \tag{2.31}$$

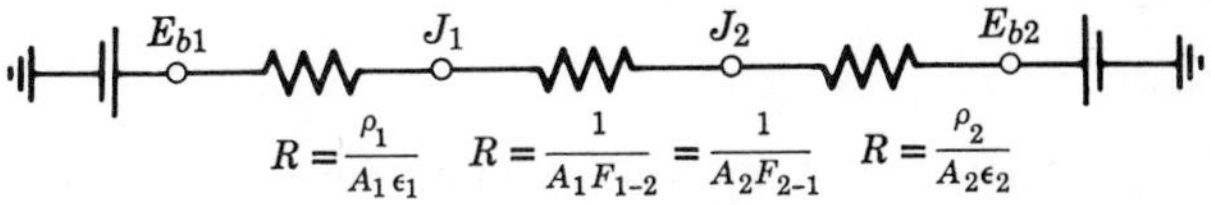

Figure 2.5 Analogous network for typical gray-body radiant heat transfer problem.

If radiation is uniformly distributed over the gray surface of area A,

$$q_{net} = \frac{\epsilon}{\rho} A(E_b - J). \qquad (2.32)$$

The radiant energy exchange between two gray surfaces A_1 and A_2, emitting radiation at the rates $J_1 A_1$ and $J_2 A_2$, respectively, can be represented by the analogous electrical network of Figure 2.5.

The resistance $1/A_1 F_{1-2}$ takes into account the geometrical relationship between the gray surfaces A_1 and A_2.

The sum of resistance between the radiant emission potentials E_{b1} and E_{b2} defines the gray-body shape factor $\mathcal{F}_{1-2}$ ($= \mathcal{F}_{2-1}$); $\mathcal{F}_{1-2}$ can be found for the case described by the network of Figure 2.5 by adding the various resistances of that network and combining the gray-body shape factor with the smaller of the two gray surfaces. Thus

$$A_1 \mathcal{F}_{1-2} = \left(\frac{\rho_1}{A_1 \epsilon_1} + \frac{1}{A_1 F_{1-2}} + \frac{\rho_2}{A_2 \epsilon_2} \right)^{-1}. \qquad (2.33)$$

Values of $\mathcal{F}_{1-2}$ for several pairs of surfaces are given in Table 2.2.

Equation 2.34 gives the rate of radiant energy exchange between two gray surfaces, considering that A_1 is the smaller of the surfaces and taking into account the Stefan-Boltzmann law.

$$q = \sigma A_1 \mathcal{F}_{1-2}(T_1^4 - T_2^4). \qquad (2.34)$$

Table 2.2 Values of $\mathcal{F}_{1-2}$ for Various Combinations of Surfaces

$\mathcal{F}_{1-2}$	Combination of surfaces
$\dfrac{\epsilon_1 \epsilon_2}{\epsilon_2 + (1 - \epsilon_2)\epsilon_1}$	Parallel plates
$\dfrac{\epsilon_1 \epsilon_2}{\epsilon_2 + (A_1/A_2)(1 - \epsilon_2)\epsilon_1}$	Long coaxial cylinders
$\dfrac{\epsilon_1 \epsilon_2}{\epsilon_2 + (A_1/A_2)(1 - \epsilon_2)\epsilon_1}$	Concentric spheres
(where A_1 = area of inner surface, A_2 = area of outer surface.)	
ϵ_1	Completely enclosed body, small compared with enclosure

REFERENCES

[1] Dunn, T. S., J. C. Richmond, and J. F. Parmer, "Survey of Infrared Measurement Techniques and Computational Methods in Radiant Heat Transfer," *J. Spacecraft and Rockets*, **3**, No. 7. (July, 1966).

[2] Gamov, G., *Thirty Years That Shook Physics*, Anchor (Double-day), Garden City, N.Y., 1966.

[3] Greene, J. E., ed., *100 Great Scientists*, Washington Square Press (Simon and Schuster), New York, 1964.

[4] Hottel, H. C., "Radiant Heat Transmission," *Mech. Eng.* **52** (1930).

[5] Jakob, M., *Heat Transfer*, Vol. I, Wiley, New York, 1949.

[6] Kreith, F., *Principles of Heat Transfer*, International Textbook, Scranton, Pa., 1958.

[7] McAdams, W. H., *Heat Transmission*, McGraw-Hill, New York, 1954.

[8] Hamilton, D. C., and W. R. Morgan, "Radiant-Interchange Configuration Factors," *NACA Tech. Note* 2836, December, 1952.

[9] Stevenson, J. A., and J. C. Grafton, "Radiation Heat Transfer Analysis for Space Vehicles," *ASD Tech. Rept.* 61–119, Part 1.

3

Convection Heat Transfer

3.1 FLUID MOTION

Fluid motion is induced either when a mass of fluid at a certain temperature in a gravity field is introduced to a wall at another temperature and there occur differences in density between hotter and cooler fluid particles that give rise to circulation currents, or when a pressure head is created in a piping system by an externally driven mechanical device such as a pump or a fan. The process of heat transfer resulting in buoyancy-impelled flow is called *natural convection*; the process of heat transfer occurring under the influence of externally driven flow is called *forced convection*.

The quality of fluid flow is substantially of two regimes, laminar and turbulent. In laminar flow the fluid moves steadily in parallel layers, called streamlines; there are no components of fluid velocity normal to the direction of flow. When fluid in laminar flow moves past a solid surface, a parabolic distribution of velocity of the streamlines, such as that of Figure 3.1, occurs with the velocity zero at the solid surface.

In turbulent flow the streamlines are broken up and the pattern of motion is random; the over-all velocity of fluid propagation, however, is constant across the fluid cross section.

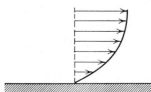

Figure 3.1 Parabolic velocity distribution for fluid in laminar flow past a wall.

3.2 THE BOUNDARY LAYER

In both laminar and turbulent flow over an initial portion of a solid surface the particles of fluid in the immediate vicinity of the surface are slowed down by shear forces. The particles adjacent to the solid adhere to it and have zero velocity relative to it. Moving away from the wall, the flow pattern becomes one of successively faster-moving layers of fluid particles. The shearing stress τ between adjacent layers of fluid moving relative to one another is determined in laminar flow by the viscosity μ of the fluid and is completely defined by the equation

$$\tau = \mu \frac{dV}{dy},$$

where dV/dy is the velocity gradient in the direction normal to the wall. The effects of viscous shearing forces extend into the body of the fluid but

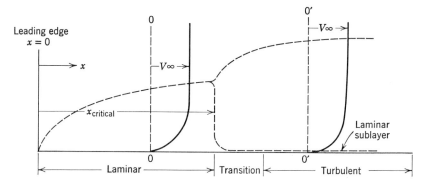

Figure 3.2   Velocity profiles for laminar and turbulent boundary layers in flow over a flat plate. (Vertical scale enlarged for clarity.)

diminish steadily. At a short distance from the wall the magnitude of velocity of the retarded fluid particles approaches that of particles in the free stream.

In laminar flow, viscous shear occurs between molecules on a microscopic scale. In turbulent flow, an interaction between lumps of fluid, called turbulent shear, is superimposed on the viscous shear.

The region where fluid flow is slowed substantially by viscous shearing forces is called the *hydrodynamic boundary layer*.* The effects of viscosity outside the boundary layer are negligible. The distance from the solid wall at which the fluid velocity reaches 99% of that of the free stream has been defined as the thickness of the boundary layer.

As flow proceeds across a plane wall, as in Figure 3.2, the shearing forces retard increasing amounts of flow, and the thickness of the boundary layer increases from zero at the wall's leading edge. As long as the viscous forces there are large, the small disturbances normally present in laminar flow are

* Ludwig Prandtl (1875–1953), whose work is the basic material of aerodynamics, expounded the existence of the boundary layer in 1904.

prevented from growing. As the boundary layer thickens, however, the ratio of shear forces to inertia forces declines. A point on the solid surface is reached where the disturbances can no longer be restrained, the boundary layer becomes unstable, and transition from the well-ordered laminar flow of the boundary layer to turbulent flow ensues. Eddies and vortices which destroy the boundary layer are formed, but quasi-laminar flow persists in a very thin layer adjacent to the wall. The point of transition depends on the contour of the solid surface, on the surface roughness, on the disturbance level in the flow, and on the rate of heat transfer between surface and fluid.

The boundary layer causes flow to separate from a curved surface: in overcoming the shear stresses in the boundary layer, the fluid consumes energy. The fluid particles reach a region of high pressure and do not contain enough energy to move against the pressure gradient; they stop, accumulate, and are given rotary motion by the surrounding fluid. An eddy of increasing size is developed. Its momentum is so great that it cannot be restrained by the surface but must break away, allowing another eddy to form.

3.3 DEFINITION OF THE FILM COEFFICIENT

Heat is transferred between a solid and a fluid sweeping a surface of the solid, at a rate according to the relation proposed by Isaac Newton in 1701:

$$q_c = \bar{h}_c A (T_s - T_\infty), \tag{3.1}$$

where q_c = the rate of heat transfer, in Btu/hr,

A = the area swept by the fluid, in ft²,

T_s = the surface temperature, in °F,

T_∞ = the fluid temperature (usually at a point far from the surface), in °F,

and $\bar{h}_c$ = the average unit coefficient of heat transfer or film coefficient, in Btu/hr ft² °F.

Equation 3.1 is a definition of the average value of conductance $\bar{h}_c$ over the heat transfer surface. The numerical value of $\bar{h}_c$ in a given situation depends on the orientation and geometry of the heat transfer surface, on the velocity and the physical and thermal properties of the fluid, and sometimes on the temperature difference, $T_s - T_\infty$.

3.4 CONVECTION HEAT TRANSFER

The process of heat transfer between a surface and a fluid sweeping it, which is called convection, is accomplished as follows. If, for example, the temperature of the solid surface is higher than that of the fluid, heat is transferred by conduction from the surface to the fluid in the immediate vicinity. If the flow regime is laminar, heat is transferred within the fluid by molecular conduction; if the regime is turbulent, the conduction mechanism is modified and assisted by the mixing motions of fluid particles. In either case, the heat transmitted increases the internal energy of the fluid and is carried away by the motion of the fluid.

Values of thermal conductivity of liquids (except liquid metals) and gases are relatively low; the rapidity of convective heat transfer in a particular situation, therefore, is largely dependent on the vigor of the mixing motion of the fluid particles. When the fluid velocity and turbulence are low, the

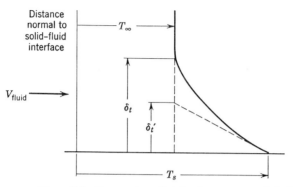

Figure 3.3   Temperature distribution near a cooled plate.

energy transport rate is not aided materially by any mixing currents on a macroscopic scale; when fluid velocity and turbulence are high, however, there are strong mixing currents between portions of fluid at different temperatures, and the mechanism of conduction is less important than that of mixing in effecting a high rate of heat transfer.

Consider the temperature distribution in a turbulent flow boundary layer for a fluid sweeping a heated plate, as shown in Figure 3.3. In the immediate vicinity of the plate heat flows in the fluid only by conduction because the fluid particles are stationary relative to the plate. Since the values of thermal conductivity are low for fluids, the temperature gradient normal to the plate is rather steep. As the distance normal to the plate increases, the movement of fluid particles relative to the plate and the mixing of warmer and colder portions of fluid both increase and the temperature gradient becomes decreasingly steep, finally leveling out in the main stream of flow.

The temperature gradient in the fluid is confined to a rather thin layer, of thickness δ_t, in the vicinity of the solid-fluid interface. If the actual temperature distribution is replaced by a linear distribution representing a layer of stagnant liquid of thickness δ_t', the thermal resistance offered by this hypothetical boundary layer is the same as that presented by the actual boundary layer. (The slopes of both temperature gradients are equal at the solid-fluid interface.) The rate of conduction heat transfer per unit area is given by

$$\frac{q}{A} = k_f \frac{T_s - T_\infty}{\delta_t'}, \tag{3.2}$$

where k_f is the thermal conductivity of the fluid.

From the definition of the coefficient of heat transfer, or film coefficient, $\bar{h}_c$, the following equality is obtained:

$$\frac{q}{A} = k_f \frac{T_s - T_\infty}{\delta_t'} = \bar{h}_c(T_s - T_\infty). \tag{3.3}$$

The film coefficient $\bar{h}_c$ may be expressed by

$$\bar{h}_c = \frac{k_f}{\delta_t'}. \tag{3.4}$$

A significant dimension of the system, L, is introduced to specify the geometry of the object from which heat flows:

$$\frac{\bar{h}_c L}{k_f} = \frac{L}{\delta_t'}. \tag{3.5}$$

The dimensionless quantity $\bar{h}_c L/k_f$ is known as the Nusselt modulus (or Nusselt number), Nu. Equation 3.4 shows that the thinner the hypothetical boundary layer is, the larger the coefficient of convective heat transfer. Boundary layer thickness is reduced by increasing fluid velocity and turbulence.

3.5 DIMENSIONAL ANALYSIS

The principal method of evaluating convective heat transfer coefficients is that of dimensional analysis combined with experiments. Dimensional analysis is performed in order to determine the independent dimensionless groups, such as the Nusselt number, by which experimental data of heat transfer by convection can be correlated. Dimensional analysis provides an empirical relationship that expresses the effect of each of the independent parameters on the dependent variable whose value in the given situation is desired.

Consider, for example, a fluid flowing through a heated tube. The convective heat transfer coefficient is dependent on the dimensions of the tube, on the fluid velocity, and on the following fluid properties: thermal conductivity,

Table 3.1   Primary Dimensions

Quantity	Dimensions	Units
Heat	Q	Btu
Length	L	ft
Mass	M	lb
Temperature	T	°F
Time	θ	hr

viscosity, density, and specific heat. The preceding parameters are expressed in Table 3.2 by the primary dimensions of Table 3.1.

The heat transfer coefficient is likely to be a function of all of the parameters listed in Table 3.2 and can be written as the product of these variables, each raised to an unknown power:

$$\bar{h}_c = A\rho^a D^b C_p^{\,c} k^d V^e \mu^f. \tag{3.6}$$

The dimensions of the parameters are substituted:

$$\frac{Q}{L^2\theta T} = A\left(\frac{M}{L^3}\right)^a (L)^b \left(\frac{Q}{MT}\right)^c \left(\frac{Q}{L\theta T}\right)^d \left(\frac{L}{\theta}\right)^e \left(\frac{M}{\theta L}\right)^f. \tag{3.7}$$

The exponents of each dimension are equated:

$$
\begin{array}{rl}
Q: & 1 = c + d, \\
L: & -2 = -3a + b - d + e - f, \\
\theta: & -1 = -d - e - f, \\
T: & -1 = -c - d, \\
M: & 0 = a - c + f.
\end{array} \tag{3.8}
$$

Equations 3.8 constitute a system of four simultaneous equations with six unknowns, which can be solved in terms of two of the unknowns. Let $d = d$

Table 3.2   Parameters

Quantity		Dimensions	Units
ρ,	Density	M/L^3	lb/ft³
D,	Diameter of tube	L	ft
$\bar{h}_c$,	Heat transfer coefficient	$Q/L^2\theta T$	Btu/ft² hr °F
C_p,	Specific heat	Q/MT	Btu/lb °F
k,	Thermal conductivity	$Q/L\theta T$	Btu/ft hr °F
V,	Velocity	L/θ	ft/hr
μ,	Viscosity	$M/\theta L$	lb/hr-ft

and $e = e$. Thus

$$
\begin{aligned}
a &= e, \\
b &= -1 + e, \\
c &= 1 - d, \\
d &= d, \\
e &= e, \\
f &= 1 - d - e.
\end{aligned}
$$

Therefore

$$
\bar{h}_c = A \rho^e D^{(-1+e)} C_p^{(1-d)} k^d V^e \mu^{(1-d-e)},
$$

$$
\bar{h}_c D = A \left(\frac{\rho V D}{\mu}\right)^e (C_p \mu)^{1-d} k^d. \tag{3.9}
$$

Multiplying both sides of (3.9) by k^{-1}, we have

$$
\frac{\bar{h}_c D}{k} = A \left(\frac{\rho V D}{\mu}\right)^e \left(\frac{C_p \mu}{k}\right)^{1-d}, \tag{3.10}
$$

where $\dfrac{\rho V D}{\mu}$ = a dimensionless group known as the Reynolds* number,

$\dfrac{C_p \mu}{k}$ = a dimensionless group known as the Prandtl number.

3.6 FORCED CONVECTION IN CONDUITS

The Nusselt modulus for flow in conduits is usually evaluated from empirical equations based on experimental results. The Nusselt number has been shown to be proportional to the product of functions of the Reynolds number and the Prandtl number, as in (3.11):

$$
\mathrm{Nu} \sim \Phi(\mathrm{Re}) \Psi(\mathrm{Pr}). \tag{3.11}
$$

In long ducts (with entrance effects neglected) flow regimes are defined as follows:

$$
\begin{aligned}
\mathrm{Re} &< 2100, \quad \text{laminar flow,} \\
2100 &< \mathrm{Re} < 10{,}000, \text{ transitional flow,} \\
\mathrm{Re} &> 10{,}000, \text{ turbulent flow.}
\end{aligned}
$$

---

* Osborne Reynolds (1842–1912) studied the similarities in the flow of different fluids moving with various velocities in tubes of different diameters. In a famous paper published in 1883 he showed that the flow of fluids is dynamically similar when a certain dimensionless group of variables is the same for all fluids.

The convective heat transfer coefficient $\bar{h}_c$ in laminar flow is rather low because the mechanism of heat transfer is solely conductive and the values of thermal conductivity of all fluids except liquid metals are rather low. There is a marked increase in the values of $\bar{h}_c$ in the transition flow regime, because some mixing, by means of eddies, occurs between warmer and cooler regions of fluid.

The flow pattern for a fluid traveling turbulently through a pipe is shown in Figure 3.4. The major portion of the over-all thermal resistance offered to heat transfer between the surface of the pipe and the fluid is that presented

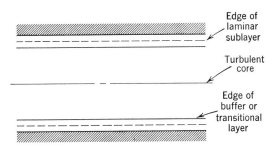

Figure 3.4   Flow of a fluid in a pipe.

by the laminar sublayer. The turbulent portion of the flow offers little resistance to heat transfer. The only effective method of increasing $\bar{h}_c$ is to reduce the effect of the laminar sublayer by increasing the turbulence in the main stream so that the turbulent eddies can penetrate deeper into the sublayer. Increase in flow rate yields higher values of $\bar{h}_c$, therefore, but magnification of turbulence is accompanied by large energy losses that increase frictional pressure drop (and pumping cost).

Equations and curves are presented for evaluating convective heat transfer coefficients $\bar{h}_c$ for flow in conduits. The bulk temperature used for evaluating values of parameters in the equations is defined as the temperature that the fluid passing a particular station in a conduit would attain if it were mixed perfectly in a cup. The mean bulk temperature is employed in preliminary calculations.

The convective heat transfer coefficient $\bar{h}_c$ is found from the Nusselt modulus, $\mathrm{Nu} = \bar{h}_c D_H/k_f$, where D_H, the hydraulic diameter, is given by

$$D_H = 4r(\text{hydraulic}) = \frac{4(\text{cross-sectional area})}{\text{perimeter}} . \qquad (3.12)$$

In a circular tube of diameter D, then,

$$D_H = D.$$

In an annulus of inside diameter D_i and outside diameter D_o,

$$D_H = D_o - D_i,$$

and in a rectangle of sides a and b,

$$D_H = 2\frac{ab}{a+b}.$$

3.7 EQUATIONS FOR TURBULENT AND LAMINAR FLOW IN CIRCULAR CONDUITS*

For heating or cooling of any fluids in fully developed turbulent motion (Re $>$ 2300) through pipes with $L/D > 60$ and moderate temperature differences, the following preliminary equation relates various moduli:

$$\frac{h_c D_H}{k} = 0.02\left(\frac{VD_H\rho}{\mu}\right)_b^{0.8}\left(\frac{\mu C_p}{k}\right)_b^n, \tag{3.13}$$

where $n = 0.4$ for heating and 0.3 for cooling, and the parameters are evaluated at the bulk temperature.

McAdams [5] recommends the following equation for the circumstances mentioned above:

$$\left(\frac{h_c}{C_p V\rho}\right)_b\left(\frac{C_p\mu}{k}\right)_f^{\frac{2}{3}} = \frac{0.023}{(\rho VD/\mu)_f^{0.2}}, \tag{3.14}$$

where $h_c/C_p V\rho$ is the Stanton modulus, and $\frac{1}{2}[T(\text{wall}) + T(\text{bulk})]$ is the temperature at which the Prandtl and Reynolds moduli are evaluated.

For large temperature differences and for fluid properties that are highly sensitive to temperature the following equation is recommended:

$$\left(\frac{h_c}{C_p\rho V}\right)_b\left(\frac{C_p\mu}{k}\right)_b^{\frac{2}{3}}\left(\frac{\mu_w}{\mu_b}\right)^{0.14} = \frac{0.023}{(\rho VD_H/\mu)_b^{0.2}}, \tag{3.15}$$

where all properties except μ_w have been evaluated at the fluid bulk temperature.

The Prandtl number for gases changes very little. A simplified equation for h_c for common gases in turbulent flow through circular ducts is obtained by substituting $(C_p\mu/k)_b = 0.78$ and $\mu_b = 0.0455$ lb/hr ft into (3.13):

$$h_c = 0.014 C_p\frac{(\rho V)^{0.8}}{(D)^{0.2}}. \tag{3.16}$$

The following equation is used for air and for large temperature differences:

$$\frac{h_c D_h}{k_b} = 0.020\left(\frac{D_h\rho V}{\mu}\right)_f^{0.8}\left(\frac{C_p\mu}{k}\right)_b^{0.4}. \tag{3.17}$$

* (See References 4 and 5 for a more complete discussion.)

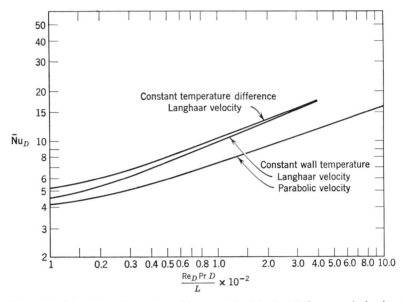

Figure 3.5 Mean Nusselt number with respect to tube length for gases in laminar flow. (Extracted from [8], "Numerical Solutions for Laminar Flow Heat Transfer in Circular Tubes," by W. M. Kays, published in *Trans. ASME, 77* (1955), with permission of the publishers, the American Society of Mechanical Engineers.

For the laminar flow of liquids in circular ducts, the equation of Sieder and Tate [6] has been proposed:

$$\frac{\bar{h}_c D_h}{k} = 1.86 \left(\frac{\rho V D}{\mu}\right)^{\frac{1}{3}} \left(\frac{\mu C_p}{k}\right)^{\frac{1}{3}} \left(\frac{D}{L}\right)^{\frac{1}{3}} \left(\frac{\mu_b}{\mu_s}\right)^{0.14}, \tag{3.18}$$

where h is related to the mean surface temperature T_s and the arithmetic mean T_m of the bulk temperature of liquid at the entrance and exit of the duct, and L is the heated length of the duct.

Kays' [8] numerical solution for gases in laminar flow is given by Figure 3.5.

3.8 NATURAL CONVECTION

If a heated surface is exposed to a relatively colder fluid, the fluid in the vicinity of the surface is heated and acquires a density less than that of the main body of fluid. This lighter fluid, near the surface, flows upward under the impetus of buoyant forces. If, on the other hand, the surface were colder than the fluid, the portion of fluid near the surface would lose heat, become heavier than the main body of fluid, and flow downward.

The process of heat exchange by which the currents described above are created is called *natural,* or *free, convection.* The characteristics of the buoyancy-driven flow in the vicinity of the heat transfer surface are similar to those in forced convection: the characteristics of the boundary layers in both processes are similar; the flow may be either laminar or turbulent in both cases. Although the temperature profiles are the same in fluids accomplishing heat exchange by either natural or forced convection processes, the

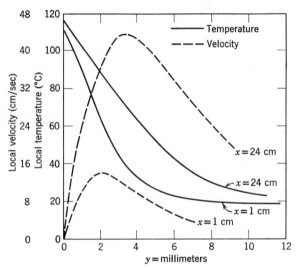

Figure 3.6 Temperature and velocity distributions at two locations near the surface of a vertical heated plate cooling in air (according to Schmidt). (From [2], by permission of D. Van Nostrand Co.)

velocity profiles in these fluids are not the same. The velocity and temperature profiles in air to which a heated plate has been exposed are shown in Figure 3.6.

When buoyancy is the only driving force, the fluid velocity is determined entirely by the quantities contained in the Grashof modulus,

$$N_{GR} = \frac{g\beta x^3(T_s - T_\infty)}{\nu^2},$$

where g = acceleration due to gravity, 4.17×10^8 ft/hr^2,
 $\quad\beta$ = coefficient of volumetric expansion, in (°F)$^{-1}$,
 $\quad x$ = geometrical factor, in ft,
 $\quad T_s$ = temperature of heated or cooled wall, in °F,
 $\quad T$ = temperature of main body of fluid, in °F,
 $\quad\nu = \mu/\rho$, kinematic viscosity, in ft^2/hr.

The following are equations for determining convective heat transfer coefficient $\bar{h}_c$ in free convection [1] and [5].

For horizontal heated plates facing upward or cooled plates facing downward (side dimension used):

Laminar range: $(Gr\ Pr)_f$ from 10^5 to 2×10^7,

$$(Nu)_f = 0.54[(Gr\ Pr)_f]^{0.25}. \tag{3.19}$$

Turbulent range: $(Gr\ Pr)_f$ from 2×10^7 to 3×10^{10},

$$(Nu)_f = 0.14[(Gr\ Pr)_f]^{1/3}. \tag{3.20}$$

For horizontal heated plates facing downward or cooled plates facing upward, flow in the laminar range, $(Gr\ Pr)_f$ from 3×10^5 to 3×10^{10},

$$(Nu)_f = 0.27[(Gr\ Pr)_f]^{0.25}. \tag{3.21}$$

Simplified equations for $\bar{h}_c$ of air can be obtained by manipulating the standard free-convection equation as follows:

$$\bar{h}_c = C\frac{k}{L}\left(\frac{g\beta L^3(T_s - T)}{\nu^2}\frac{\nu}{a^*}\right)^{0.25} \tag{3.22}$$

is rearranged to give

$$\bar{h}_c = Ck\left(\frac{g\beta}{\nu a}\right)^{0.25}\left(\frac{\Delta T}{L}\right)^{0.25}. \tag{3.23}$$

If average values of air properties are selected,

$$\bar{h}_c = C'\left(\frac{\Delta T}{L}\right)^{0.25}. \tag{3.24}$$

Simplified equations for $\bar{h}_c$ of air are as follows:

For heated plates facing up or cooled plates facing down in air at atmospheric pressure and room temperature:

Laminar range: $(Gr\ Pr)_f > 10^4$ or 10^5,

$$\bar{h}_c = 0.27\left(\frac{\Delta T}{L}\right)^{0.25}. \tag{3.25}$$

Turbulent range: $(Gr\ Pr)_f > 10^8$ or 10^9,

$$\bar{h}_c = 0.22(\Delta T)^{1/3}. \tag{3.26}$$

For cooled plates facing up or heated plates facing down flow in the

---

* a is thermal diffusivity, $\dfrac{k}{C_p \rho}$.

laminar range, $(Gr \, Pr)_f > 10^4$ or 10^5,

$$\bar{h}_c = 0.12 \left(\frac{\Delta T}{L}\right)^{0.25}. \tag{3.27}$$

For vertical plates and large diameter vertical cylinders (height the characteristic length):

Gases.

Laminar range: $(Gr \, Pr)_f < 10^8$,

$$Nu = 0.56[(Gr \, Pr)_f]^{0.25}. \tag{3.28}$$

Turbulent range: $(Gr \, Pr)_f > 10^8$

$$Nu = 0.12[(Gr \, Pr)_f]^{1/3}. \tag{3.29}$$

Water.

Turbulent range: $(Gr \, Pr)_f > 2 \times 10^9$,

$$Nu = 0.17[(Gr \, Pr)_f]^{1/3}. \tag{3.30}$$

Simplified equations for air.

Laminar range: $(Gr \, Pr)_f$ from 10^4 to 10^9,

$$\bar{h}_c = 0.29 \left(\frac{\Delta T}{L}\right)^{0.25}. \tag{3.31}$$

Turbulent range: $(Gr \, Pr)_f$ from 10^9 to 10^{12},

$$\bar{h}_c = 0.19(\Delta T)^{1/3}. \tag{3.32}$$

Free-convection heat transfer between surfaces S_1 and S_2 of enclosed air spaces is now considered. A heat transfer coefficient h_c' is defined, based on the over-all coefficient between surfaces S_1 and S_2 a distance x apart but with any radiant heat transfer neglected,

$$\frac{1}{h_c'} = \frac{1}{h_{c1}} + \frac{x}{k_f} + \frac{1}{h_{c2}}, \tag{3.33}$$

and, therefore, on the temperature difference $T_{S1} - T_{S2}$,

$$q_c = h_c' A (T_{S1} - T_{S2}). \tag{3.34}$$

If, however, the clearance x between surfaces S_1 and S_2 were made sufficiently small to suppress natural convection, heat would be transported between S_1 and S_2 only by gaseous conduction. The rate of heat transfer by gaseous conduction q_k is given by

$$q_k = \frac{kA(T_{S1} - T_{S2})}{x}. \tag{3.35}$$

The ratio

$$\frac{q_c}{q_k} = \frac{h_c'A(T_{S1} - T_{S2})}{kA(T_{S1} - T_{S2})/x} = \frac{h_c'x}{k} \tag{3.36}$$

defines the Nusselt number used in the correlation of natural convection coefficients in enclosed air spaces. The Grashof number used in that correlation is $[x^3\rho^2g\beta(T_{S1} - T_{S2})/\mu^2]_f$.

In vertical enclosed air spaces, data for natural convection have been correlated by the equation

$$\frac{h_c'x}{k_f} = \frac{C}{(L/x)^{1/9}}\left[\left(\frac{x^3\rho^2g\beta T}{\mu^z}\right)_f\left(\frac{C_p\mu}{k}\right)_f\right]^n. \tag{3.37}$$

For Grashof numbers (based on clearance x) below 2×10^3, natural convection is suppressed, gaseous conduction controls the rate of heat transfer, and the equation does not apply. For Grashof numbers from 2.1×10^3 to 2×10^4, $C = 0.20$ and $n = \frac{1}{4}$. (For a given L/x, $h_c' \sim x^{-1/4}$.) For Grashof numbers from 2.1×10^5 to 1.1×10^7, $C = 0.071$ and $n = \frac{1}{3}$. (For a given L/x, h_c' is independent of x.)

In horizontal enclosed air spaces (horizontal parallel plates with heat flow upward),

$$\frac{h_c'x}{k_f} = C\left[\left(\frac{x^3\rho^2g\beta T}{\mu^2}\right)_f\left(\frac{C_p\mu}{k}\right)_f\right]^n. \tag{3.38}$$

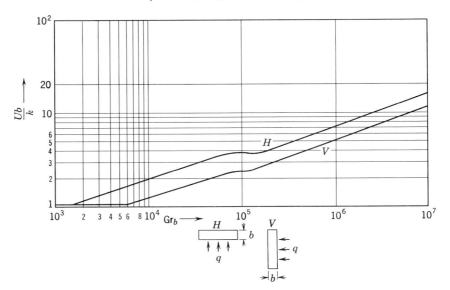

Figure 3.7 Free-convection heat transfer through enclosed-plane air layer. (By permission of International Textbook Co.)

For Grashof numbers below 10^3, gaseous conduction controls the rate of heat transfer, and $h_c' = h/x$. For Grashof numbers from 10^4 to 3.2×10^5, $C = 0.21$ and $n = \frac{1}{4}$. For Grashof numbers from 3.2×10^5 to 10^7, $C = 0.075$ and $n = \frac{1}{3}$.

Kreith [4] has summarized the results for free-convection heat transfer through an enclosed-plane air layer in the graph of Figure 3.7.

REFERENCES

[1] Fishenden, M., and O. A. Saunders, *An Introduction to Heat Transfer*, Oxford University Press, London, 1950.
[2] Giedt, W. H., *Principles of Engineering Heat Transfer*, Van Nostrand, Princeton, N.J., 1957.
[3] Jakob, M., and G. A. Hawkins, *Elements of Heat Transfer*, Wiley, New York, 1947.
[4] Kreith, F., *Principles of Heat Transfer*, International Textbook, Scranton, Pa., 1958.
[5] McAdams, W. H., *Heat Transmission*, McGraw-Hill, New York, 1954.
[6] Sieder, E. N., and G. E. Tate, "Heat Transfer and Pressure Drop of Liquids in Tubes," *Ind. Eng. Chem.*, **28**, 1429 (1936).
[7] Vennard, J. K., *Elements of Fluid Mechanics*, Wiley, New York, 1947.
[8] Kays, W. M., "Numerical Solutions for Laminar Flow Heat Transfer in Circular Tubes," *Trans. ASME*, **77** (1955).

4

Methods for Changing Thermal Conductance

4.1 INTRODUCTION

In preceding chapters we have discussed ways in which heat is transferred and have presented basic equations of heat transfer. This chapter is a transition from those fundamentals to methods of fixing desired rates of heat transfer and heat exchange. It describes three common situations for which analytical and experimental work indicates how rates of heat transfer can be changed. Also, the chapter illustrates the basic equations of heat exchanger design.

The following topics are considered in this chapter:

1. Parameters for rating heat transfer fluids.
2. The efficiencies and optimum dimensions of extended surface elements.
3. The estimation and control of contact thermal conductance.*
4. Heat exchanger design.

Heat transfer by any combination of conduction, convection, and radiation proceeds according to the equation, $q = (1/R) \Delta T$, where $1/R$ is the conductance between two points, ΔT is the difference between their temperatures, and q is the rate of heat transfer between them. For steady-state, one-dimensional conduction through a substance, $q = (KA/\Delta x) \Delta T$, where the value of $KA/\Delta x$ is the conductance. The rate of heat transfer across the interface between two solid surfaces in contact is given by $q = hA \Delta T$, where

---

* *Conductance* is the inverse of *resistance*. The two terms are used interchangeably. Typical units for conductance are Btu/hr °F.

the conductance, hA, is the product of the over-all coefficient of heat transfer between the surfaces and the total interface area. Conductance in conduction heat transfer through a structure depends on the values of thermal conductivity of the materials and gases present, the geometry of the heat transfer paths, the properties and dimensions of the surfaces in contact, and the properties of any substances trapped between those surfaces.

For convection between a solid surface and a fluid, $q = hA \, \Delta T$, where the value of hA is the conductance. This value depends on properties of both the surface and the fluid. Important properties of a surface are the amount of it available for heat transfer, its orientation, and its quality. For radiation between nonblack surfaces in the same temperature range,

$$q = \sigma A F_\epsilon F_A (T_1^4 - T_2^4) = \sigma A F_\epsilon F_A (T_1^2 + T_2^2)(T_1 + T_2)(T_1 - T_2)$$
$$= \sigma A F_\epsilon F_A 4 T_1^3 \, \Delta T,$$

where the value of $4\sigma A F_\epsilon F_A T_1^3$ is the conductance. The value of radiation conductance arises from the area available for radiation, the thermal properties of the surfaces emitting and receiving radiation, their view factors, and their temperature levels.

Hence, if q is the rate of heat transfer between two points, the value of conductance between them determines their temperature difference. Therefore if it is possible to adjust the conductance between two points transferring heat at a given rate, their temperature difference can be changed. If both the rate of heat dissipated at a heat source and the temperature at a heat sink are fixed, the temperature of the heat source is a function of the value of thermal conductance between source and sink. This chapter describes several ways to change values of thermal conductance in certain heat transfer situations.

The rating parameters for heat transfer fluids, treated in Section 4.2, provide a means of comparing the convection properties of fluids. The fluids considered for a particular convection situation are compared in order to maximize the heat transfer coefficient and, in forced convection, to reduce pumping power.

Section 4.3 discusses how rates of heat transfer at surfaces can be increased by adding extensions to the surfaces. Extended surface elements consume space and increase weight, however. Also, they are not completely efficient in heat transfer. Efficiences of extended surface elements are determined by dimensionless ratios of their material properties, heat transfer parameters, and sizes. Charts of efficiencies of several extended surface elements and equations for optimizing the dimensions of these elements are given in Section 4.3.

Contact thermal conductance is that occurring between two solid surfaces in contact. Its value may be expressed as hA, where A is the total surface area and *h* is the conductance heat transfer coefficient, expressed in typical units, Btu/hr °F ft². The conductance coefficient is a combination of the heat transfer coefficient for the places where the two surfaces are in actual contact and the conductance coefficient across the substance trapped between them. For the important case in which the contact occurs in vacuum and no filler material is sandwiched between the surfaces, there is virtually no conductance across the voids where the surfaces are not in contact. Section 4.4 is an introduction to a subject vital to anyone analyzing heat transfer in structures. Even if the parts of the structure have high values of conductance, the over-all values of conductance in the structure will be low if the thermal connections between the parts provide low contact conductance values. In a structure where interior temperatures must not exceed certain levels, as in an electronics package, for example, thermal conductances across joints and contacting surfaces are critical when the package is operated in a vacuum and cannot be cooled internally by radiation.

The work on contact thermal resistance outlined in Section 4.4 indicates how the properties of the contacting surfaces and of the substances trapped between them affect the values of conductance. The references cited correlate surface and filler substance properties and methods of joining surfaces with values of contact conductance.

Section 4.5 reviews the basic equations of heat exchanger and cold plate design. A heat exchanger is a device in which two media come into thermal contact with one another and transfer heat between themselves. A cold plate is a specific type of heat exchanger through which a medium is forced that removes heat from a structure to which the cold plate is mounted. The equations in Section 4.5 are concerned with fluid temperatures and heat-absorbing capabilities in a heat exchanger. Knowledge of the methods for increasing thermal conductance is essential to improve the capabilities of heat exchangers and cold plates. The use of these devices involves work in the particular heat transfer situations described in this chapter. Of the utmost concern are the means of attaching a cold plate to a cooled structure, and the thermal resistance across the interface; the choice of fluids used in a heat exchanger or cold plate, both to reduce pumping power and to increase heat transfer rates; and the use of extended surface elements inside a cold plate in order to increase heat transfer rates.

4.2   PARAMETERS FOR RATING HEAT TRANSFER FLUIDS

We now derive rating parameters for heat transfer fluids in two typical cases of natural and forced convection. In natural convection the rating parameter is the heat transfer coefficient; in forced convection the heat transfer coefficient, the pumping power, and their quotient are rating parameters. The ratings show that the heat transfer capabilities of a fluid are dependent on the values of more than any single property. They are not all-encompassing for choices of fluids, however; when selecting a fluid, freezing and boiling points, flash and ignition temperatures, lubricity, chemical compatibility, toxicity, availability and cost are among the other factors to be considered. Furthermore, the rating parameters may not be used for comparing different types or applications of convection heat transfer.

An equation for natural convection (heat transfer) with turbulent flow from heated plates facing upward or from cooled plates facing downward has been given by Fishenden and Saunders [1] (of Chapter 3):

$$\frac{hL}{k} = K_1 \left[\left(\frac{L^3 \rho^2 g \beta \, \Delta T}{\mu^2} \right) \left(\frac{C_p \mu}{k} \right) \right]^{\frac{1}{3}}, \tag{4.1}$$

where h = free convection heat transfer coefficient,
   L = a characteristic length,
   k = fluid thermal conductivity,
   K_1 = a constant,
   ρ = fluid density,
   g = acceleration of gravity,
   β = fluid coefficient of thermal expansion,
   ΔT = maximum temperature rise of wetted surface above bulk fluid or
        fluid inlet temperature,
   μ = fluid dynamic viscosity,
   C_p = fluid specific heat.
The rating parameter for the heat transfer fluid is formed by comparing values of h for identical values of L, g, and ΔT. Thus, relative values of N_1:

$$N_1 = \left(\frac{\rho^2 k^2 \beta C_p}{\mu} \right)^{\frac{1}{3}} \tag{4.2}$$

are used to compare fluids for the same dimensions and under the same conditions as for (4.1).

The following equation for forced-convection heat transfer with turbulent flow in tubes has been suggested by Dittus and Boelter [4]:

$$\frac{hD}{k} = K_2 \left(\frac{\rho VD}{\mu} \right)^{0.8} \left(\frac{C_p \mu}{k} \right)^{0.4}, \tag{4.3}$$

where all fluid properties are evaluated at fluid bulk temperature, and
   D = a characteristic diameter,
   K_2 = a constant (= 0.023),
   V = mean fluid velocity.

The fluid pressure drop for turbulent flow in tubes is given by

$$\Delta p = f \frac{L}{D} \rho \frac{V^2}{2g}, \tag{4.4}$$

where $f = \dfrac{F_1}{(\rho V D/\mu)^{0.2}}$ is a friction factor with F_1 a constant.

Also, the fluid pumping power is given by $\Delta p W/\rho$, where W, the fluid mass flow rate, is equal to $K_3 \rho V$.

The heat transfer coefficients of fluids flowing through tubes of identical size may be compared by using the following relation from (4.3):

$$h = K_4 \frac{\rho^{0.8} V^{0.8} k^{0.6} C_p^{0.4}}{\mu^{0.4}}. \tag{4.5}$$

Using (4.4) and its associated definitions, pumping powers for various fluids flowing through identical tubes may be compared as follows:

$$\frac{\Delta p W}{\rho} = K_5 \mu^{0.2} \rho^{0.8} V^{2.8}. \tag{4.6}$$

The mean velocities of fluids propelled through identical tubes by the same magnitude of pumping power may be compared by rearranging (4.6):

$$V^{2.8} = \frac{K_6}{\mu^{0.2} \rho^{0.8}}. \tag{4.7}$$

Hence for both identical tubes and equal pumping power (4.5) may be amended to

$$h = K_7 \frac{\rho^{0.57} k^{0.6} C_p^{0.4}}{\mu^{0.46}}. \tag{4.8}$$

For equal values of h, mean fluid velocities may be compared by rearranging (4.5):

$$V^{0.8} = K_8 \frac{\mu^{0.4}}{\rho^{0.8} k^{0.6} C_p^{0.4}}. \tag{4.9}$$

In order to compare pumping power requirements for identical tubes and equal values of h, (4.6) is amended to

$$\frac{\Delta p W}{\rho} = K_9 \frac{\mu^{1.6}}{\rho^{2.0} k^{2.1} C_p^{1.4}}. \tag{4.10}$$

The optimum fluid would have a high value of h and require a minimum level of $\Delta p W/\rho$. For turbulent flow in tubes of identical dimensions, the parameter for rating heat transfer fluids may be given by the ratio of (4.8) to (4.10):

$$N_2 = \frac{\rho^{2.57} k^{2.7} C_p^{1.8}}{\mu^{2.0}}. \tag{4.11}$$

4.3 EXTENDED SURFACE ELEMENTS: FINS*

Extended surface elements, such as fins, may be used to increase the amounts of surface area available for heat transfer. A fin operates imperfectly, however. Because the temperature level at its root is not maintained along its length, heat is not transferred to or from a fin at a uniform rate along its length. The rate at the root is greater than at any other section. The efficiency of a finned surface, η_0, is given by

$$\eta_0 = 1 + (\eta_f - 1)\frac{A_f}{A}, \tag{4.12}$$

where η_f = fin efficiency,

A_f = heat transfer area of the fins,

A = total heat transfer area (that of the fins combined with the available base surface).

The efficiency of a fin is computed by resolution of the equation that describes the energy balance of an incremental volume of that fin, with these assumptions:

1. Steady-state conditions obtain.
2. The fin material is homogeneous and its thermal conductivity is uniform and constant.
3. No heat is generated in the fin.
4. The convective heat transfer coefficient is uniform and constant over the heat-transfer surface of the fin.
5. The temperature of the medium surrounding the fin is uniform and constant.
6. The temperature at the base of the fin is uniform and constant.
7. A negligible amount of heat is transferred from the edges and the end of the fin.
8. There are no temperature gradients in the fin other than along a direction leading away from the base surface to which the fin is attached.

The energy balance of the incremental volume $Lt\,dx$ of the fin of Figure 4.1 is

$$-ktL\frac{dT}{dx} = -ktL\frac{d}{dx}\left(T + \frac{dT}{dx}\,dx\right) + 2hL\,dx(T - Ta). \tag{4.13}$$

Equation 4.13 is solved as follows: After rearranging and substituting $m^2 = 2h/kt$,

$$\frac{d^2T}{dx^2} - m^2(T - T_a) = 0. \tag{4.14}$$

---

* A fin is an extended surface whose thermal conductivity is of sufficient magnitude to prevent temperature gradients in any direction other than that leading away from the base surface to which the fin is attached.

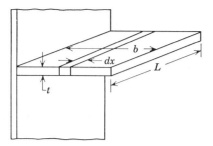

Figure 4.1 A rectangular fin.

The solution for $(T - T_a)$ is given by

$$T - T_a = C_1 e^{mx} + C_2 e^{-mx}. \tag{4.15}$$

The fin boundary conditions are the following:

$$\text{at } x = 0, \qquad T = T_0,$$

$$\text{at } x = b, \qquad \frac{dT}{dx} = 0.$$

From those boundary conditions

$$C_1 = \frac{(T_0 - T_a)e^{-mb}}{e^{+mb} + e^{-mb}}, \tag{4.16}$$

$$C_2 = \frac{(T_0 - T_a)e^{+mb}}{e^{+mb} + e^{-mb}}, \tag{4.17}$$

where T_a = ambient temperature,
T_0 = base surface temperature.

Therefore

$$T - T_a = \frac{(T_0 - T_a)}{e^{+mb} + e^{-mb}} [e^{m(x-b)} + e^{-m(x-b)}], \tag{4.18}$$

or,

$$T - T_a = (T_0 - T_a)\frac{\cosh m(b - x)}{(\cosh mb)}.$$

The amount of heat conducted through the base of the fin is given by

$$q_0 = -ktL \left.\frac{dT}{dx}\right|_{x=0}, \tag{4.19}$$

$$q_0 = -ktL(T_0 - T_a)m \tanh (mb). \tag{4.20}$$

The fin efficiency is given by the ratio of the actual heat conducted through the fin base, q_0 to that which would have been transferred from the fin were its entire surface at the base temperature, q_I:

$$\eta_f = \frac{q_0}{q_I} = \frac{ktL(T_0 - T_a)m \tanh (mb)}{h(2bL)(T_0 - T_a)}.$$

Since $m^2 = 2h/kt$,

$$\eta_f = \frac{\tanh(mb)}{mb}. \tag{4.21}$$

Similarly, the efficiency of the triangular fin of Figure 4.2 (computed from Bessel's form of the energy balance equation) is given by

$$\eta = \frac{I_1(2mb)}{mbI_0(2mb)}, \tag{4.22}$$

where $m^2 = 8h/kt_b$.

Also, the efficiency of a cylindrical spine is

$$\eta = \frac{\tanh(mb)}{mb}, \tag{4.23}$$

where $m^2 = 4h/k$ (diam.).

Efficiencies of rectangular, triangular, and cylindrical fins are plotted in Figure 4.3 as functions of mb.

We can determine the fin thickness and height for maximum heat dissipation with a given profile area A_p. For a rectangular-profile fin the optimum thickness is

$$t_{A_p} = 0.791 \left(\frac{2hA_p^2}{k} \right)^{1/3}. \tag{4.24}$$

The optimum height is

$$b_{A_p} = \frac{A_p}{t} = 1.262 \left(\frac{kA_p}{2h} \right)^{1/3}. \tag{4.25}$$

For a triangular-profile fin the optimum thickness is

$$t_{b_{A_p}} = 1.328 \left[A_p^2 \left(\frac{2h}{k} \right) \right]^{1/3}. \tag{4.26}$$

The optimum height is

$$b_{A_p} = \frac{2A_p}{t_b} = 1.506 \left(\frac{kA_p}{2h} \right)^{1/3}. \tag{4.27}$$

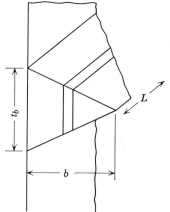

Figure 4.2 A triangular fin.

For the optimum thickness the rectangular-profile area for a given base heat flow q_0 and base-to-ambient temperature difference $(T_b - T_a)_0$ is given by

$$A_p = \frac{0.500}{h^2 k} \left[\frac{q_0}{(T_b - T_a)_0} \right]^3. \tag{4.28}$$

Similarly, for a triangular profile,

$$A_p = \frac{0.347}{h^2 k} \left[\frac{q_0}{(T_b - T_a)_0} \right]^3. \tag{4.29}$$

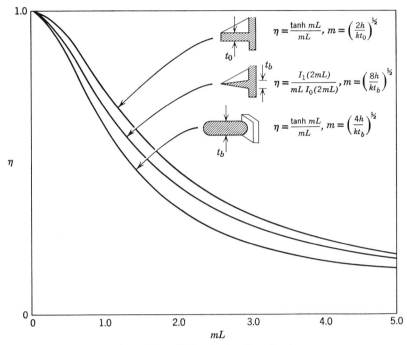

Figure 4.3   Efficiencies for three fin shapes.

Comparison of (4.28) and (4.29) indicates that for the same materials, heat flow, and base-to-ambient temperature difference a smaller amount of material is needed for a triangular-profile fin than for a rectangular-profile one.

In either case, note that in order to increase heat flow an amount Δ it is necessary to use either fins $(\Delta)^3$ times as large or Δ times the number of fins.

4.4   DETERMINING THERMAL CONTACT RESISTANCE

The two surfaces shown in magnification in Figure 4.4, their peaks and valleys the products of typical machining operations, have been brought together for the purpose of transferring heat from one to the other. Initial contact is made only between the combination of highest peaks, and thus over a rather small portion of the available surface area. Since the resistance to heat flow across the void fluid is large relative to that where the surfaces are in contact, the over-all intersurfaces thermal resistance at the line of mutual contact is high. As the surfaces are pressed together, however, and the peaks of the softer surface material are crushed, the number of points of contact increases, and the over-all thermal resistance is lowered. Thus, the higher the pressure between surfaces, the higher is the intersurface conductance h_c. (Also, h_c increases with rising mean intersurface temperature.)

The lowest intersurface thermal conductance for two metals in contact is generally observed in vacuum if no filler material is employed in the voids. With filler material in the voids, the conductance in vacuum is raised to values approaching those obtained at atmospheric pressure. Typical filler materials must be used carefully, however. For example, the thermal

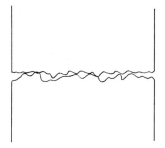

Figure 4.4 Two surfaces in contact.

conductivities of commercial silicone-based heat transfer compounds are much lower than those of metals and alloys. These compounds must be worked into surfaces so that they fill up the valleys between the peaks that remain after the surfaces are pressed together but do not cover these peaks with a layer of insulation. Metallic foils, such as indium, are also employed between heat transfer surfaces; their use is not recommended, however, when the material of one surface is softer than the foil.

The following expression for the intersurface conductance between two surfaces in contact has been derived by Fenech et al. [6], [8], from the idealized model of Figure 4.5:

$$h_c = \frac{\dfrac{k_f}{\delta_1 + \delta_2}\left[(1-\epsilon^2)\left(\dfrac{4.26\sqrt{n}\,\dfrac{\delta_1}{\epsilon}+1}{k_1} + \dfrac{4.26\sqrt{n}\,\dfrac{\delta_2}{\epsilon}+1}{k_2}\right) + 1.1\epsilon\left(\dfrac{1}{k_1}+\dfrac{1}{k_2}\right)\right] + 4.26\epsilon\sqrt{n}}{(1-\epsilon^2)\left[1-\dfrac{k_f}{\delta_1+\delta_2}\left(\dfrac{\delta_1}{k_1}+\dfrac{\delta_2}{k_2}\right)\right]\left[\dfrac{4.26\sqrt{n}\,\dfrac{\delta_1}{\epsilon}+1}{k_1} + \dfrac{4.26\sqrt{n}\,\dfrac{\delta_2}{\epsilon}+1}{k_2}\right]}$$

$$(4.30)$$

where
h_c = contact conductance,
δ = void thickness,
k = thermal conductivity,
ϵ^2 = contact area ratio,
n = contacts per unit area (number per inch),

subscript 1 = surface 1,
2 = surface 2,
f = void fluid.

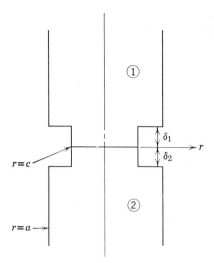

Figure 4.5   Idealized contact.

The first term in the numerator denotes the thermal conduction through the voids; the second term measures conduction through the surface contacts.

Equation 4.30 is simplified in several applications.

1. The surface states or the thermal conductivities of the materials in contact do not vary greatly. The surface parameters obey the criterion

$$\left|\left(\frac{\sigma_1 + \sigma_2}{\sigma_1 - \sigma_2}\right)\left(\frac{k_1 + k_2}{k_1 - k_2}\right)\right| > 4, \tag{4.31}$$

where σ = surface roughness, in microinches.

The location of the contact plane may be placed in the middle of the interface, and therefore $\delta = \delta_1 + \delta_2$, $\delta_1 = \delta_2 = \frac{1}{2}\delta$. Thus

$$h_c = \frac{k_s}{\delta}\left[\frac{1}{1 - (k_f/k_s)}\right]\left\{\frac{k_f}{k_s} + \left(\frac{\epsilon^2}{1 - \epsilon^2}\right)\left[\frac{1.1(k_f/k_s) + \eta}{\epsilon + \eta}\right]\right\}, \tag{4.32}$$

where
$$\eta = 2.13\delta\sqrt{n},$$

$$\frac{1}{k_s} = \frac{1}{2}\left(\frac{1}{k_1} + \frac{1}{k_2}\right).$$

2. The surface states or material thermal conductivities are greatly different. The surface parameters obey the criterion

$$\frac{\sigma_1 k_2}{\sigma_2 k_1} > 5. \tag{4.33}$$

Surface 2 may be considered flat, and the small resistance of its idealized cylinder may be neglected. The thickness of the fluid void, however, remains $\delta_1 + \delta_2 = \delta$. Thus

$$\eta_c = \frac{k_s}{\delta}\left[\frac{1}{1 - (k_f/k_1)}\right]\left\{\frac{k_f}{k_s} + \left(\frac{\epsilon^2}{1 - \epsilon^2}\right)\left[\frac{1.1(k_f/k_s) + \eta_1}{\eta_1(k_s/k_1) + \epsilon}\right]\right\}, \qquad (4.34)$$

where $\eta_1 = 2.13\delta_1\sqrt{n}$.

3. For contacts under heavy loading or in rarified atmospheres, the void-fluid conductance is neglected.

Using the approximation, $k_f/k_s < \epsilon^2/2$, and for $k_f = 0$

$$h_c = \frac{\epsilon^2/(1 - \epsilon^2)}{\delta_1/k_1 + \delta_2/k_2 + 0.46\sqrt{\epsilon^2/n}/k_s}. \qquad (4.35)$$

Methods of determining the parameters of these equations are given in [6] and [8]. Other work on contact thermal conductance is discussed in [1], [2], [15], and [17]. They are especially interesting for designers and packagers of electronic equipment.

4.5 FUNDAMENTAL RELATIONS OF HEAT EXCHANGERS AND COLD PLATES

A heat exchanger is a device in which two media, each at a different temperature, come into thermal contact with one another and transfer heat between themselves.

The basic thermal relationships in a heat exchanger are as follows:

1. The heat transfer rate at any section is proportional to temperature difference between the media at that section.

2. Each element of a moving medium involved in heat exchange experiences a change in temperature along the direction of flow proportional to its rate of heat dissipation or absorption.

We divide the several types of heat exchangers into two broad categories, *tubular* and *compact core*.

In *tubular* heat exchangers two moving fluids, one or both of which may be pumped through tubes, exchange heat. Heat is transferred by forced convection from the hotter fluid to the walls separating the fluids; by conduction through these walls; and by forced convection from the walls to the colder fluid.

A basic form of tubular heat exchanger is the single-pass type shown in Figure 4.6. If the two heat transfer fluids are flowing in the same direction, the exchanger is termed *parallel flow*; if the two fluids are traveling in opposite

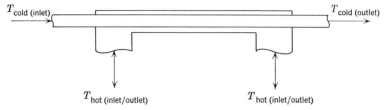

Figure 4.6 Schematic of single-pass heat exchanger.

directions, the device is called *counterflow*. The temperature difference between the fluids is not constant along the length of the exchanger; the over-all steady-state heat transfer rate is computed by resolution of the energy balance equations for any section of the exchanger.

Also in the tubular category there are *crossflow* exchangers, in which the two heat transfer fluids flow past one another at right angles. There are several arrangements of these devices. They differ in the conditions of their fluids: whether, and in what combination, they are mixed or unmixed. Figure 4.7 shows a crossflow exchanger with one fluid mixed, the other unmixed. Note that the fluid flowing through the tubes, which is unmixed, does not leave the exchanger at a uniform temperature; the temperature of the mixed fluid, however, is uniform at any cross section and varies only in the direction of flow.

In addition, there are multiple-pass shell and tube exchanges, such as the one shown schematically in Figure 4.8. Baffles in the shell route a mixed fluid over tubes carrying an unmixed fluid. Such exchangers may be found with any number of shells and with any multiple of two passes per shell.

A *compact core* heat exchanger called a *cold plate* is affixed to a heat-dissipating body as in Figure 4.9. The core is fitted with extended surface

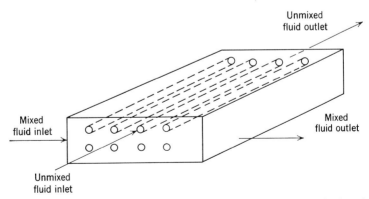

Figure 4.7 Schematic of crossflow heat exchanger with one fluid mixed and the other unmixed.

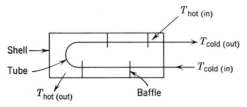

Figure 4.8 Schematic of shell and tube heat exchanger.

elements for forced-convection heat transfer to a fluid pumped past them. Heat flow from a point on the cooled surface of the body to the heat transfer fluid proceeds across the intersurface between body and cold plate, usually mainly by conduction; by conduction through the cold plate contact wall and extended surface elements; and by forced convection from the cold plate walls and extended surface elements to the heat transfer fluid.

The basic heat exchanger relations are now outlined. They are useful when one is reading manufacturers' manuals, in which heat exchangers are sized according to values of parameters (including pressure drop of fluid flowing through the device, the determination of which leads to evaluation of necessary auxiliary pumping equipment) given by empirical data.

We consider the temperature distribution in a single-pass parallel-flow heat exchanger (Figure 4.10). The equations describing the steady-state energy balance over an element of area dA are, with negligible heat losses from the exchanger and constant fluid flow rates,

$$dq = U(T_h - T_c)\,dA, \tag{4.36}$$

$$dq = -C_h\,dT_h = C_c\,dT_c, \tag{4.37}$$

where dq is the amount of heat exchanged, U is the over-all thermal conductance between the hot and cold fluids (and is constant over dA), and C_h and C_c are the thermal capacities of the hot and cold fluids, respectively (these capacities are constant).

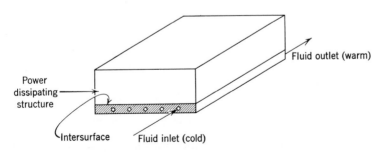

Figure 4.9 Use of a cold plate.

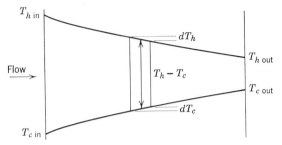

Figure 4.10   Temperature profile for a single-pass parallel flow heat exchanger.

The relationship that describes the total amount of heat gained by the cold fluid, which is the heat exchanged or lost by the hot fluid q, is,

$$C_h[T_{h(\text{in})} - T_{h(\text{out})}] = C_c[T_{c(\text{out})} - T_{c(\text{in})}] = q. \tag{4.38}$$

Combining (4.36) and (4.37),

$$\frac{d(T_h - T_c)}{(T_h - T_c)} = -\left(\frac{1}{C_h} + \frac{1}{C_c}\right) U \, dA. \tag{4.39}$$

Integration between the heat exchanger inlet and outlet, and thus over the total exchanger area, gives

$$\int_{T\text{in}}^{T\text{out}} \frac{d(T_h - T_c)}{T_n - T_c} = -\left(\frac{1}{C_h} + \frac{1}{C_c}\right) \int_0^{A\text{total}} U \, dA. \tag{4.40}$$

Thus

$$\ln\left(\frac{\Delta T_{\text{out}}}{\Delta T_{\text{in}}}\right) = -\left(\frac{1}{C_h} + \frac{1}{C_c}\right) UA. \tag{4.41}$$

Substituting (4.38),

$$\ln\left(\frac{\Delta T_{\text{out}}}{\Delta T_{\text{in}}}\right) = -\left[T_{h(\text{in})} - T_{h(\text{out})} + T_{c(\text{out})} - T_{c(\text{in})}\right]\frac{UA}{q}.$$

Rearranging,

$$q = \frac{\Delta T_{\text{out}} - \Delta T_{\text{in}}}{\ln(\Delta T_{\text{out}}/\Delta T_{\text{in}})} UA = \frac{\Delta T_{\text{in}} - \Delta T_{\text{out}}}{\ln(\Delta T_{\text{in}}/\Delta T_{\text{out}})} UA \tag{4.42}$$

or

$$q = \frac{T_{h(\text{in})} - T_{c(\text{in})} - T_{h(\text{out})} + T_{c(\text{out})}}{\ln\{[T_{h(\text{in})} - T_{c(\text{in})}]/[T_{h(\text{out})} - T_{c(\text{out})}]\}} UA;$$

$(\Delta T_{\text{in}} - \Delta T_{\text{out}})/\ln(\Delta T_{\text{in}}/\Delta T_{\text{out}})$ is called the logarithmic mean temperature, difference and henceforth will be denoted by $\overline{\Delta T_M}$.

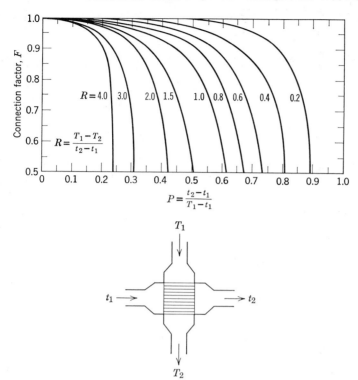

Figure 4.11 Correction-factor plot for single-pass crossflow exchanger, one fluid mixed, other unmixed. (By permission of the American Society of Mechanical Engineers.)

In a counterflow heat exchanger the log mean temperature difference is expressed as

$$\overline{\Delta T_M} = \frac{[T_{h(out)} - T_{c(in)}] - [T_{h(in)} - T_{c(out)}]}{\ln\{[T_{h(in)} - T_{c(out)}]/[T_{h(out)} - T_{c(in)}]\}}. \quad (4.43)$$

For crossflow heat exchangers, the log mean temperature difference is modified by a correction factor F, supplied by Bowman, Mueller, and Nagle [3], for example. Those authors point out that for identical inlet and outlet temperatures

$$\Delta T_M(\text{counterflow}) > \Delta T_M(\text{crossflow}) > \Delta T_M(\text{parallel flow}).$$

They present correction-factor plots for single- and two-pass crossflow exchangers, with shell and tube fluids in various mixed and unmixed combinations (Figures 4.11 through 4.14 are examples). They also present correction-factor plots for exchangers with various numbers of shell passes and any even multiple of tube passes.

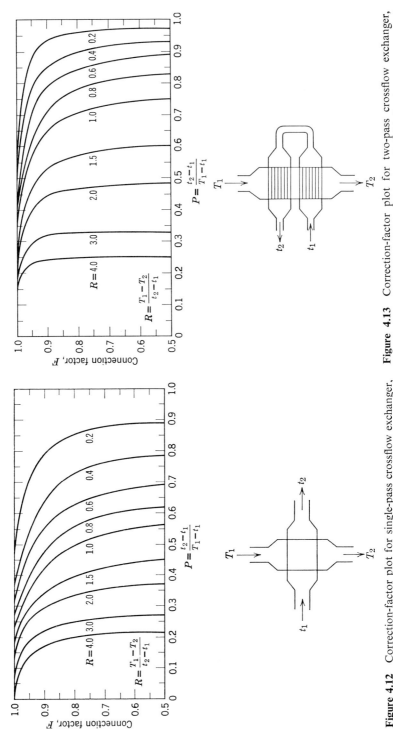

Figure 4.12 Correction-factor plot for single-pass crossflow exchanger, both fluids mixed. (By permission of the American Society of Mechanical Engineers.)

Figure 4.13 Correction-factor plot for two-pass crossflow exchanger, shell fluid mixed, tube fluid unmixed (shell fluid flowing across second and first passes in series). (By permission of the American Society of Mechanical Engineers.)

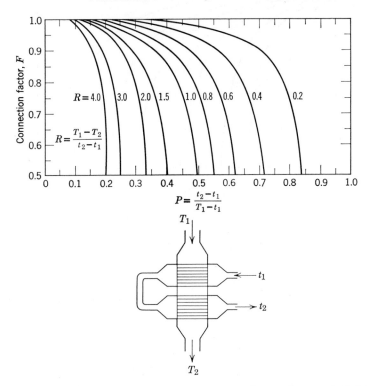

Figure 4.14 Correction-factor plot for two-pass crossflow exchanger, shell fluid mixed, tube fluid unmixed (shell fluid flowing across first and second pass in series). (By permission of the American Society of Mechanical Engineers.)

In the plots presented by Bowman et al. (Figures 4.15 though 4.17 are samples) the correction factor F is plotted against the dimensionless quantity $P = \Delta T_c / [T_{h(in)} - T_{c(in)}]$ for various magnitudes of the dimensionless quantity $R = \Delta T_h / \Delta T_c$. In order to avoid a trial-and-error analysis both the fluid outlet and the fluid inlet temperatures must be known.

A system for rating heat exchangers, without the necessity of knowing the outlet temperatures of the heat transfer fluids, is now developed. A counterflow heat exchanger is considered, with the assumptions and nomenclature employed in the preceding section. The equations describing the energy balance over an element of area dA are

$$dq = U(T_h - T_c)\, dA, \tag{4.44}$$

$$dq = C_h\, dT_h = C_c\, dT_c. \tag{4.45}$$

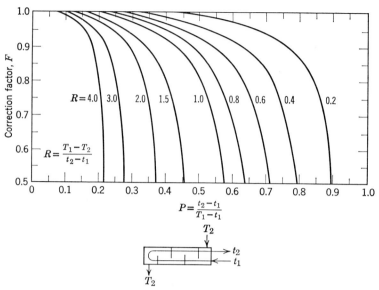

Figure 4.15 Correction-factor plot for exchanger with one shell pass and two, four, or any multiple of tube passes. (By permission of the American Society of Mechanical Engineers.)

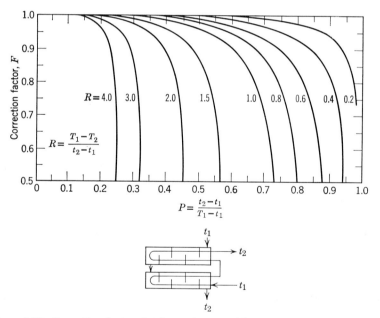

Figure 4.16 Correction-factor plot for exchanger with two shell passes, and four, eight, or any multiple of tube passes. (By permission of the American Society of Mechanical Engineers.)

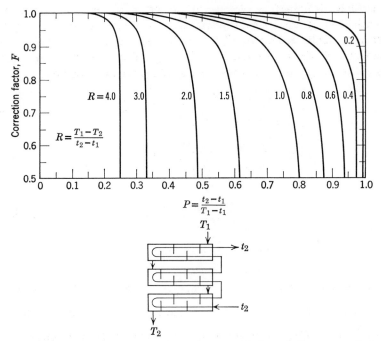

Figure 4.17 Correction-factor plot for exchanger with three shell passes, and six, twelve, or any multiple of tube passes. (By permission of the American Society of Mechanical Engineers.)

From (4.45)

$$dg\left(\frac{1}{C_h} - \frac{1}{C_c}\right) = dT_h - dT_c = d(T_h - T_c). \tag{4.46}$$

Combining (4.35) and (4.45),

$$\frac{U\,dA}{C_h}\left(1 - \frac{C_h}{C_c}\right) = \frac{d(T_h - T_c)}{(T_h - T_c)}. \tag{4.47}$$

Integrating between the ends of the exchanger, we have

$$\frac{UA}{C_h}\left(1 - \frac{C_h}{C_c}\right) = \ln\left[\frac{T_{h(\text{in})} - T_{c(\text{out})}}{T_{h(\text{out})} - T_{c(\text{in})}}\right] \tag{4.48}$$

or

$$\exp -\left(1 - \frac{C_h}{C_c}\right)\frac{UA}{C_h} = \left[\frac{T_{h(\text{out})} - T_{c(\text{in})}}{T_{h(\text{in})} - T_{c(\text{out})}}\right]. \tag{4.49}$$

In order to eliminate the outlet temperatures from the preceding equation, a dimensionless parameter, the heat exchanger effectiveness ϵ, is introduced.

This parameter is defined as the ratio of the actual rate of heat transfer in a given exchanger to the thermodynamically maximum possible rate. (The transfer area would be infinite.) Thus, if the capacity of the colder fluid is less than that of the hotter fluid, $T_{c(\text{out})} = T_{h(\text{in})}$; if the capacity of the hotter fluid is lower, $T_{h(\text{out})} = T_{c(\text{in})}$. These relationships are expressed by

$$\epsilon = \frac{C_h[T_{h(\text{in})} - T_{h(\text{out})}]}{C_{\text{min}}[T_{h(\text{in})} - T_{c(\text{in})}]}, \quad \text{if } C_c < C_h, \tag{4.50}$$

$$\epsilon = \frac{C_c[T_{c(\text{out})} - T_{c(\text{in})}]}{C_{\text{min}}[T_{h(\text{in})} - T_{c(\text{in})}]}, \quad \text{if } C_h < C_c. \tag{4.51}$$

Also

$$\epsilon = \frac{T_{c(\text{out})} - T_{c(\text{in})}}{T_{h(\text{in})} - T_{c(\text{in})}}, \quad \text{if } C_c < C_h, \tag{4.52}$$

$$\epsilon = \frac{T_{h(\text{in})} - T_{h(\text{out})}}{T_{h(\text{in})} - T_{c(\text{in})}}, \quad \text{if } C_h < C_c. \tag{4.53}$$

A parameter for sizing the heat exchanger, the number of transfer units (NTU), equal to $(1/C_{\text{min}}) \int_0^A U \, dA$, is introduced. For the exchanger that we are considering, $C_h < C_c$, so that $UA/C_h = \text{NTU}^*$ and the effectiveness is given by (4.53). Rearranging the latter,

$$T_{h(\text{out})} = \epsilon(T_{c(\text{in})} - T_{h(\text{in})}) + T_{h(\text{in})}. \tag{4.54}$$

From the total fluid enthalpy changes,

$$T_{c(\text{out})} = T_{c(\text{in})} + \frac{C_h}{C_c}(T_{h(\text{in})} - T_{h(\text{out})}) \tag{4.55}$$

Substituting the definition of effectiveness from (4.53),

$$T_{c(\text{out})} = T_{c(\text{in})} + \frac{C_h}{C_c}\epsilon(T_{h(\text{in})} - T_{c(\text{in})}). \tag{4.56}$$

Finally, substituting (4.54) and (4.56) into (4.49), canceling the common term, and rearranging, we have

$$\epsilon = \frac{1 - \exp\left[-NTU(1 - C_h/C_c)\right]}{1 - C_h/C_c \exp\left[-NTU(1 - C_h/C_c)\right]}. \tag{4.57}$$

Kays and London [11] have provided graphs to illustrate this result as well as graphs that show the relationships between ϵ, NTU, and C_h/C_c for

---

* U is invariant throughout the exchanger.

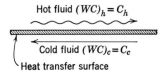

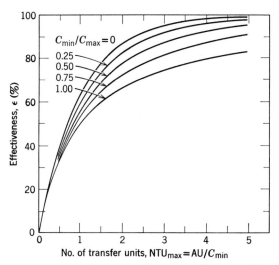

Figure 4.18 Counterflow exchanger performance. (By permission of McGraw-Hill Book Co.)

parallel flow heat exchangers and for various styles of crossflow exchangers. Figures 4.18 through 4.21 are examples.

In a finned cold plate core the heat-transfer area swept by the coolant is not perfectly efficient due to the temperature gradient along the fins and, if the fins extend the width of the core, the further temperature gradient along the cold-side wall. The over-all fin efficiency is expressed in the equation,

$$\eta_0 \, ds = ds_h + \eta_f \, ds_f + \eta_c \, ds_c, \qquad (4.58)$$

where η_0 = the over-all efficiency of the heat transfer surface of the exchanger core,

ds = the area swept by the coolant,

ds_h = the hot-side core wall-coolant intersurface,

η_f = the fin efficiency,

ds_f = the fin-coolant intersurface,

η_c = the cold-side core wall efficiency,

ds_c = the cold-side core wall-coolant intersurface.

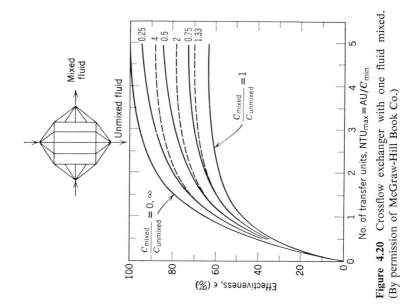

Figure 4.20 Crossflow exchanger with one fluid mixed. (By permission of McGraw-Hill Book Co.)

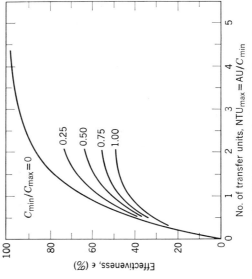

Figure 4.19 Parallel-flow exchanger performance. (By permission of McGraw-Hill Book Co.)

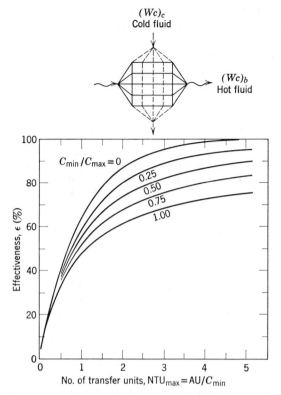

Figure 4.21 Crossflow exchanger with fluids unmixed. (By permission of McGraw-Hill Book Co.)

Noting that $ds_h = ds - ds_f - ds_c$, and after some manipulation,

$$\eta_0 = 1 - (1 - \eta_f)\frac{ds_f}{ds} - (1 - \eta_c)\frac{ds_c}{ds}. \tag{4.59}$$

Kraus [13] illustrates fin and cold-side core wall efficiencies for the case of plain plate fins and fin thickness equal to core wall thickness.

Kays and London [11] discuss several types of plate fins (plain plates, plates with louverlike projections, and plain pins) and show performance data (for air flow; heat transfer coefficients and friction factors may be obtained therefrom) for selected surface and core geometries. Their conclusions about these data are as follows:

·The performance of plain fins is similar to that of long circular tubes.

·Louvered fins break up the thermal boundary layer and provide higher heat transfer than do plain fins under the same flow conditions. Generally, the more frequent the thermal boundary layer interruption the higher the film coefficient h is; the friction factor f is higher also. However, performance is better.

•A thin boundary layer is maintained on *pin fins*. The heat transfer coefficient is high, as is the friction factor, but the performance rating offsets the latter effect.

REFERENCES

[1] Aron, W., and G. Colombo, "Controlling Factors of Thermal Conductance Across Bolted Joints in Vacuum,' *ASME Paper* 63-SA-196.

[2] Barzelay, M. E., K. N. Tong, and G. F. Holloway, "Effect of Pressure on Thermal Conductance of Contact Joints," *NACA Tech. Note* 3295.

[3] Bowman, R. A., A. E. Mueller, and W. M. Nagle, *Trans. ASME*, **62**, 283–294 (1940).

[4] Dittus, F. W., and L. M. K. Boelter, *Univ. Calif. Pub. Eng.* 2, p. 443, 1930.

[5] Fairbanks, D. R., "Parameters for Rating Heat Transfer Fluids," *Proc. Natl. Conf. Aeronautical Electronics*, 1958.

[6] Fenech, H., and W. M. Rohsenow, "Prediction of Thermal Conductance of Metallic Surfaces in Contact," *J. Heat Transfer*, **85** (February, 1963).

[7] Gardner, K. A., "Efficiency of Extended Surfaces," *Trans. ASME*, **67**, 621–631 (1945).

[8] Henry, J. J., and H. Fenech, "The Use of Analog Computers for Determining Surface Parameters Required for Prediction of Thermal Contact Conductance," *J. Heat Transfer*, **86** (November, 1964).

[9] Hunsaker, J. C., and B. G. Rightmire, *Engineering Applications of Fluids Mechanics*, McGraw-Hill, New York, 1947.

[10] Katz, L., "Heat Transfer Design for Electronic Equipment," *Electromech. Design*, October, November, December, 1963.

[11] Kays, W. M., and A. L. London, *Compact Heat Exchangers* (2nd ed.), McGraw-Hill, New York, 1964.

[12] Kraus, A. D., *Cooling Electronic Equipment*, Prentice-Hall Englewood Cliffs, N.J, 1965.

[13] Kraus, A. D., *Extended Surfaces*, Spartan Books (Books, Inc.), New York, 1967.

[14] Kreith, F., *Principles of Heat Transfer*, International Textbook, Scranton, Pa., 1958.

[15] *Proc., Natl. Electronic Packaging and Production Conf.*, Industrial and Scientific Conference Management, Chicago.

[16] Sieder, E. N., and G. E. Tate," Heat Transfer and Pressure Drop of Liquids in Tube." *Ind. Eng. Chem.*, **28**, 1429–1435 (1936).

[17] Stubstad, W. R., "Measurements of Thermal Contact Conductance in Vacuum," *ASME Paper* 63-WA-160.

[18] Welsh, J. P., "Design Manual of Cooling Electronic Equipment," *Bureau Ships Rept.* HF-845-D-9.

5

Temperature Control:
Methods, Analysis, Systems

5.1 INTRODUCTION

This chapter introduces the methods used to control the temperatures of masses contained within structures and the analytical and practical techniques for achieving such control. The chapter begins with some basic definitions, followed by descriptions of basic methods of temperature control, a presentation of several types of control systems, and a review of certain aspects of their operation and arrangement of their components. The prime analytical techniques for designing a temperature control system and for predicting and improving its performance are then presented. Finally, an example that illustrates the performance of a temperature-controlled mass is discussed.

5.2 DEFINITIONS

Thermal design may be defined as the analytical and practical methods used to regulate rates of heat transport in a structure. Important factors in the thermal design of a structure include the materials, the geometry of the structure, the construction techniques, the arrangement of the masses to be controlled and of the associated temperature control equipment within the structure, the type of environment by which the structure is surrounded, and the temperature and pressure of that environment.

Temperature control is the method by which one or more masses are held within a certain temperature range. If a mass is controlled at a particular temperature level, that level is called the *control point*.

The *control cycle* is the temperature excursion of a controlled mass about the control point when the structure in which the mass is contained is at equilibrium.

The *set point* is the temperature at which the sensing element of the system controller performs its regulating or switching function.

Thermal lag is that condition whereby a change in the rate of heat dissipated at one point in a structure is felt at other points after delays in time.

A *temperature control system* is the physical and mathematical combination of one or more temperature-controlled masses, the structure in which they are contained, the disturbances to which they are subjected, and the electrical and mechanical components used to regulate their temperatures.

5.3 BASIC METHODS OF TEMPERATURE CONTROL

There are, in general, three approaches to controlling the temperatures of masses mounted in structures:

1. The thermal resistance between a heat source and a heat sink is controlled; the control can be accomplished by either a permanent or a time-varying change for any combination of conduction, convection, or radiation heat transfer.

2. The heat dissipation at a controlled mass or on a thermal path between the controlled mass and its heat sink is regulated, either by a permanent change or in a continuously or discontinuously varying way.

3. The temperature or the heat absorption capacity of a heat sink is controlled. (The heat capacitance of the controlled mass can be changed also.)

The basic approaches may be used alone or in any combination. They are interrelated by the equation $qR = \Delta T$, where, if ΔT is the temperature difference between a mass and its heat sink and if R is the thermal resistance to heat flowing between them, then q is the rate of heat dissipated at the controlled mass. If one of the items in the equation varies, one or both of the others must vary also. Time-variable adjustments in thermal resistance, in power dissipation, or in heat sink temperature or absorption capacity usually are triggered automatically by temperature-sensing devices.

In Figure 5.1 power generated at a controlled mass is constant and thermal resistance between the mass and its heat sink is controlled in order to reduce to some desired value the difference between the set-point temperature at the control element and the indicated temperature at the controlled mass. This temperature difference determines the thermal resistance that sets the temperature potential appropriate for the rate of heat transferred between the controlled mass and its heat sink.

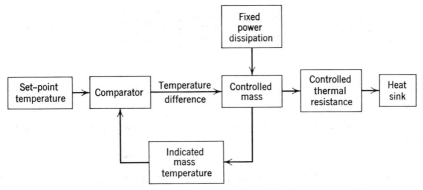

Figure 5.1 Temperature control by thermal resistance control.

In Figure 5.2 the value of thermal resistance between the controlled mass and its heat sink is constant and the amount of power dissipated at the controlled mass or between the controlled mass and its heat sink is regulated by the set-point to indicated temperature difference so that the temperature potential between the two locations is appropriate for the given value of thermal resistance.

Figure 5.3 indicates how the two control schemes are combined in cases where it is necessary to extend the range of control for wide variations in heat sink (or environment) conditions. In a given structure, for example, there may be limits on the possible ranges of values of thermal resistance and of amounts of control power. Only a combination of resistance and power controls will guarantee the proper temperature potential between the controlled mass and its heat sink over the complete range of environmental temperatures. Resistance change could provide the proper potential for hot heat sink conditions, while added power dissipation could take care of cold extremes.

Passive temperature control is the control method which, either on a permanent or on a time-variable basis, changes thermal resistance without

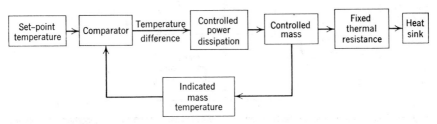

Figure 5.2 Temperature control by power dissipation control.

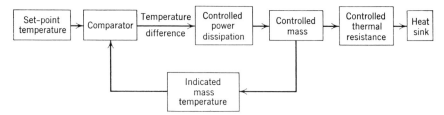

Figure 5.3 Temperature control by a combination of power dissipation and thermal resistance control.

expending mechanical or electrical energy. Permanent passive control may be employed in a situation such as that of Figure 5.4, where the possible temperature excursion of a controlled mass exceeds the expected steady-state temperature range of its heat sink, and the low steady-state temperature limit of the mass is higher than that of the sink. A structural change affecting a critical thermal barrier could satisfy such passive temperature control requirements. Examples of such a change are the use of mounts to decrease thermal contact between abutting surfaces, the employment of additional fasteners or filler materials to increase thermal contact between abutting surfaces, the application of certain surface finishes to alter the thermal resistance between surfaces involved in radiant heat transfer, the alteration of orientations of surfaces being cooled or heated by convection, the variation of the amount of area available for convection or radiation, and the modification of the view factor between surfaces involved in radiant heat transmission.

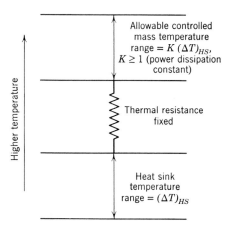

Figure 5.4 Conditions permitting passive temperature control by permanent thermal resistance change.

As an example of the efficacy of changing the thermal resistance between two surfaces involved in radiant heat transfer, consider the effect of placing a wall of negligible thickness to block completely one surface from the other, as in Figure 5.5. For equal heat dissipation, $q_I = q_{II}$, note that thermal resistance has doubled from case I to case II and that $(T_1 - T_2)$ in case II is double $(T_1 - T_2)$ in case I.

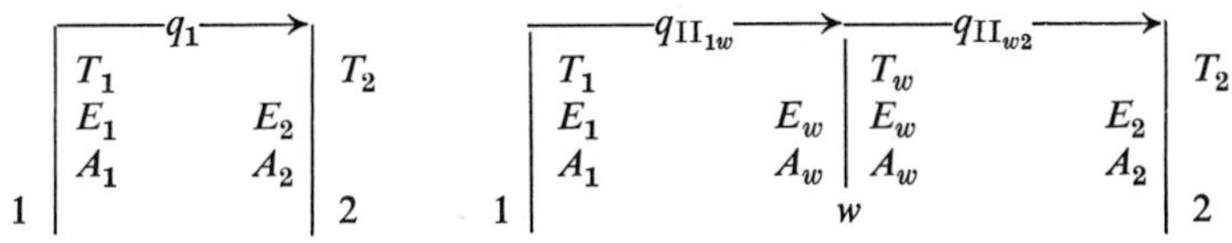

Case I: No interference between surfaces 1 and 2. Thermal emissivities E_1 and $E_2 = 1$; areas are parallel and $= 1$.

Case II: A wall of zero thickness is interposed between surfaces 1 and 2. All thermal emissivities $= 1$; areas are parallel and $= 1$.

$$E = \left[\frac{1}{E_1} + \frac{1}{E_2} - 1\right]^{-1} = 1. \qquad E_{1w} = \left[\frac{1}{E_1} + \frac{1}{E_w} - 1\right]^{-1} = 1;$$

$$E_{w2} = \left[\frac{1}{E_w} + \frac{1}{E_2} - 1\right]^{-1} = 1.$$

For simplicity, T_1 and T_2 are given nearly equal.

$q_I = 4\sigma T_1{}^3(T_1 - T_2).$

$q_{II_{1w}} = 4\sigma T_1{}^3(T_1 - T_w);$
$q_{II_{w2}} = 4\sigma T_w{}^3(T_w - T_2).$
At steady state, $q_{II_{1w}} = q_{II_{w2}}$
$T_1{}^3 \cong T_w{}^3$, as given
By addition,
$q_{II} = 2\sigma T_1{}^3(T_1 - T_2).$

Let $4\sigma T_1{}^3 = R^{-1}.$

$q_I R = (T_1 - T_2)$
$2q_{II} R = (T_1 - T_2).$

Figure 5.5 Change in radiation thermal resistance caused by interposing between the original surfaces an intermediate body.

Active temperature control is the method for regulating temperature by the time-variable control of thermal resistance, heat dissipation, or heat absorption with the expenditure of energy. Active or passive time-variable temperature control is required if the steady-state temperature range of a heat sink exceeds that of a controlled mass, as in Figure 5.6, or if oscillations in heat sink temperatures cause excessive oscillations in the uncontrolled mass's temperatures. Thus, for example, to control the temperature of a mass expending a constant level of power, thermal resistance between the mass and its heat sink would be lowered if heat sink temperatures were close to those of the sensitive mass and would be raised if the temperature potential were greater.

As a general rule, the designer may find it most convenient to bring about a variable thermal resistance change when he forces a particular mode of heat transfer to take precedence over others. He then need control only the value of thermal resistance which is relevant to that specific mode. Such control could be accomplished, for example, by erecting the thermal barrier

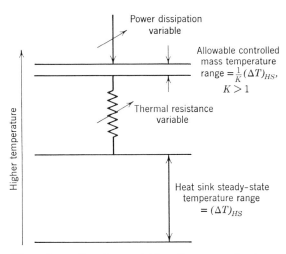

Figure 5.6 Conditions demanding time-variable active or passive temperature control.

of Figure 5.5 and placing a gate in the barrier. The gate could be a fluid-circulating device (actively actuated) for regulating forced convection or simply an opening for controlling natural convection (passively actuated as described in Section 8.8). The gate would be opened automatically when a low resistance was called for and closed when a high resistance was required.

As mentioned below, active temperature control of the mass of Figure 5.6 may be accomplished by installing a heater on the mass or between the mass and its heat sink and controlling the power dissipation of the heater. The amount of change of heater power dissipation required when there is a change in heat sink temperature is a function of the thermal resistance between heater location and heat sink: the higher the resistance, the lower the required power change. Also, the range of heat sink temperatures over which the mass of Figure 5.6 can be controlled may be extended if both the thermal resistance between the mass and the heat sink and the power dissipation of an installed heater can be regulated. The combination of increased heater power dissipation and increased thermal resistance extends

The situation in Figure 5.6, whereby a time-variable control scheme is necessary to hold the controlled mass within its possible temperature range, may be altered if the heat sink temperature oscillates between the limits T_1 and T_2 so that T_1 and T_2 are not steady-state limits. For despite the fact that the allowable temperature range of the controlled mass is exceeded by the limits of the heat sink temperature variation, time-variable temperature control of the mass is not required if there is sufficient attenuation of the sink temperature oscillations at the mass. Attenuation is caused by the combination of the weight of the controlled body, its specific heat, and the magnitude of thermal resistance between it and its heat sink. Adding weight to the controlled mass or changing the material of the mass from one with a relatively low value of specific heat to one with a relatively high value reduces the temperature oscillation at the mass for a given oscillation at its heat sink. Also, if the control point level can be raised, the additional thermal resistance necessary to dissipate power from the controlled mass to its heat sink will lower the temperature oscillations of the mass.

Consider a mass of heat capacity C_m, which is dissipating power at a rate q_m and is connected by thermal resistance R_{ms} to its heat sink. The heat sink temperature T_s oscillates sinusoidally with amplitude t_0 about a level T_{s0}. T_s is given by

$$T_s = T_{s0} + t_0 \sin \omega\theta \tag{5.1}$$

The energy balance for the mass at temperature T_m is given by

$$q_m - \frac{T_m - T_s}{R_{ms}} = C_m \frac{dT_m}{d\theta}. \tag{5.2}$$

Substituting (5.1) into (5.2) and transposing, we have

$$q_m R_{ms} + t_0 \sin \omega\theta + T_{s0} = C_m R_{ms} \frac{dT_m}{d\theta} + T_m. \tag{5.3}$$

The following steady-state solution for T_m is assumed:

$$T_{mss} = A \sin \omega\theta + B \cos \omega\theta + q_m R_{ms} + T_{s0}. \tag{5.4}$$

Substitution of (5.4) into (5.3) yields

$$t_0 \sin \omega\theta = C_m T_{ms}(A\omega \cos \omega\theta - B\omega \sin \omega\theta) + A \sin \omega\theta + B \cos \omega\theta. \tag{5.5}$$

Equating coefficients of like terms gives, eventually,

$$A = \frac{t_0}{1 + (C_m R_{ms}\omega)^2} ;$$

$$B = -\frac{t_0 C_m R_{ms}\omega}{1 + (C_m R_{ms}\omega)^2}. \tag{5.6}$$

Therefore

$$T_m = \frac{t_0}{[1 + (C_m R_{ms}\omega)^2]^{1/2}} (\sin \omega\theta - \tan^{-1} C_m R_{ms} \omega) + q_m R_{ms} + T_{s0}. \tag{5.7}$$

The variation in T_m is given by

$$\Delta T_m = \pm \frac{t_0}{\sqrt{1 + (C_m R_{ms}\omega)^2}} \tag{5.8}$$

Thus the larger the magnitudes of C_m and R_{ms}, the smaller will be the amplitude of the oscillation of T_m for a given amplitude of oscillation at the heat sink.

the lower limit of heat sink temperatures; similarly, with the heater off and thermal resistance reduced, the upper heat sink temperature limit is extended.

5.4 BASIC RELATIONS FOR THERMAL DESIGN FOR TIME-VARIABLE TEMPERATURE-CONTROL SYSTEMS

In Figure 5.7, a temperature-sensitive mass, m, is thermally connected to a heat sink which varies in steady-state temperature from T_1 to T_2, where $T_1 > T_2$. If the thermal resistance between the mass and the heat sink can range from R_1 to R_2, where $R_1 < R_2$, and where the subscript indicates the heat sink temperature with which that value of resistance is associated,

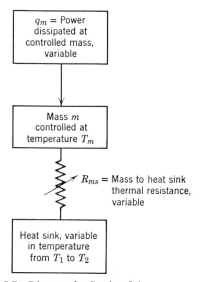

Figure 5.7 Diagram for Section 5.4.

the limits of power q_m dissipated at the mass and required to maintain it at temperature T_m are given by the equations

$$q_{m1} = \frac{T_m - T_1}{R_1} \tag{5.9}$$

and

$$q_{m2} = \frac{T_m - T_2}{R_2}, \tag{5.10}$$

where q_m is partly the basic level of heat dissipated at the sensitive mass, q_{mb}, partly temperature control power, and partly any power used for effecting a value of thermal resistance. (In this discussion, all power is dissipated at the controlled mass.)

Temperature control of mass m, over the range of heat sink steady-state temperatures T_1 to T_2 $(T_1 > T_2)$, is accomplished with minimum, constant power, equal to the basic power level, q_{mb}, if the thermal resistance between the mass and the heat sink can be varied from R_1 to R_2 with no expenditure of power and if R_1 and R_2 are given by

$$R_1 = \frac{q_{mb}}{T_m - T_1} \tag{5.11}$$

and

$$R_2 = \frac{q_{mb}}{T_m - T_2}. \tag{5.12}$$

The ratio of resistances R_1 and R_2 is

$$\left(\frac{R_1}{R_2}\right)_{q_{mb}} = \frac{T_m - T_1}{T_m - T_2}. \tag{5.13}$$

The difference between R_1 and R_2 is

$$(R_2 - R_1)_{q_{mb}} = \frac{T_1 R_2 - T_2 R_1}{T_1 - T_2}. \tag{5.14}$$

The variation of T_m with q_{mb} is linear:

$$\frac{dT_m}{dq_{mb}} = \frac{T_1 R_2 - T_2 R_1}{T_1 - T_2}. \tag{5.15}$$

The limits of power, q_1 and q_2, required for maintaining mass m at temperature T_m, over the range of heat sink temperatures T_1 to T_2 $(T_1 > T_2)$, with no variation in thermal resistance between the mass and heat sink, R_c, are given by

$$q_1 = \frac{T_m - T_1}{R_c} \tag{5.16}$$

and

$$q_2 = \frac{T_m - T_2}{R_c}. \tag{5.17}$$

The ratio of the power limits is

$$\left(\frac{q_1}{q_2}\right)_{R_c} = \frac{T_m - T_1}{T_m - T_2}. \tag{5.18}$$

The difference between power limits is

$$(q_2 - q_1)_{R_c} = \frac{T_1 - T_2}{R_c}. \tag{5.19}$$

The variation of T_m with R_c is linear:

$$\frac{dT_m}{dR_c} = \frac{T_1 q_2 - T_2 q_1}{T_1 - T_2}. \tag{5.20}$$

5.5 COMMANDING COMPONENTS OF CONTROL SYSTEMS; ON-OFF AND PROPORTIONAL CONTROL

Examples of commanding components in a temperature control system where heater power is regulated are the thermostat and the resistance-element sensor. Desired temperature ranges and indicated temperatures are set and sensed within the single thermostatic component. The control provided by this device is discontinuous, or ON-OFF, and is shown in Figure 5.8. When

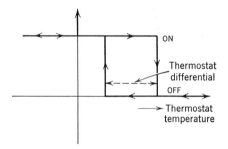

Figure 5.8   Control action with thermostat: ON-OFF.

the temperature of the thermostat has dropped to a particular level, the electric heater which the device controls is activated; when the thermostat temperature has increased to a higher, set level, the electric heater is deactivated. At any temperature below the ON value, the control power remains on; at any temperature above the OFF value, the control power stays off. The difference between these ON and OFF temperatures is called the instrument's differential. The steady-state value of power commanded by the switch is the integrated average amount of power dissipated over a given time period while the controlled mass's temperature oscillates about an equilibrium value. In the control range of the thermostat (i.e., between the temperature limits at which the thermostat turns the heater on or off), during the ON time there is a rise in temperature of the switch caused by the step change in power which it has commanded. During the OFF time there is a decay in temperature, effected by removal of the step change in power. The swiftness of the temperature rise is dependent on the thermal location,* relative to the switch, of the commanded power, the amount of that power,

* *Thermal location* refers to thermal resistance and thermal capacitance.

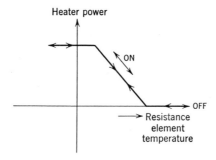

Figure 5.9 Control action with resistance element: Proportional.

and the thermal capacitance and method of mounting of the switch. Similarly, the speed of switch temperature decay depends on the thermal location of the heat sink of the device and on the thermal capacitance of its element.

The resistance element is generally employed as part of the commanding component in a proportional control circuit. Proportional control action is shown in Figure 5.9. In this type of circuit the amount of control power expended is proportional to the amount of displacement of the actual temperature of the commanding element from the comparator component's set point. In Figure 5.10 a resistance element appears as a leg of a Wheatstone bridge circuit (see Chapter 6) whose signal regulates the amplitude of control power by varying the ratio of ON to OFF time during a base reference cycle.

Discontinuous control with a multiposition switch as the commanding element tends toward proportional control as the number of switching points

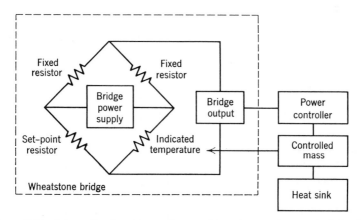

Figure 5.10 Schematic of resistance-element-driven temperature control circuit.

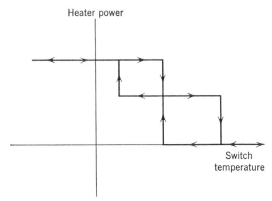

Figure 5.11   Control action with a three-position switch.

is increased. Figure 5.11 illustrates discontinuous control action with a three-position switch.

5.6   ARRANGING THE ELEMENTS OF A TEMPERATURE CONTROL SYSTEM

The arrangement of the elements of a temperature control system and the thermal lags between them will (in the absence of feedback compensation) dictate the performance of the system. For example, the relative positions of a heater, an ON-OFF temperature controller, and a controlled mass determine the amplitudes of the mass's temperature excursions during control cycles. The arrangement of the elements is also crucial to the maintenance of control when there are variations in the structure's environment. The location of an element which must control the temperatures of several masses simultaneously is equally critical. In the following discussion, the elements of the temperature control system whose locations are under consideration are a controlled mass, an ON-OFF controller, and a small heater.

Thus, for example, a change in the rate of heat dissipated by a control heater will not be felt immediately by a distant controlling element and a remote-controlled mass to which the heat must be transferred by conduction or convection. The temperature excursions of the latter two elements will be different in magnitude and phase from that of the heater, as in Figure 5.12 and as described by the calculation in Section 5.3. Furthermore, if the controlling element and the temperature indicator of the controlled mass are separated, the controller set point and the mass's control point will be displaced. As two elements transferring heat by conduction or convection are moved closer together, the thermal lag between them will be smaller and their temperature levels and excursions will become more coincident.

Also, if the conduction or convection heat transfer medium between two remote elements is changed from one with a relatively low value of thermal diffusivity to one with a higher value, thermal lag between the elements will be reduced.

As a controlling element and a heater are moved closer and closer to a controlled mass, the system's control capabilities will be improved. As a heater is moved further and further away from a tightly coupled control element and controlled mass combination, the temperature excursions of

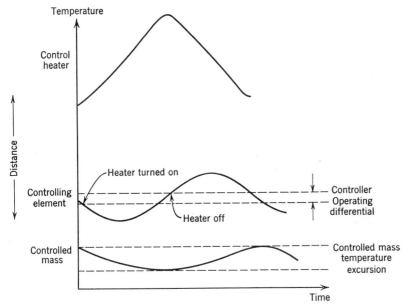

Figure 5.12   Temperature excursions of control system components.

the controlled mass during control cycles grow larger and larger. Changes in heat dissipation requirements at the controlled mass can be sensed rapidly, however. Now, if a controlling element and a heater are grouped together at a location remote from a controlled mass, the mass will undergo small temperature excursions during control cycles. Because of the large thermal lag between the controlling element and the controlled mass, however, response of the control system to thermal disturbances is poor. Placing a controlling element midway between a controlled mass and a heater may solve the problem of providing both moderate temperature excursions during control cycles and fast response to thermal disturbances.

Finally, suppose that an adjacent heater and controlled mass are remote from the controlling element. The distance between the heater-controlled mass unit and the controlling element causes a lag in response that makes for inefficient control of the temperature of the mass.

If the arrangement of the elements cannot be altered, feedback compensation, discussed in Section 5.9, should be considered to improve the situation.

5.7   THERMAL ANALOGUES

Effective thermal design in a structure is the result of appropriate construction and analysis of its thermal analogue. A structure's thermal analogue is the mathematical representation of the heat transfer paths within it, of the thermal capacities of its parts, of the heat dissipations within it, and of its environment. The analogue is one of the thermal designer's most important and practical instruments. He can use it to calculate the levels and the distribution of temperatures in a structure in a particular thermal environment, as well as to predict changes in the temperature level and distribution under changing environmental conditions; he may also use the analogue to observe how changes in the thermal and mechanical parameters of the structure or its parts cause shifts in temperatures at various points in the structure. The designer employs the analogue to determine the values of thermal resistance and of heating (or cooling) power required for controlling temperatures in a given situation. With the analogue he can compute the response of a mass to a remote thermal disturbance. He can determine then the alterations necessary to control that response.

Analogues are pertinent to all varieties of temperature control methods and situations. They can be used to make observations about the placement of heaters and sensors. An analogue is required, for example, in designing for efficient multiple mass control by manipulating the relative magnitudes of thermal resistances between the controlled masses and the sources of control heat and by proportioning control power according to these relationships.

We have observed that the equations describing the modes of heat transfer are written in a form analogous to Ohm's law. The analogous quantities are heat flow q and current I, temperature difference ΔT and voltage potential or electromotive force E, and the factors expressing thermal resistance and electrical resistance R. Thus, for steady-state conduction in the one-dimensional case, $q = KA \, \Delta T/L$ is of the form $I = E/R$ with $R = L/KA$; for convective heat flow from a surface to a fluid, $q = hA \, \Delta T$ is analogous to $I = E/R$ with $R = 1/hA$; for heat flow by radiation between nonblack surfaces $q = \sigma AF_\epsilon F_A(T_1^4 - T_2^4)$ may be rewritten $q = 4\sigma AF_\epsilon F_A T_1^3(\Delta T)$ if T_1 is approximately equal to T_2; the latter equation is of the form $I = E/R$ with $R = 1/4\sigma AF_\epsilon F_A T_1^3$.

Consider now, for example, a rod insulated on the sides and conducting heat in the x direction in the transient condition. The partial differential equation describing this situation is

$$k \frac{\partial^2 T}{\partial x^2} = \rho C_p \frac{\partial T}{\partial \theta}. \qquad (5.21)$$

This equation can be approximated by the finite difference equation 5.22, given with reference to Figure 5.13, the insulated rod divided into finite lumps:

$$(T_{n-1} + T_{n+1} - 2T_n) \frac{kA_c}{\Delta x} = \frac{dT_n}{d\theta_{\text{thermal}}} \rho C_p \Delta x A_c. \qquad (5.22)$$

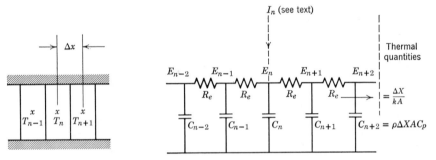

Figure 5.13 Temperature gradient in an insulated rod, and the thermal analogue representation.

In the circuit shown in Figure 5.13, the current balance at node n is given by the equation

$$\frac{E_{n-1} + E_{n+1} - 2E_n}{R_{\text{elec}}} = \frac{dE_n}{d\theta_{\text{elec}}} C_n. \qquad (5.23)$$

The two previous equations are analogous with $R_e = \Delta x / k A_c$ and $C_n = \rho \, \Delta x A_c C_p$.

The rod is simulated exactly if

$$R_e = \frac{\Delta x}{k A_c} F_R \quad \text{and} \quad C_n = \rho \, \Delta x A_c C_p F_C,$$

where F_R and F_C are arbitrary scale factors, and if a time factor, $F_\theta = \theta_{\text{elec}}/\theta_{\text{therm}} = F_R F_C$, and a voltage factor, $F_v = E/T$, are used.

Thus, the thermal functioning of a structure can be analyzed through the use of the thermal analogy to electrical networks. An analogue in the form of a resistance-capacitance network describes the thermal characteristics of the structure. Isothermal masses and volumes are rendered points of temperature potential, or nodes, and are connected along heat transfer paths by thermal resistances. The various heat dissipation sources provide current inputs or temperature potentials at these nodes. Heat added at node E_n of the analogue of Figure 5.13 is represented by the current input I_n.

The analogue is drawn in accordance with the thermal energy balances at the temperature-potential nodes. The heat capacities of the isothermal masses and volumes denoted by these nodes are represented by capacitors (whose units are Btu's or watt-hours), all grounded to the same potential. The analogue applies to both steady-state and transient conditions. A delay in the form of a time constant, whose units are (time)$^{-1}$, may be substituted for a resistance-capacitance combination.

The equations describing the analogue itself are based on an application of Kirchhoff's laws: the algebraic sum of the temperature drops around a closed loop is zero; the sum of the energies flowing into a node is equal to the sum of those flowing away from it.

In the steady-state condition, the analogue is described by a set of simultaneous linear equations. Cramer's rule, leading to the solution of such sets by taking a ratio of determinants, may be useful in some cases. Simultaneous linear equations may also be solved by the less elegant method of successive elimination of unknowns by algebraic manipulation. Indeed, Crandall [3] shows that, when the number of equations is large, the elimination process is faster than the method of determinants. (This is the case for hand computations; computer solutions of systems of equations may conveniently employ large determinants.) Another method of hand computation of solutions to simultaneous linear equations is the relaxation technique, which is discussed at length in Crandall [3, 10].

In the transient condition, the analogue is described by a system of first-order differential equations. Laplace transform solutions of simultaneous linear differential equations with constant coefficients are easily applied by the use of Cramer's rule. Computerized solutions of large systems of differential equations are accomplished by finite difference techniques.

Unfortunately, a thermal analogue cannot always be developed on a purely theoretical basis. Often, experiments must be conducted in order to determine a resistance-capacitance network model that explains the thermal operation of a structure. These experiments may consist of selectively imposing a large number of different thermal situations on the structure, such as altering the pressure and temperature of its environment, changing the amounts of heat dissipation in the structure, or forcing certain thermal resistances, external and internal to it, to take on predictable values.

It must be emphasized that, although certain experiments can yield values for the various over-all thermal resistances in an analogue, more tests and calculations may be required to determine the individual parameters operating in the relevant heat transfer mode. Without this additional work it may not be possible to predict how a variation in a particular heat transfer parameter will affect one or more resistances. Thus, if we seek to determine one or more parameters relevant to transfer in only one of the modes, the remaining transfer modes must be forced to predictable values, probably zero, by forcing the thermal conductances contributed by these modes to zero.

It is important to define the thermal resistances in an analogue completely, both by determining the over-all levels of resistance offered to heat flowing between various nodes and by assigning values to the parameters comprising these resistances. Only a complete definition illuminates ways of fixing desired rates of heat transfer.

5.8 THÉVENIN'S THEOREM

Consider an analogue network consisting of a number of thermal resistances and heat inputs. In order to determine the effect of altering any particular resistance or combination of connected resistances, or the amount of heat flowing through it, for the same temperature potential across the resistance of resistances, we employ Thévenin's theorem.*

The analogue circuit is replaced by an equivalent circuit composed of the following items connected in series:

1. The open-circuit temperature potential between the terminals exposed upon removal of the considered resistance, or group of resistances, from the analogue circuit.

---

* Leon Charles Thévenin (1875–1926) joined the Paris Administration of Post, Telephone and Telegraph in 1878 as an engineer in the department of long-distance cables; he later held a number of managerial positions in the administration until retirement in 1914. In addition to his administrative duties, Thévenin taught mechanics and applied mathematics. At the age of 26 he made an exhaustive study of Kirchhoff's laws on electrical networks. In 1883 Thévenin stated his theorem in the *Annales Telegraphiques:* "Assuming any system of linear conductors connected in such a manner that to the extremities of each one of them there is connected at least one other, a system having some electromotive force, $E_1, E_2, \ldots,$ E_3, no matter how distributed, we consider two points A and A' belonging to the system and having the potentials V and V'. If the points A and A' are connected by a wire ABA' which has a resistance r, with no electromotive forces, the potentials of points A and A' assume different (other?) values of V and V', but the current i flowing through this wire is given by the equation $i = V + V'/r + R$, in which R represents the resistance of the original system, this resistance being measured between the points A and A', which are considered to be electrodes."

To Thévenin's surprise he was considered wrong in some quarters; a controversy about the theorem ensued. Thévenin is said to have been a humble man and to have failed to realize the importance of his discovery. Fortunately, his biographer notes, shortly before his death he was told by a friend that his law was in use the world over. Proof of Thévenin's theorem can be found in Reference 19.

2. The resistance of that remaining circuit, its potential sources short-circuited and its current sources open-circuited.

3. The resistance value of the elements or group of elements being studied.

As an example of the use of Thévenin's theorem, consider the analogue network of Figure 5.14, with the following problem: find the relationship between heat flow q_0 and thermal resistance R_0.

The solution proceeds as follows. The open-circuit potential $T_0 - T_s$, resistance R_0 having been removed, is determined: Kirchhoff's law applied to the outer loop of Figure 5.14 yields the equation

$$q_1(R_2 + R_3 + R_4) - q_2 R_1 = 0. \tag{5.24}$$

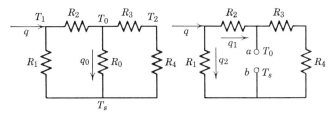

Figure 5.14   A thermal analogue network.

For the upper-left-corner node, Kirchhoff's law gives $q = q_1 + q_2$. Thus

$$q_1 = \frac{qR_1}{R_1 + R_2 + R_3 + R_4}. \tag{5.25}$$

The open-circuit potential $T_0 - T_s$ is, therefore,

$$T_0 - T_s = q_1(R_3 + R_4) = \frac{qR_1(R_3 + R_4)}{R_1 + R_2 + R_3 + R_4}. \tag{5.26}$$

The equivalent resistance of the analogue network, R_e, looking backward into the circuit from the terminals a and b, with the current source q open-circuited, is found with Figure 5.15:

$$R_e = \frac{(R_1 + R_2)(R_3 + R_4)}{R_1 + R_2 + R_3 + R_4}. \tag{5.27}$$

The Thévenin circuit equivalent to the circuit of Figure 5.14 between the terminals a and b is given as Figure 5.16.

Thus the relationship between R_0 and q_0 is found from substitution in the equation

$$\frac{T_0 - T_s}{R_e + R_0} = q_0. \tag{5.28}$$

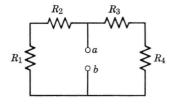
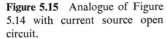
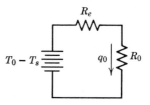

Figure 5.15 Analogue of Figure 5.14 with current source open circuit.

Figure 5.16 Thévenin equivalent of Figure 5.14.

The change in the rate of heat flow q_0 with thermal resistance R_0 is perceived from the following sequence. With $R_0 = R_{01}$, the rate of heat flowing across this thermal resistance is

$$q_{01} = \frac{T_0 - T_s}{R_e + R_{01}}. \tag{5.29}$$

After R_0 is changed to R_{02}, the rate of heat flow, for the same temperature drop $(T_0 - T_s)$, is

$$q_{02} = \frac{T_0 - T_s}{R_e + R_{02}} = q_{01}\left(\frac{R_e + R_{01}}{R_e + R_{02}}\right). \tag{5.30}$$

In order to observe the change in temperature potential with a change in thermal resistance, for the same rate of heat flow across that resistance, Norton's theorem is employed. Norton's equivalent circuit is similar to that of Thévenin: the constant open-circuit temperature potential ΔT_0 in series with the equivalent resistance $R_e = \Delta T_0/q_0$ is replaced by a constant heat source q_0 in parallel with the resistance R_e, as in Figure 5.17. With $R_0 = R_{01}$, the temperature potential across that resistance is given by

$$T_{01} = q_0\left(\frac{R_e R_{01}}{R_e + R_{01}}\right). \tag{5.31}$$

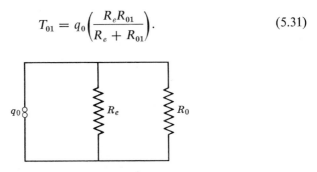

Figure 5.17 Norton equivalent circuit.

After R_0 is changed to R_{02}, the temperature potential ΔT_{02}, for the same rate of heat flow q_0, is

$$\Delta T_{02} = q_0\left(\frac{R_e R_{02}}{R_e + R_{02}}\right) = \Delta T_{01}\left[\frac{R_{02}(R_e + R_{01})}{R_{01}(R_e + R_{02})}\right]. \tag{5.32}$$

5.9 TEMPERATURE CONTROL SYSTEMS

Analysis of control systems explains functionally and mathematically the behavior of a combination of a temperature-sensitive mass, the structure and environment in which it exists, the various disturbances to which the mass and the structure are subjected, and the physical and electrical arrangements of the thermal and electronic elements used to regulate the temperature of the mass. The analysis can be used to predict whether temperature can be controlled in a given situation under expected thermal load and environmental conditions and, as well, in the face of extraordinary circumstances. The techniques of the analysis can serve to show what sort and amount of control equipment must be provided or adjusted to compensate for fixed, adverse thermal conditions of masses whose temperatures are to be controlled and for a fixed, adverse arrangement of thermal elements in a particular structure.

A typical temperature control system is a group of components, or subsystems, combined to regulate the temperature of a mass. The system may be described by a functional block diagram, such as that shown in Figure 5.18, where the blocks represent black boxes that receive certain indicated inputs and emit designated outputs. In this block diagram, the *controlled variable* represents the temperature of the controlled mass measured at a particular time and place by the *feedback element*. The signal from that element is sent to a comparator component, where, as the *feedback signal*, it is compared with a signal called the *reference input* which portrays the desired or set-point temperature. The result of the comparison is the *actuating signal*, which excites the *control elements* of the temperature control system. These control elements process the actuating signal so that their output, known as the *manipulated variable*, affects elements in the *controlled system* (which includes heating elements, controlled masses, and the structure containing them) in such away that despite *disturbances* the temperature measured at the controlled mass (the *controlled variable*) moves toward the set-point value. The thermally sensitive aspect or function of the regulated mass, called the *indirectly controlled variable*, is related to the measured temperature by the *indirectly controlled system*. (The indirectly controlled variable may be the size of the controlled mass, the temperature at another point in the mass, or a temperature-sensitive mechanical or electrical output of the operation of the mass.) The desired value of the considered aspect, or output, of the regulated mass commands the level of the *reference input signal* through

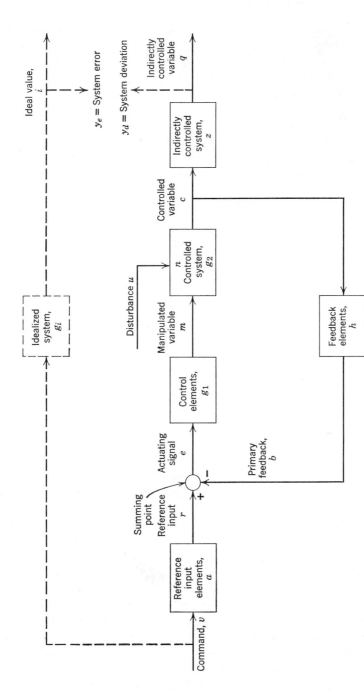

Figure 5.18 Control system functional block diagram. (From AIEE Committee Report in Electrical Engineering, 70 (1951), by permission of the Institute of Electrical and Electronics Engineers.)

the *reference input elements*, which may be the resistance elements of a Wheatstone bridge or the adjustment devices in a mechanical thermostat. The *system error* or *system deviation* describes the accuracy and stability of control and is the ultimate criterion for evaluating the performance of the temperature control system; a particular value of this error or deviation is the performance criterion that the control system is designed to meet.

The transient and steady-state response of a certain variable to the stimulus of another variable is affected by the operations of other elements in the control system. Similarly, the response of the controlled variable to disturbances in the controlled system can be varied by changing the elements of

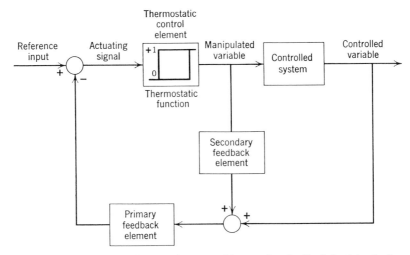

Figure 5.19   Thermostatic control system with secondary feedback (anticipation).

any of the subsystems: the feedback, the control, or the controlled. Elements used to effect such changes may be called *compensation* elements.

If the behavior of the control system can be described mathematically, the responses of the system variables can be determined quantitatively. Furthermore, the designer can dictate the operations of the elements of the system that will effect certain desired responses. He can also determine where in the system there should be the flexibility that will allow for compensation to be applied.

If thermal conditions in a controlled system are fixed (if a thermally sensitive mass has been mounted within a structure in an unalterable way, for example, or if the arrangement of the various heating and sensing elements cannot be changed) and the temperature of a mass in that system is not controlled properly, electrical or mechanical compensation may be used in either the feedback or the control elements of the controlling system. If, for instance, there is excessive lag in the controlled system between heat sources and other thermal elements, lead can be built electrically into the control elements to compensate; if a mechanical thermostat, acting as a combined feedback, comparator, and control element, is too far away from a control heater, a small heater wired in parallel with the main control heater is affixed to the thermostat to provide any necessary lead compensation. The size of this compensating, or anticipating, heater controls the amount of lead provided by the thermostat operation. In the system block diagram the compensation would appear in a secondary feedback loop, as in Figure 5.19. Various papers by Roots et al. [18] provide a full discussion of the theory of anticipation.

5.10   INTRODUCTION TO LINEAR-SYSTEM MATHEMATICS

The response of a linear system is proportional to its stimulus. Also, the response of a linear system to several stimuli acting together is the sum of its responses to each stimulus acting alone. This property of *superposition* permits the determination of the output of a linear system in response to a complex input signal, as follows: the input signal is resolved into a set of more simple time functions; the output signals resulting from each of the simple functions acting alone are found; summation of those signals yields the output corresponding to the total input signal.

The unit impulse shown in Figure 5.20*a* is a convenient simple time function. It is defined as the limit of a rectangular pulse obtained when the amplitude is increased toward infinity and the width is decreased toward zero while the area remains equal to one unit of time. The response of a linear system to an impulse stimulus is of a shape characteristic of the system, as in Figure 5.20*b*. The ordinates of the impulse response are proportional to the strength of the impulse, that is, to the area underneath it. Figure 5.20*c* shows an input signal represented by a sequence of unit impulses of appropriate strengths. The development of the proper response to the given input signal is illustrated in Figure 5.20*d*.

The ratio of the impulse response to the strength of its impulse stimulus is the normalized impulse response and is called the *system weighting function*. Its dimensions are always output units/input units $\times$ 1/time units. In a linear system the system weighting function is independent of the strength of the exciting impulse but characterizes the system uniquely. Also, because an effect cannot precede its cause in time, weighting functions for physical systems are zero for negative time.

Consider, then, the contribution to a linear system output at time θ attributable to an input of amplitude $f_1(\theta)$ at some time θ_1 before θ: that is,

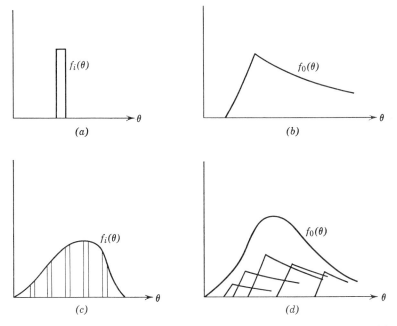

Figure 5.20 Superposition. (*a*) Impulse stimulus. (*b*) Impulse response. (*c*) Arbitrary stimulus described by a sequence of impulses. (*d*) Response to an arbitrary function approximated by the summation of responses to an appropriate sequence of impulses.

at $\theta - \theta_1$. The input amplitude at $\theta - \theta_1$ is given by $f_1(\theta - \theta_1)$. The infinitesimal output over the time interval $d\theta_1$, $df_0(\theta)$, is related to an infinitesimal impulse, corresponding to time span $d\theta_1$ and input amplitude $f_i(\theta - \theta_1)$ by the system weighting function $w(\theta_1)$ evaluated at θ_1:

$$df_0(\theta) = w(\theta_1) f_i(\theta - \theta_1) \, d\theta_1. \tag{5.33}$$

Integration over all time yields the system output at time θ:

$$f_0(\theta) = \int_{-\infty}^{\infty} w(\theta_1) f_i(\theta - \theta_1) \, d\theta_1 \tag{5.34}$$

The integral of (5.34) is known as the convolution integral. Because, for actual systems, $w(\theta_1)$ is zero for $\theta < 0$, the limit $-\infty$ may be replaced by zero for actual systems.

The relationship in the frequency domain between input and output of a linear system is found by formally transforming the terms of (5.34) from the time to the frequency domain. The Laplace transform can be applied conveniently. It is defined by the equation

$$F(s) = \int_0^\infty e^{-s\theta} f(\theta) \, d\theta,$$
(5.35)

where $f(\theta)$ = a function of time,
$\quad F(s)$ = the Laplace transform of $f(\theta)$,
$\quad\quad s$ = the Laplace operator.
If $f(\theta)$ is of exponential order and sectionally continuous, it can be transformed. (Most functions encountered in engineering practice satisfy these criteria.) The transformation itself is linear and usually a rational algebraic function of s.* The steady-state sinusoidal response of a system may be obtained by letting $s = j\omega$.

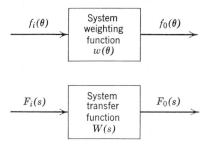

Figure 5.21 Block diagrams of time and frequency representations.

The Laplace transformation of (5.34) is given by

$$F_0(s) = \int_0^\infty \int_0^\theta e^{-s\theta} f_i(\theta - \theta_1) w(\theta_1) \, d\theta_1,$$
(5.36)

which becomes,

$$F_0(s) = W(s) \, F_i(s)$$
(5.37)

The Laplace transformation of the system weighting function is called the system *transfer function*. The weighting function written in a block diagram representing a linear system illustrates the relationship in the time domain between the input and output of the system; the transfer function shows the relationship in the frequency domain between the input and output of the system (Figure 5.21).

* A linear differential equation with constant coefficients produces a rational algebraic function when transformed. Application of the Laplace transform to a general equation of the form

$$a_n \frac{d^n f_0(\theta)}{d\theta^n} + a_{n-1} \frac{d^{n-1} f_0(\theta)}{d\theta^{n-1}} + \cdots + a_0 f_0(\theta) = b_m \frac{d^m f_i(\theta)}{d\theta^m} + b_{m-1} \frac{d^{m-1} f_i(\theta)}{d^{m-1}} + \cdots + b_0 f_i(\theta)$$

yields the following expression, assuming zero initial conditions:

$$F_0(s) = \frac{b_m s^m + b_{m-1} s^{m-1} + \cdots + b_0}{a_n s^n + a_{n-1} s^{n-1} + \cdots + a_0} Fi(s).$$

The over-all input-output relationship of a linear combination of linear subsystems can be determined by manipulating algebraically the individual subsystem transfer functions. Consider the mathematical block diagram of Figure 5.22, where the symbols inside the blocks are the transfer functions of the various subsystems. The transformed equations relating the parameters of the block diagram are

$$E = R - B, \qquad M = EW_1, \qquad C = MW_2,$$

$$C = \frac{W_1 W_2}{1 + W_1 W_2 W_3} R, \qquad E = \frac{1}{1 + W_1 W_2 W_3} R.$$

Transfer functions are the means of characterizing a linear system.

A wealth of literature exists on the theoretical and experimental techniques of control systems analysis. Standard works, for example, offer several

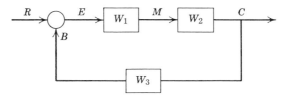

Figure 5.22   Mathematical block diagram.

theoretical and experimental methods for determining system transfer functions. The theoretical method is dependent on the analyst's ability to write a differential equation describing the operation of a particular system. The equation is transformed, and the resulting fraction, the ratio of output to input in terms of s, is the system transfer function. The well-known experimental method involves measuring the frequency response of the system to sinusoidal excitation. Frequency response data are presented in the *Bode diagram*, which consists of logarithmic plots of the magnitude* and phase angle of the frequency function versus the excitation frequency. The logarithmic magnitude scale permits the construction of the magnitude of a rational frequency function as a linear combination of the magnitudes of its component factors. The magnitude plot either yields a straight line or approaches straight-line asymptotes; the intersections of such asymptotes are related to some of the coefficients in the transfer function. Furthermore, because a rational function can be factored into first- and second-order

---

* Either the magnitude is plotted on a logarithmic scale or the logarithm of the magnitude is plotted on a linear scale. The shape of the curve is the same in either case. The linear scale is given in decilogs (dg) or decibels (db). The value of a number N in decilogs is $10 \log N$; that of N in decibels is $20 \log N$. Phase angle is plotted in degrees on a linear scale.

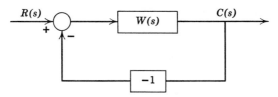

Figure 5.23   Unity feedback block diagram.

factors, the entire function can be constructed from a set of standard curves representing the magnitudes and phase angles of these factors.

Consider next the unit-feedback system of Figure 5.23, where $W(s)$ is a ratio of rational polynomials in s. The block diagram is described by the equation

$$\frac{C(s)}{R(s)} = \frac{W(s)}{1 + W(s)}.$$ (5.38)

The *Nichols chart* relates characteristics of the open-loop transfer function $W(s)$ to those of the closed-loop transfer function $W(s)/[1 + W(s)]$. The chart is valuable because the form of the open-loop function is invariably simpler than that of the closed-loop function. Furthermore, use of the Nichols chart facilitates compensation design.

The Bode diagram is helpful for providing analyses for compensation design in control and feedback elements. The use of elements in series with existing control components can improve the stability of a system, for example. (A linear, time-invariant system is stable if its impulse response approaches a constant value and remains constant long after the impulse has occurred.) A feedback loop internal to the over-all system feedback, as in Figure 5.24, can stabilize the characteristics of the forward part of a control system.

In contrast to frequency-response analysis, the *root locus* method examines the system behavior in the entire $s = \sigma + jw$ complex plane. Thus additional information on the system's transient behavior can be obtained.

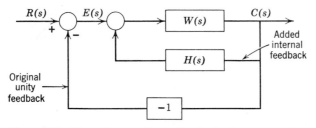

Figure 5.24   Block diagram illustrating feedback compensation.

Consider Figure 5.25, a block diagram of a linear time-invariant system, where g and h are constants and $G(s)$ and $H(s)$ are ratios of rational polynomials in s. The block diagram is described by the equation

$$\frac{C(s)}{R(s)} = \frac{gG(s)}{1 + kG(s)H(s)}, \tag{5.39}$$

where $k = gh =$ open-loop gain. The characteristic equation

$$1 + kG(s)H(s) = 0$$

is a complex function in s and is the equation upon which the system stability criterion is based. System stability can be established by finding the roots of

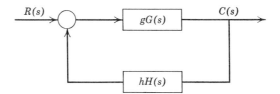

Figure 5.25   Block diagram.

the characteristic equation; similarly, the behavior of the closed-loop transfer function $C(s)/R(s)$ is determined by the location of its poles, that is, the roots of the characteristic equation.

A plot in the complex plane of the relationship $kG(s)H(s) = -1$, as a function of k, is the locus of the closed-loop poles. A number of rules in Reference 21 simplify the plotting procedure.

The degree of stability of a system can be determined by observing the motion of the closed-loop poles as k is varied.

5.11   INTRODUCTION TO NONLINEAR-SYSTEM MATHEMATICS

A nonlinear system is a mathematical model for which the superposition principle does not hold. A temperature control system containing a saturable element such as an ON-OFF switch is nonlinear (although piecewise linear). Such a system, described by a block diagram of the type shown in Figure 5.26, is amenable to several methods of rapid analytical solution that provide insights into system behavior and preliminary approaches to system design. (Final design should be subjected to extensive testing and computer simulation.)

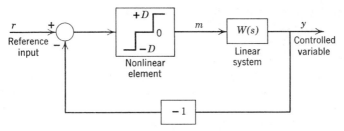

Figure 5.26 Block diagram of ON-OFF system.

The *phase plane* method [21, 4, 6] is useful for studying the transient behavior of systems that can be described by differential equations of the form

$$\frac{d^2y}{d\theta^2} + f\left(y, \frac{dy}{d\theta}\right) = m, \tag{5.40}$$

where y = a dependent variable,
         θ = an independent variable,
$f(y, dy/d\theta)$ = a nonlinear (or linear) function of the dependent variable and
         its derivative,
         m = a system forcing function (a constant or zero).

The method consists of observing the behavior of $dy/d\theta$ as a function of y. This functional relationship is derived by rewriting (5.40) as follows. First,

$$\frac{d^2y}{d\theta^2} = \frac{d}{dy}\left(\frac{dy}{d\theta}\right)^2.$$

Substitution in (5.40) yields

$$\frac{d}{dy}\left(\frac{dy}{d\theta}\right) = \frac{1}{dy/d\theta}\left[m - f\left(y, \frac{dy}{d\theta}\right)\right], \tag{5.41}$$

and thus the second-order equation has been reduced to a first-order equation in y and $dy/d\theta$.

Equation 5.41 can be solved analytically for y in terms of $dy/d\theta$ for all linear systems and a limited number of nonlinear ones, including the ON-OFF closed-loop system with deadband shown in Figure 5.26. There are only three possible states for m, yielding three forms of (5.41):

$$m = D: \quad \frac{d}{dy}\left(\frac{dy}{d\theta}\right) = \left(\frac{dy}{d\theta}\right)^{-1}\left[D - f\left(y, \frac{dy}{d\theta}\right)\right],$$

$$m = D: \quad \frac{d}{dy}\left(\frac{dy}{d\theta}\right) = (dy/d\theta)^{-1}\left[-f\left(y, \frac{dy}{d\theta}\right)\right]; \tag{5.42}$$

$$m = -D; \quad \frac{d}{dy}\left(\frac{dy}{d\theta}\right) = \left(\frac{dy}{d\theta}\right)^{-1}\left[-D - f\left(y, \frac{dy}{d\theta}\right)\right].$$

In these equations $f(y, dy/d\theta)$ is a linear function of time.

Starting with a given reference input and given initial conditions $y(0)$ and $(dy/d\theta)(0)$, we find that it is possible to iterate quasilinearly through the above equations to obtain the phase portrait of $dy/d\theta$ versus y.

The method of isoclines is employed generally for nonlinear systems which cannot be treated quasi-linearly. The use of this method arises from the observation that the right side of (5.41) takes on explicit constant values in the $y - dy/d\theta$, or phase, plane and the left side of the equation is the slope of the phase trajectory. Slopes, or isoclines, are plotted in the phase plane,

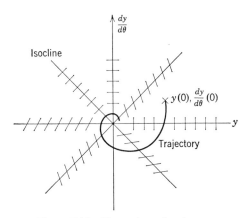

Figure 5.27   Phase-plane sketch.

as in Figure 5.27, and, given the initial conditions, the trajectory is drawn. Time is contained implicitly in the phase portrait, for

$$d\theta = \frac{dy}{(dy/d\theta)} .$$

Thus

$$\int_{\theta_1}^{\theta_2} d\theta = \int_{y_1}^{y_2} \frac{dy}{(dy/d\theta)} = \theta_2 - \theta_1, \tag{5.43}$$

which can be integrated analytically sometimes. The approximation

$$\theta_2 - \theta_1 = \Delta\theta \simeq \frac{\Delta y}{(dy/d\theta)_{\text{average}}} \tag{5.44}$$

can be employed to extract the time graphically.

The phase-plane method can be used to examine higher order systems (in which case the term phase space is appropriate), but it loses much of its utility and convenience under such circumstances.

The *describing function* method is a quasi-linear approach to the treatment of nonlinear systems. Because of the quasi-linear nature of the analysis, the actual nonlinear behavior in response to a given input is approximated by a linear operation or a series of linear operations. The performance of the approximator so derived displays the nonlinear character in that its gain depends on the input amplitude.

Describing function analysis was pioneered in the United States by Kochenburger [9] in connection with relay-driven servomechanisms. The method is most applicable to systems which contain only one time-invariant nonlinearity. A block diagram for such a system can be drawn as shown in Figure 5.28. The usual procedure is to assume that the input is a sinusoid

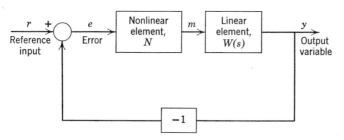

Figure 5.28   Block diagram of nonlinear system with unity feedback.

and to make the further crucial assumption that the linear element, $W(s)$, passes only the fundamental component of the input sinusoid. In a practical sense this requires that $W(s)$ act as an attenuator to the higher harmonics of the input.

Having satisfied these limiting, but not debilitating, assumptions, we proceed to approximate the response of the nonlinear element to the driving sinusoid by a Fourier analysis that includes only the fundamental term, the higher order terms being filtered by $W(s)$. Thus the describing function N is defined as the ratio of the first Fourier harmonic of the nonlinear element's output, $m(j\omega)$, to the driving sinusoid:

$$N = \frac{m(j\omega)}{E \sin \omega t}.$$

Describing functions have been calculated for many commonly encountered nonlinearities. The frequency behavior of the system is obtained by treating N as a linear transfer function and proceeding in the manner of linear-systems analysis.

Work by Vander Velde [23] has advanced a unified treatment of nonlinear systems using the quasi-linear approach. This new treatment provides an analytical attack which considers signals other than sinusoids at the input to the nonlinearity. A describing function that minimizes a system error is derived. The transient behavior of nonlinear systems can be predicted readily.

5.12 EXAMPLE ILLUSTRATING THE PERFORMANCE OF A CONTROLLED MASS

Thermal Response of an Uncontrolled Mass to Heat Sink Disturbances

The energy balance of an object of mass m and specific heat c, with heat input Q, heat available for temperature control $F(\theta, T)$, and thermal resistance R to heat sink at temperature T_0, is illustrated by Figure 5.29. The equation describing this process is

$$Q_1 + F(\theta, T) - \frac{T - T_0}{R} = mc \frac{dT}{d\theta}. \tag{5.45}$$

At temperature T and for steady-state conditions these definitions obtain:

$$F(\theta, T) = 0; \qquad R = R_1.$$

At T_1, therefore,

$$Q_1 = \frac{T_1 - T_0}{R_1} \text{ (steady state).} \tag{5.46}$$

The thermal response of mass m to a step change (at time $\theta = 0$) in thermal resistance R, from R_1 to R_2, with $R_2 = R_1/(1 + \delta)$ and with control power zero, is now computed.

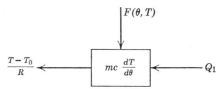

Figure 5.29 Energy balance of mass m.

The appropriate form for the energy balance equation (5.45) at time $\theta = 0+$ is

$$mc \frac{dT}{d\theta} + \frac{T}{R_2} = \frac{T_0}{R_2} + Q_1. \tag{5.47}$$

The solution for T is

$$T = A \exp\left(-\frac{\theta}{mcR_2}\right) + T_0 + R_2 Q_1, \tag{5.48}$$

where A is a constant of integration, to be found from the initial condition that, at $\theta = 0$, $T = T_1$. Thus

$$A = T_1 - T_0 - R_2 Q_1 \tag{5.49}$$

and

$$T = T_1 \exp\left(-\frac{\theta}{mcR_2}\right) + (T_0 + R_2 Q_1)\left[1 - \exp\left(-\frac{\theta}{mcR_2}\right)\right]. \tag{5.50}$$

By use of the relations $Q_1 = (T_1 - T_0)/R_1$ and $R_2 = R_1/(1 + \delta)$,

$$T_0 + R_2 Q_1 = T_0 + \frac{T_1 - T_0}{1 + \delta} = \frac{T_0 \delta + T_1}{1 + \delta} \qquad (5.51)$$

and

$$\frac{1}{mcR_2} = \frac{Q_1(1 + \delta)}{mc(T_1 - T_0)}. \qquad (5.52)$$

With substitution and rearrangement,

$$T = T_1 - \frac{\delta}{1 + \delta}(T_1 - T_0)\left\{1 - \exp\left[\frac{-Q_1(1 + \delta)\theta}{mc(T_1 - T_0)}\right]\right\}. \qquad (5.53)$$

At time $\theta = \infty$, $T = T_2$:

$$T_2 = T_1 - \frac{\delta}{1 + \delta}(T_1 - T_0). \qquad (5.54)$$

The change of temperature T with time θ, for $R_2 < R_1$, is shown in Figure 5.30.

The thermal response of mass m to a step change (at time $\theta = 0$) in heat sink temperature, from T_0 to T_F, with the thermal resistance R constant and equal to R_1 and temperature control power zero, is now computed.

The appropriate form for the energy balance equation (5.45) at time $\theta = 0+$ is

$$mc\frac{dT}{d\theta} + \frac{T}{R_1} = \frac{T_F}{R_1} + Q_1. \qquad (5.55)$$

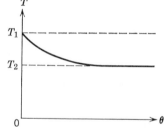

Figure 5.30 Response of temperature of mass m to decrease of resistance between the mass and its heat sink.

Using the initial condition $T = T_1$ at $\theta = 0$, and the relation $R_1 Q_1 = T_1 - T_0$, we find that the solution for T is

$$T = T_1 + (T_F - T_0)\left\{1 - \exp\left[-\frac{Q_1}{mc(T_1 - T_0)}\theta\right]\right\}. \qquad (5.56)$$

Thermal Response of a Mass to Discontinuous Control Power

The thermal response of mass m to two-position, ON-OFF temperature control is now investigated. With such control, the heat input $Q_1 + F(\theta)$ is defined by

$$Q_1 + F(\theta) = Q_{max}, \quad \text{when } T = T_{min} \text{ or below;}$$
$$Q_1 + F(\theta) = Q_{min}, \quad \text{when } T = T_{max} \text{ or above.} \qquad (5.57)$$

Thermal response for operation during the control cycle (between T_{min} and T_{max}) is derived as follows. Given that $T = T_{max}$ at time $\theta = 0$, the energy balance equation is

$$mc \frac{dT}{d\theta} + \frac{T}{R_1} = \frac{T_0}{R_1} + Q_{min}. \tag{5.58}$$

Using the initial condition above and rearranging, we find the solution for T:

$$T = T_{max} - (T_{max} - T_0 - R_1 Q_{min})\left[1 - \exp\left(-\frac{\theta}{mcR_1}\right)\right]. \tag{5.59}$$

The time θ_D required for the excursion from T_{max} to T_{min} may be found from a rearranged form of (5.53):

$$\frac{T_{min} - T_0 - R_1 Q_{min}}{T_{max} - T_0 - R_1 Q_{min}} = +\exp\left(-\frac{\theta_D}{mcR_1}\right). \tag{5.60}$$

Taking logarithms and changing sign,

$$\theta_D = mcR_1 \ln\left(\frac{T_{max} - T_0 - R_1 Q_{min}}{T_{min} - T_0 - R_1 Q_{min}}\right). \tag{5.61}$$

With constant temperature control limits T_{min} and T_{max}, the total time for a control excursion, $\theta_D + \theta_I$, increases with increasing values of either m, c, or R_1. The temperature-rise time decreases with increasing values of Q_{max}; the temperature-fall time decreases with decreasing values of Q_{min}.

If, alternatively, $T = T_{min}$ at time $\theta = 0$, the energy balance equation is

$$mc \frac{dT}{d\theta} + \frac{T}{R_1} = \frac{T_0}{R_1} + Q_{max}; \tag{5.62}$$

the solution for T is

$$T = T_{min} - (T_{min} - T_0 - RQ_1)(1 - e^{-\theta/mcR_1}); \tag{5.63}$$

and the time θ_I required for the excursion from T_{min} to T_{max} is

$$\theta_I = mcR_1 \ln\left(\frac{T_{min} - T_0 - R_1 Q_{max}}{T_{max} - T_0 - R_1 Q_{max}}\right). \tag{5.64}$$

The change of temperature with time, for operation between the control-temperature limits or in the control cycle, is shown in Figure 5.31. The asymptotes of the decreasing and increasing portions of the temperature cycle are defined, respectively, by

$$T_{\alpha D} = T_0 + R_1 Q_{min}$$

and

$$T_{\alpha I} = T_0 + R_1 Q_{max}. \tag{5.65}$$

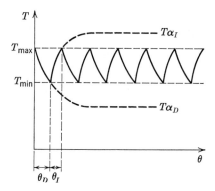

Figure 5.31 Response of temperature of mass m to discontinuous control power.

Phase Plane Portrait of Control Cycle

Because during the control cycle the variation of temperature with time is exponential, the representation in the phase plane of the temperature of the controlled mass is linear. Given (5.53) for the temperature decrease of the controlled mass with power dissipation equal to Q_{min}, the equation is

$$\frac{dT}{d\theta} = -(T_{max} - T_0 - RQ_{min})\left(\frac{\theta}{mcR_1} e^{-\theta/mcR_1}\right). \qquad (5.66)$$

The variation of $dT/d\theta$ with T in the phase plane is given by the ratio

$$\frac{d/d\theta(dT/d\theta)}{(d/d\theta)(T)} = \frac{-(T_{max} - T_0 - R_1Q_{min})[-(\theta/mcR_1)^2 e^{-\theta/mcR_1}]}{-(T_{max} - T_0 - R_1Q_{min})[(\theta/mcR_1)e^{-\theta/mcR_1}]}$$

$$= -\frac{\theta}{mcR_1}. \qquad (5.67)$$

Thus the graph of $dT/d\theta$ as a function of T for that part of the control cycle is a straight line with negative slope given by (5.67). The variation of $dT/d\theta$ with T for the part of the control cycle with power dissipation equal to Q_{max} and temperature T increasing is given by (5.67) also. Thus the phase plane portrait of the temperature cycle of Figure 5.31 is composed of linear segments, as in Figure 5.32.

In Figure 5.32 the vertical lines da and bc represent the maximum and minimum temperatures of the control cycle. These are the temperatures of the controlled mass at which power switching occurs. The lines ab and cd represent, respectively, the rises and falls of mass temperature during the

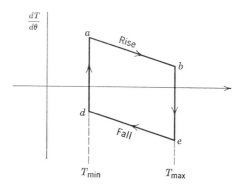

Figure 5.32   Phase portrait of discontinuous control cycle.

control cycle. Point *a* is at the beginning of the rise: $dT/d\theta$ decreases as the line *ab* is traversed. Point *c* is at the beginning of the fall; $dT/d\theta$ increases as the line *cd* is traversed.

REFERENCES

[1] Broida, V., *Heat Inertia in Problems of Automatic Control of Temperature*, Instruments Publishing Co, Pittsburgh, Pa., 1950.
[2] Churchill, R. V., *Operational Mathematics*, McGraw-Hill, New York, 1958.
[3] Crandall, S. H., *Engineering Analysis*, McGraw-Hill, New York, 1956.
[4] Den Hartog, J. P., *Mechanical Vibrations*, McGraw-Hill, New York, 1956.
[5] Donovan, J. C., "How to Compensate Temperature Loops," *Control Eng.*, December, 1965.
[6] Gibson, J. E., *Nonlinear Automatic Control*, McGraw-Hill, New York, 1963.
[7] "How to Get Better Temperature Control," Fenwal, Inc., 1961.
[8] James, H. M., N. B. Nichols, and R. S. Phillips, *Theory of Servomechanisms*, Dover, New York, 1965.
[9] Kochenburger, R. J., "A Frequency Response Method for Analyzing and Synthesizing Contactor Servomechanisms," *Trans. AIEE*, **69** (1950).
[10] Kreith, F., *Principles of Heat Transfer*, International Textbook, Scranton, Pa., 1958.
[11] Ku, Y. H., *Analysis and Control of Nonlinear Systems*, Ronald Press, New York, 1958.
[12] Kutz, M. P., "Minimum Power Thermal Design for Inertial Guidance Systems," *Mass. Inst. Technology Instrumentation Lab. Rept.* E-1900, 1965.
[13] Lloyd, S. G., "Frequency Response for Process Control Elements," TM-13, Fisher Governor Co.
[14] Miles, V. C., *Thermostatic Control*, George Newnes Ltd., London, 1965.
[15] Newton, G. C., Jr., L. A. Gould, and J. F. Kaiser, *Analytical Design of Linear Feedback Controls*, Wiley, New York, 1961.
[16] Paschkis, V., "The Heat and Mass Flow Analyzer A Simulator for the Study of Heat Conduction," *Ann. Assoc. Intern. pour le Calcul Analogique*, No. 1, Janvier, 1963.
[17] Peskin, E., *Transient and Steady-State Analysis of Electric Networks*, Van Nostrand Princeton, N.J., 1961.

[18] Roots, W. K., and J. M. Nightingale, "Closed-Loop Controlled Electric Space-Heating and Space-Cooling Processes," *IEEE Trans. Appl. Ind.*, September–October, 1966.

[19] Skilling, H. H., *Electrical Engineering Circuits*, Wiley, New York, 1958.

[20] Suchet, C., "Leon Charles Thévenin," *Elec. Eng.*, **68**, 843 (October, 1949.)

[21] Truxal, J. G., *Automatic Feedback Control System Synthesis*, McGraw-Hill, New York, 1955.

[22] Truxal, J. G., ed., *Control Engineers' Handbook*, McGraw-Hill, New York, 1958.

[23] Vander Velde, W. E., and A. Gelb, *Multiple Input Describing Function Theory*, McGraw-Hill, New York, 1967.

6

Electrical Resistance Elements

6.1 INTRODUCTION

In this chapter we are concerned with several components of electric systems used to control temperatures of masses. We discuss ways whereby the components measure temperature and a method by which such measurements are translated into signals to system controllers. The block diagram of Figure 6.1 shows the mathematical arrangement of components of a typical

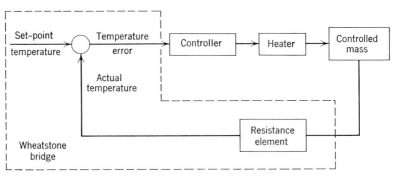

Figure 6.1   Block diagram of temperature control system.

control system. The process of properly exciting the system controller is accomplished as follows. The temperature-measuring component contains a *resistance element* of characteristic sensitivity so that a change in its temperature is accompanied by a change in its electrical resistance; the element's instantaneous level of resistance is compared in a component such as a Wheatstone bridge with other resistances that are fixed; the output of the Wheatstone bridge, the control system error signal, or the difference between a set-point and an indicated temperature is the input to the system controller.

We discuss both conductive and semiconductive resistance elements and compare the properties and capabilities of the two types. The two main styles of components that use conductive elements are examined and their suitable applications indicated; also, various constructions of semiconductive elements are illustrated. The discussion of resistance elements emphasizes the following operational requirements.

A measuring component used to control temperatures of small masses should be highly sensitive (its electrical output should change noticeably with small temperature variation) and quickly responsive to temperature change. The sensitive element within the component must function reproducibly and be mounted free from any error-producing disturbances. The element will always be operated in an excited state, furthermore, and the level of excitation should not cause appreciable energy dissipation within the element (resulting in an undesirable temperature rise of the element above the actual temperature of the measured mass).

The Wheatstone bridge, for reasons of sensitivity and widespread use, is considered as the comparison component of the control system. Because in actual operation the bridge may be physically remote from the measuring component, elimination of lead wire resistances (when they are detrimentally large) is discussed.

6.2 THE WHEATSTONE BRIDGE

An instrument used to measure a temperature error and to supply excitation to a temperature controller is the Wheatstone bridge circuit. It was invented in 1833 by Samuel Hunter Christie [8] but was allowed to lie unused until 1843 when it was publicized by Sir Charles Wheatstone, who showed its applicability to electrical measurements.*

* Wheatstone (1802–1875), the son of a Gloucester, England, music seller, was at twenty-one a maker of musical instruments in London. His first scientific experiments were in the field of sound. In 1827, he fashioned a kaleidoscope, a thin steel rod of rectangular cross section, fixed vertically, its upper end carrying a silver bead. Where the rod is vibrated, the bead describes beautiful curves resulting from the combination of perpendicular simple harmonic motions of unequal frequencies. Returning to business, in 1829 Wheatstone invented the concertina. In 1834, he was appointed an experimental physicist at King's College, London. He achieved fame the next year, when his paper, "The Prismatic Analysis of Electric Light," was presented to the British Association. He demonstrated that the light given off when an arc is passed between two metal electrodes produces a unique spectrum for each different metal when refracted by a prism, and thus small quantities of any metal can be detected. At about the same time, Wheatstone attempted to measure the velocity of electric current in a

The Wheatstone bridge is a configuration of four resistance elements connected to a source of electrical energy and yielding an electrical output as shown in Figure 6.2. The bridge is in balance when the output is zero and is out of balance otherwise. In using the bridge for either the measurement or control of temperature, three of the elements have resistance values which are invariant with temperature change while that of the fourth is temperature

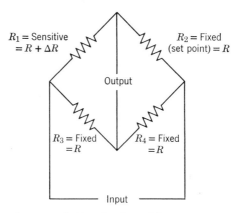

Figure 6.2   Wheatstone bridge circuit used for temperature measurement.

sensitive. Thus, the bridge out-of-balance output, which is the input to the controller, is sensitive to the change in resistance of the temperature-sensitive element.

6.3 THE BASIC WHEATSTONE BRIDGE EQUATIONS

In order to determine the relationship between bridge output and input voltages, Kirchhoff's laws, which state that the algebraic sum of the voltage

conductor. He suspended half a mile of wire in the vaults under the college for his experiment and measured a speed of 250,000 miles per second. In 1838 he invented the stereoscope: an object is photographed at two slightly different angles; the pictures are viewed simultaneously, one by each eye, and the total image appears three-dimensional.

After a long visit by the American Physicist Joseph Henry, Wheatstone collaborated with William Fothergill Cooke (in anticipation of Morse) to render the telegraph available to the public for transmission of messages. The two men worked on many associated instruments; Wheatstone also performed pioneer research on laying undersea cable.

Sir Charles was knighted for his work on the British telegraph system and for his method of generating constant electric current. His other accomplishments are legion. The father of five children, he was a shy man, morbidly afraid of audiences. His friend Michael Faraday saw to it that Wheatstone's papers were published. He was also an authority on his hobby, cryptography, and invented a secret-dispatch writer that is supposedly indecipherable [1, 15].

drops around a closed loop is zero and that the sum of the currents flowing into a junction is equal to the sum of those flowing away from it, are used. The latter law yields the following relationships for the currents flowing through resistances R_2 and R_4 (Figure 6.3):

$$i_2 = i_1 - i_o,$$
$$i_4 = i_3 + i_o, \tag{6.1}$$

where i_o is the current through the output detector.
The former law indicates these equations:

$$0 = -E_i + i_1R_1 + (i_1 - i_o)R_2,$$
$$0 = -E_i + i_3R_3 + (i_3 + i_o)R_4, \tag{6.2}$$
$$0 = E_o + i_1R_1 - i_3R_3.$$

Combining (6.2),

$$E_o = \left(\frac{R_1}{R_1 + R_2} - \frac{R_3}{R_3 + R_4}\right)E_i$$
$$+ i_o\left(\frac{R_1R_2}{R_1 + R_2} + \frac{R_3R_4}{R_3 + R_4}\right). \tag{6.3}$$

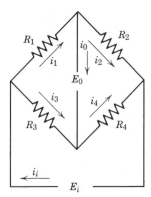

Figure 6.3 The Wheatstone bridge circuit showing directions of current flow.

If the bridge is in balance, the output current i_o is zero, and the equation for the output voltage (which is also zero) is

$$E_o = \frac{R_1R_4 - R_2R_3}{(R_1 + R_2)(R_3 + R_4)}E_i. \tag{6.4}$$

Thus, when the bridge is balanced and $E_o = 0$, $R_1R_4 = R_2R_3$. In order to change the level at which the bridge (with R_1 the variable resistor) is balanced, the value of R_2 is changed. The bridge un-balance voltage caused by a resistance change in R_1 and with the output impedance infinite (it can be shown that maximum output of a bridge with resistance change in one leg is achieved with infinite output resistance) is reached from (6.4) and the relation $R_1R_4 = R_2R_3$. After rearranging,

$$E_o = \frac{R_4}{(R_1 + R_2)(R_3 + R_4)}\left[\frac{\Delta R}{1 + (\Delta R/R_1 + R_2)}\right]E_i, \tag{6.5}$$

where ΔR is the change in resistor R_1. The bridge output is nonlinear with resistance change ΔR. If at balance $R_1 = R_2 = R_3 = R_4$,

$$E_o = \frac{\Delta R}{4R + 2\Delta R}E_i. \tag{6.6}$$

If ΔR is large compared to R (20%, say), for a 20% change in R the bridge nonlinearity can be as much as 10%. This nonlinearity can be reduced by making R_2 and R_4 large compared to R_1 and R_3, as shown in Figure 6.4, where R_2 or R_4 is each K times larger than R_1 or R_3. The equation for bridge output voltage is

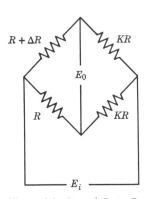

$$E_o = \frac{K\,\Delta R}{(1+K)^2 R + (1+K)\,\Delta R}\,E_i,\quad K \geq 1,\tag{6.7}$$

and the reduction in nonlinearity is evident from observing that in the denominator the coefficient of R increases more rapidly than that of ΔR as K increases.

Figure 6.4 R_2 and $R_4 > R_1$ and R_3.

This improvement in bridge linearity, however, is expensive in terms of bridge sensitivity, or gain, which is defined as $E_o/\Delta R$. Maximum sensitivity is achieved when the resistances of all legs are equal at balance (and K in Figure 6.4 is 1). The equation for bridge gain is

$$\frac{E_o}{\Delta R} = \frac{KE_i}{(1+K)^2 R + (1+K)\,\Delta R}\tag{6.8}$$

If the resistance R_o of the bridge output detector is less than infinite, the equation for output current i_o as a function of input voltage E_i is

$$i_o = \frac{(R_1 R_4 - R_2 R_3)E_i}{R_0(R_1 + R_2)(R_3 + R_4) + R_1 R_2(R_3 + R_4) + R_3 R_4(R_1 + R_2)}.\tag{6.9}$$

If $R_1 = R_2 = R_3 = R_4$, and ΔR is the resistance change in R_1,

$$i_o = \frac{\Delta R E_i}{4R(R_0 + R) + (2R_0 + 3R)\,\Delta R}.\tag{6.10}$$

6.4 ERRORS CAUSED BY LEAD WIRE RESISTANCE

If the resistance element is connected to the rest of the bridge with lead wires whose resistances are significant compared to the resistance change of the element (Figure 6.5), the output voltage E_o is related to the input E_i by the equation

$$E_o = \frac{\Delta R + 2R_L}{4R + 2\,\Delta R + 4R_L}\,E_i,\tag{6.11}$$

where R_L is the resistance of one of the lead wires. Noting the quantity $2R_L$ in the numerator, we observe that the bridge cannot be balanced in such a

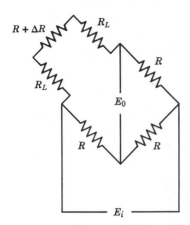

Figure 6.5 Wheatstone bridge with sensitive element connected to bridge with significant resistance in lead wires.

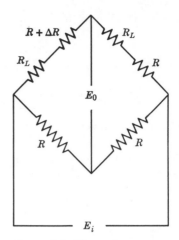

Figure 6.6 Three-wire connection,

$$E_0/R = E_i/(4R + 2\,\Delta R + 4R_i).$$

situation and, furthermore, that sensitivity is destroyed. In order to remove the difficulty, a three-wire connection is used.

6.5 THREE-WIRE CONNECTIONS

Three-wire connections used to eliminate errors caused by lead wire resistances are shown in Figures 6.6 and 6.7. The scheme in Figure 6.6 is recommended on the basis of comparison of the sensitivities of the two bridge

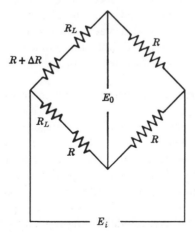

Figure 6.7 Three-wire connection, $E_0/\Delta R = E_i/[4R + 2R + 4R_L + (R_L{}^2/R) + (\Delta R/R)]$.

circuits, (6.12) and (6.13). ($R_1 = R_2 = R_3 = R_4$ at balance.)

$$\frac{E_o}{\Delta R} = \frac{E_i}{4R + 2\,\Delta R + 4R_L}\ ; \tag{6.12}$$

$$\frac{E_o}{\Delta R} = \frac{E_i}{4R + 2\,\Delta R + 4R_L + (R_L{}^2/R) + (\Delta R/R)}\,. \tag{6.13}$$

Note that in either case there is a reduction in sensitivity from the condition where lead wire resistance is negligible (6.6). When (6.12) is subtracted from (6.6) the reduction in sensitivity caused by lead wire resistances, as a percentage of input voltage, is

$$\frac{100R_L}{R_L + R + (\Delta R/2)}\,.$$

6.6 CONDUCTIVE RESISTANCE ELEMENTS

The metals most frequently used as conductive resistance elements are those which combine time stability of their temperature-resistance characteristics with good sensitivity to temperature change. Platinum and nickel best meet these criteria.

There are two physical classifications for the commercial application of metallic resistance elements: immersion sensors, called resistance thermometers, and surface-mounting sensors. In the immersion type, used to measure and control temperatures within solid and liquid masses, the metallic element, wire of small diameter, is supported wound on a cylindrical mandrel. Heat can flow to the wire either along the mandrel or radially inward from the thermometer case. The predominance of one heat flow rate over the other depends on the relative magnitudes of the thermal conductance of the mandrel material and the thermal contact conductance between the wire and the thermometer case. Thus a resistance thermometer may be designed to sense a temperature at the tip of its stem or an average of temperatures along the stem.

Some commercial resistance thermometers are rather large and have comparatively large time constants. They are not used generally to control temperatures of small masses. Beckwith and Buck [6] list responses (times to detect 90% of any temperature change in water flowing at 1 fps) for several commercially available resistance thermometers whereby heat is transferred radially inward: for example, platinum element in a stainless steel case, 10–30 seconds; copper or nickel in a brass case, 20–60 seconds. Hickes [13], however, states that with a silver or copper core of suitably small diameter the probe-style resistance thermometer responds as fast as a thermocouple.

The surface-mounting sensor employing a conductive element is similar in construction to a wire-type bonded strain gage. Wire grid (about 1 mil diameter) is cemented between two thin pieces of paper, phenolic or the like. Larger lead wires are welded to the ends of the grid. These wires may be connected to the lead wires of a Wheatstone bridge with material that will not break down over anticipated temperature excursions. Responses of the different surface-mounting sensors vary from 0.050 to 1 second. These sensors have the added advantage of providing area coverage and, therefore, the capability of sensing an average of temperatures over an area. On the other hand, a sensor should be small enough so that it does not interfere with heat transfer from the surface whose temperature it is measuring.

For special circumstances metal wire temperature control sensors can also be constructed so that the wire is wound integrally with electric resistance wire heaters. The advantage inherent in such an application is the reduction of thermal lag between sensor and heater. The lag can be eliminated entirely if the sensor wire is the heater (but there will still be lag between a sensor used for control and one used for indication if they are not one and the same).

The induction of mechanical strain by improper wire-mounting and gage-bonding techniques is treated theoretically below. In manufacturing and using temperature sensors two related thermal problems obtain: mounting the resistance element within the sensor, and attaching or immersing the sensor so that there is excellent thermal contact between it and the temperature-sensed mass. Solutions to both problems are subject to similar theoretical interpolations. The special problem of the surface preparation and application of adhesives and of their effects on the performance of strain gage types of sensors is treated extensively in the literature, especially by Stein in Dean and Douglas [9], by Perry and Lissner [16], and in a brochure available from Baldwin-Lima-Hamilton [4]. The importance of this question may be best summarized by paraphrasing Stein: if there is not faithful transmission of temperature change from the specimen surface to the sensitive filament, no amount of expensive instrumentation attached to the gage terminals will give correct results.

6.7 RESISTANCE-TEMPERATURE CHARACTERISTIC OF CONDUCTORS

The electrical resistance of a segment of metal wire is related to its length-over-area ratio by the variable parameter, resistivity,

$$R = r\frac{L}{A}, \tag{6.14}$$

which is increased by temperature rise, greater alloy content, and mechanical distortion. If (6.14) is differentiated with respect to temperature, T, the effects of the thermal coefficient of resistivity, C_r, and the thermal coefficients of expansion, α_e, are noted:

$$\frac{dR}{R} = \left(\frac{1}{r}\frac{dr}{dT} + \frac{1}{L}\frac{dL}{dT} - \frac{1}{A}\frac{dA}{dT}\right) dT, \tag{6.15}$$

where

$$\frac{1}{r}\frac{dr}{dT} + \frac{1}{L}\frac{dL}{dT} - \frac{1}{A}\frac{dA}{dT} = C_R,$$

which is the thermal coefficient of resistance, $(1/r)(dr/dT) = C_r$, and $(1/L)(dL/dT)$ and $(1/A)(dA/dT) = \alpha_e$ and $2\alpha_e$, respectively.

The electrical resistance-temperature characteristic of a pure metal is usually defined as an equation of the form

$$R = R_0(1 + K_1 T + K_2 T^2 + K_3 T^3 + \cdots + K_n T^n). \tag{6.16}$$

By differentiating (6.16) with respect to T,

$$\frac{1}{R_0}\frac{dR}{dT} = K_1 + 2K_2 T + 3K_3 T^2 + \cdots + nK_n T^{n-1}, \tag{6.17}$$

it is observed that the quantity dR/dT is nonlinear.

The resistance-temperature characteristic of platinum can be specified sufficiently with the first two coefficients over the range* 32°F (the ice point) to 1166.9°F (the freezing point of antimony). The coefficient K_2 is negative, thus giving a downward impulse to the characteristic, as plotted in Figure 6.8, at higher temperatures.

Over the temperature range −297.346 (the oxygen point) to 32°F the platinum characteristic is defined by the equation

$$R = R_0[1 + K_1 T + K_2 T^2 + \gamma(T - 100)T^3],$$

where γ is found by a measurement at the oxygen point.

Three constants are required for indicating the characteristic of nickel, whose sensitivity exceeds that of platinum. In this case K_2 is positive, thus providing a concave-upward shape to the resistance-temperature curve (Figure 6.8). The use of nickel is limited to temperatures not exceeding 600°F, where the Curie point transformation causes a change in the resistance characteristic of the metal.

---

* The Standard Platinum Resistance Thermometer is the standard for interpolation of temperature from −297.346 to 1166.9°F.

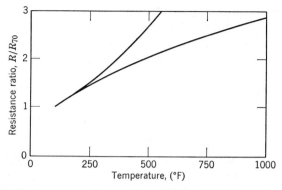

Figure 6.8   Temperature resistance characteristics of nickel and platinum.

Copper can be used at moderate temperatures; it has an almost perfectly linear characteristic from 0 to 250°F.

Table 6.1 lists thermal coefficients of resistance and absolute resistivities and resistances for a number of conductors that can be used either as temperature-sensitive resistance elements (platinum, nickel) or as the invariant legs (manganin) in the Wheatstone bridge. Also included are gage factors (strain sensitivities) and thermal coefficients of expansion, both of which will be used in the analysis below.

Figure 6.8 indicates the resistance-temperature characteristics of three metal conductors employable as resistance elements. Note that the non-linearities of the chemically pure nickel and the nickel-iron characteristics are concave upwards, whereas the chemically pure platinum characteristic is concave downward.

Table 6.1   Properties of Conductors [23], [24]

Conductor	Resistivity	Resistance	Temperature Coefficient of Resistance	Gage Factor	Temperature Coefficient of Expansion
	microhm-centimeter	ohm/mil-foot	ohm/ohm/°F		microinch/inch/°F
Platinum	9.83 @ 32°F	80	0.0017	4.8	4.6 @ 68°F
Nickel	6.84 @ 68°F	45	0.0033	−12.0	7.4
Iridium 5% Ir; 95% Pt	19	137	0.0007	+5.1	5
Nichrome 80% Ni; 20% Cr	107.9 @ 68°F	638	0.0002	+2.0	9.8
Manganin 4% Ni; 12% Mn; 84% Cu	46	260	0.000006	+0.47	
Copper	1.67 @ 68°F		0.0022		9.2 @ 68°F
Tungsten	5.5 @ 68°F		0.0025		2.4 @ 68°F

The inherent nonlinearity of the temperature-resistance characteristics of some metals, such as nickel, used as resistance elements can be turned to advantage in offsetting the nonlinearity of the bridge output. Consider the bridge output, defined in (6.6), for which the bridge is operating at midrange (the resistances of all four legs are equal):

$$E_o = \frac{\Delta R}{4R + \Delta R} E_i. \tag{6.6}$$

A plot of E_o, bridge output, as a function of R is concave downward. The nonlinearity of a nickel resistance element opposes the bridge nonlinearity and tends to linearize bridge output as a function of temperature. The non-linearities can offset each other exactly if appropriately sized padding resistors are used in concert with the nickel element. Consider that ΔR, the change in resistance of the temperature-sensitive element, is small compared to its absolute resistance, R. The bridge output is now

$$E_o = \frac{\Delta R}{4R} E_i, \quad R \gg \Delta R. \tag{6.6a}$$

Output will be linear with temperature, then, if $\Delta R/R = \Delta T$, and if this is to be, the relationship of R and T must be given by

$$R = Ke^T. \tag{6.6b}$$

The resistance-temperature characteristic of a nickel element can be forced to the necessary relationship by first attempting to effect the solution by adding a fixed resistance in series and, following that, by then combining a fixed resistance in parallel with the element. Grant and Hickes [11] have delved into the arithmetic of the effort. They have also shown that a bridge with an exponential resistance element in one leg provides a linear relationship between output voltage and input temperature when the bridge is far from balance.

Padding resistors are not employed without corresponding loss of sensitivity.

6.8 EFFECTS OF ALLOYS AND IMPURITIES

Comparison of the electrical resistances of a pure metal element and of an alloy or an element impregnated with an impurity (all elements being identical in size) indicates that the impurity acts almost like a resistance in series with that of the pure metal. The temperature-resistance curve is displaced a nearly constant resistance to considerably higher values of R for the same values of T. Therefore, if the sensitivity of an electrically conductive resistance element is $(1/R)(dR/dT)$, this sensitivity is reduced (from that of the pure metal) with increased alloying or impurity impregnation.

6.9 EFFECTS OF MECHANICAL STRAIN

In order to obtain an answer to the question of the amount of resistance change indicated by an element perfectly mounted to a strain-free surface, the following quantities must be specified: α_e, the thermal coefficient of expansion of the element $(\Delta L/L/\text{deg})$; α_s, the thermal coefficient of expansion of the surface $(\Delta L/L/\text{deg})$; S_e, the strain sensitivity of the element $(\Delta\Omega/\Omega/\Delta L/L)$; C_r, the thermal coefficient of resistivity of the element in a free state $(\Delta\Omega/\Omega/\text{deg})$. Equation 6.15 defines the thermal coefficient of resistance:

$$\frac{dR}{R_0} = C_R \, dT. \tag{6.15}$$

The thermal coefficients of expansion are defined by these equations:

$$\left(\frac{dL}{L_0}\right)_e = \alpha_e \, dT;$$
$$\left(\frac{dL}{L_0}\right)_s = \alpha_s \, dT. \tag{6.18}$$

Then (6.19) is the equation that delineates the amount of mechanical strain induced in the element because of its being perfectly attached to a body whose thermal coefficient of expansion is not equal to that of the element (and which undergoes no strain itself):

$$de = \left(\frac{dL}{L_0}\right)_s - \left(\frac{dL}{L_0}\right)_e$$
$$= (\alpha_s - \alpha_e) \, dT. \tag{6.19}$$

The total temperature-resistance coefficient for an element mounted to a surface can now be deduced. Equation 6.19 is multiplied by the element's strain sensitivity and the result is combined with (6.15):

$$\left(\frac{dR}{R}\right)_{\text{total}} = (C_R + (\alpha_s - \alpha_e)S_e) \, dT. \tag{6.20}$$

The strain sensitivity of the element can be deduced by redifferentiating (6.14), this time with respect to both temperature (T) and strain (e) [thus rewriting (6.20)]:

$$\frac{dR}{R} = \frac{1}{r}\left(\frac{\partial r}{\partial T}\right)_e dT + \frac{1}{r}\left(\frac{\partial r}{\partial e}\right)_T de + \frac{1}{L}\left(\frac{\partial L}{\partial T}\right)_e dT + \frac{1}{L}\left(\frac{\partial L}{\partial e}\right)_T de$$
$$- \frac{1}{A}\left(\frac{\partial A}{\partial T}\right)_e dT - \frac{1}{A}\left(\frac{\partial A}{\partial e}\right)_T de. \tag{6.21}$$

Combining and rearranging terms, we have

$$\frac{dR}{R} = C_R\, dT + \left(\frac{1}{r}\frac{\partial r}{\partial e} + \frac{1}{L}\frac{\partial L}{\partial e} - \frac{1}{A}\frac{\partial A}{\partial e}\right) \tag{6.22}$$

The expression

$$\left(\frac{1}{r}\frac{\partial r}{\partial e} + \frac{1}{L}\frac{\partial L}{\partial e} - \frac{1}{A}\frac{\partial A}{\partial e}\right)$$

is the strain sensitivity, or gage factor, of the metal resistance element. Here $\partial A = -2Av\,\partial e$, where v is Poisson's ratio for the gage factor of the wire; $(1/L)(\partial L/\partial e)$ equals 1, so $-(1/A)(\partial A/\partial e)$ equals $2v$. Strain sensitivity is thus defined by (6.23):

$$S_e = \frac{1}{r}\frac{\partial r}{\partial e} + 1 + 2v = \frac{1}{R}\frac{\partial R}{\partial e}. \tag{6.23}$$

6.10   SEMICONDUCTIVE RESISTANCE ELEMENTS

Semiconductors made of ceramic materials and used as temperature-sensitive resistance elements are called thermistors. They function at resistance levels many orders of magnitude higher than do conductive elements. Their responses to temperature changes are also many orders of magnitude greater, with the further difference that their thermal coefficients of resistance are negative. Figure 6.9 illustrates these differences.

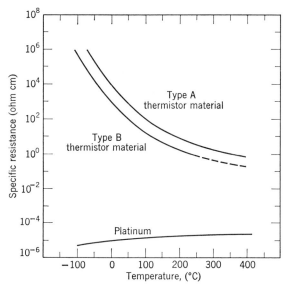

Figure 6.9   Comparison of thermistor and platinum resistance-temperature characteristics.

Thermistors are made in the shapes of beads, rods, disks, washers, and flakes, and in many sizes for each shape. Bead diameters, for example, can range from 0.006 to 0.100 in. (the corresponding resistance values can vary from 300 ohms to 100 megohms). Extended rods can vary in diameter from 0.05 to 0.17 in. and in length from 0.25 to 2 in. (with resistance values from 1000 to 150,000 ohms). Figure 6.10 illustrates various thermistor constructions.

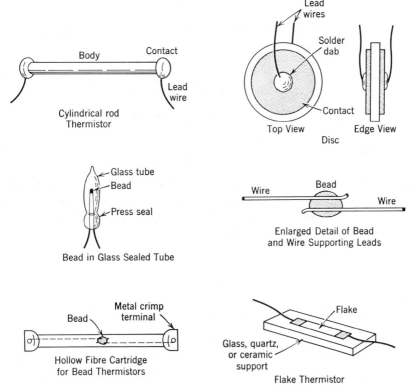

Figure 6.10 Various thermistor contructions. (From [10], by permission of D. Van Nostrand Co.)

The contacts can be affixed to the thermistors by first painting the contact surfaces with precious-metal paste and then firing to reduce the paste to a solid metallic film to which solder contacts can be attached. Beads are made by bridging two fine platinum alloy wires, held taut and parallel, 0.010 in. apart, with a small ellipsoid of thermistor material. The material is sintered at high temperature. The product may be coated with glass for protection or mounted in glass envelopes that have been either evacuated or filled with an inert gas.

6.11   RESISTANCE-TEMPERATURE CHARACTERISTIC FOR THERMISTORS

Bosson, Gutmann, and Simmons [7] have provided a most accurate equation for the relationship between resistance and temperature:

$$\log R = A + \frac{B}{T + \theta}, \tag{6.24}$$

where A, B, and θ are constants. For a temperature change from T_0 to T_1, the corresponding change in resistance is

$$T_0 - T_1 = -B\left[\frac{\log R_0/R_1}{(\log R_0 - A)(\log R_1 - A)}\right]. \tag{6.25}$$

For most purposes, however, an adequate expression is

$$\frac{R_1}{R_0} = \exp c\left(\frac{1}{T_1} - \frac{1}{T_0}\right), \tag{6.26}$$

where c is a constant dependent on the thermistor material. Typical values for c are 3500–4000. If T_2 is considered a fixed reference and T_1 is a variable, the thermal coefficient of resistance, $(1/R_1)(dR_1/dT_1)$, may be found by differentiating R_1 in (6.26) with respect to T_1:

$$\frac{1}{R_1}\frac{dR_1}{dT_1} = -\frac{c}{T_1^2}. \tag{6.27}$$

6.12   THERMISTOR SELF-HEATING

The electrical power dissipated instantaneously in a thermistor, IV (where V is the potential drop across the terminals and I is the current being passed through the instrument), is proportional to the instantaneous temperature

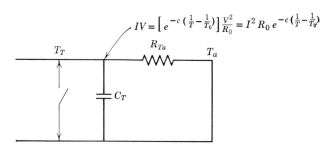

Figure 6.11   Thermal analogue of a thermistor.

difference between the thermistor and its ambient, $T_T - T_a$. This thermal situation is defined in Figure 6.11; C_T is the thermal capacity of the thermistor, and R_{T_a} is the thermal resistance between the thermistor and its environment. The equation describing the thermal behavior of the thermistor is derived from analysis of the analogue circuit (thus from thermal energy balance considerations):

$$IV - \frac{T_T - T_a}{R_{T_a}} = C_T \frac{dT_T}{d\theta}, \tag{6.28}$$

where θ is time.

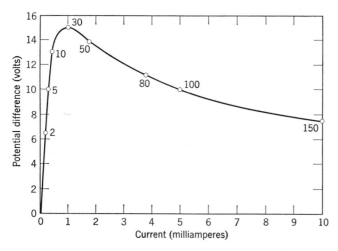

Figure 6.12   The nonohmic voltage-current characteristic of a thermistor. (From [5], by permission of the Institute of Electrical and Electronics Engineers.)

The steady-state functioning of the thermistor is considered first:

$$IV = \frac{T_T - T_a}{R_{T_a}}. \tag{6.29}$$

From (6.29), we note that an appreciable increase in current (greater than 1 milliampere) causes an increase in thermistor temperature T_T. With a thermistor's negative temperature coefficient of resistance this temperature rise commands a corresponding drop in electrical resistance of the thermistor material. The voltage across the thermistor is now less than if the resistance had remained constant.

Figure 6.12 illustrates the nonohmic voltage-current characteristic of a thermistor. If the current is sufficiently high to conspire with an unfavorable thermal resistance, there will be a large temperature potential between thermistor and ambient. When such a temperature relationship is stabilized, the result will be a false indication of the ambient temperature by the amount of the potential difference. Given such a self-heating effect, one is well advised to limit the amount of current supplied to a thermistor. Figure 6.12 also delineates temperature rise above ambient (300°K) as a function of current.

In order to determine the rate of temperature rise of the thermistor when a change occurs in its ambient temperature, reference is made to Figure 6.11 and (6.28):

$$I^2 R_0 \exp\left[+C\left(\frac{1}{T_T} - \frac{1}{T_0}\right)\right] - \frac{T_T - T_a}{R_T} = C_T \frac{dT_T}{d\theta}.$$

6.13 SOME RELATIVE MERITS OF CONDUCTIVE AND SEMICONDUCTIVE RESISTANCE ELEMENTS

The following list is a summary of the advantages and disadvantages associated with choices between temperature sensors that either have metal wire as their resistance element or are thermistors.

Stability (capability of maintaining the same temperature-resistance characteristic with time)	Metal conductor > thermistor (platinum > nickel, etc.)
Sensitivity $\left(\frac{1}{R_0}\frac{dR}{dT}\right)$	Thermistor > metal conductor.
Operating range	Platinum: from cryogenic temperatures to 2000°F. Nickel: up to 600°F. Thermistors: −150 to 500°F.
Small size	Manufacturers of thermistors or strain-gage type sensors claim that surfaces and spaces are essentially undisturbed by a gage's presence. The standard platinum resistance thermometer is at least 2 in. long and $\frac{1}{8}$ in. in diameter.
Ability to manufacture identical sensors	Metal conductors, yes; thermistors, no, except accidentally. However, thermistors cost much less than conductive elements.
Concern over lead wire resistance errors	Thermistors, no; metal conductors, yes.
Errors caused by aging	Insignificant for either type because of standard manufacturing processes.

Cost of Wheatstone bridge	Metal conductor > thermistor.
Sensitivity to changes in light intensity and pressure and to shock	Thermistors.
Current limitations	Thermistors > metal conductors.*
Rapid response	Both thermistors and strain gage types, yes; resistance thermometers, no in certain cases.
Annealing requirement to relieve residual strains	Resistance thermometers have this manufacturing requirement.
Absolute level of resistance	Thermistors > metal conductors.

REFERENCES

[1] *Asimov's Biographic Encyclopedia of Science and Engineering*, Doubleday, Garden City, N.Y., 1964.

[2] Baker, H. D., E. A. Ryder, and N. H. Baker, *Temperature Measurement in Engineering*, Wiley, New York, 1961.

[3] "Strain Gage Handbook," *Bulletin* 103–1, Baldwin-Lima-Hamilton, 1966.

[4] "Resistance Thermometers," *Product Data* 206–1 and 209, Baldwin-Lima-Hamilton, 1966.

[5] Becker, J. A., C. B. Green, and G. L. Pearson, "Properties and Uses of Thermistors," *Trans. AIEE*, **65**, 713 (1946).

[6] Beckwith, T. G., and N. L. Buck, *Mechanical Measurements*, Addison-Wesley, Reading, Mass., 1961.

[7] Bossun, G., F. Gutmann, and L. M. Simmons, "A Relationship between Resistance and Temperature of Thermistors," *J. Appl. Phys.*, **21**, 1267 (1950).

[8] Christie, S. H., *Phil. Trans. Roy. Soc. (London)*, Ser. A, **123**, 95 (1833).

[9] Dean, M., and R. D. Douglas, *Semiconductor and Conventional Strain Gages*, Academic Press, 1962.

[10] *Brochure* EMC-5 (on thermistors), Fenwal Electronics, 1966.

[11] Grant D. A. and W. F. Hickes, "Industrial Temperature Measurement with Nickel Resistance Thermometers " in *Temperature, Its Measurement and Control in Science and Industry*, C. M. Hertzfeld, ed.-in-chief, Vol. III, Part 2, Reinhold, New York, 1962.

[12] Hetenyi, M., ed., *Handbook of Experimental Stress Analysis*, Wiley, New York, 1950.

[13] Hickes, W. F., "Temperature Measurements " American Society for Metals, 1956.

[14] Meaden, G. T., *Electrical Resistance of Metals*, Plenum Press, New York, 1965.

[15] *Dictionary of National Biography* Oxford University Press.

[16] Perry, C. C., and H. R. Lissner, *The Strain Gage Primer* (2nd ed.), McGraw-Hill, New York, 1962.

[17] Pharo, L. C., "Some Characteristics of the VECO 32A8 Thermistor Operating in a Self-Heated Condition," *Rev. Sci. Instr.*, **36**, No. 2 (February, 1965).

* The self-heating effect in metal conductor resistance elements can be calibrated.

[18] "RDF Stikon Resistance Elements for Temperature Measurement and Control," *Form* T-65, RDF Corp., 1966.

[19] Scott, R. B., *Cryogenic Engineering*, Van Nostrand, Princeton, N.J., 1959.

[20] Shive, J. N., *Semiconductor Devices*, Van Nostrand, Princeton, N.J., 1959.

[21] Sinnott, M. J., *The Solid State for Engineers*, Wiley, New York, 1963.

[22] Werner, F. D., "Some Recent Developments in Applied Platinum Resistance Thermometry," in *Temperature, Its Measurement and Control in Science and Industry*, C. M. Hertzfeld, ed.-in-Chief, Vol. III, Part 2, Reinhold, New York, 1962.

[23] Carmichael, C., ed., *Kent's Mechanical Engineers Handbook*, Wiley, New York, 1955.

[24] Lyman, T., ed., *Metals Handbook*, American Society for Metals, 1948.

7

Electronic Temperature Control Equipment

7.1 INTRODUCTION

Proportional temperature control of a mass is effected when, for example, the level of power expended by a heating element thermally connected to the mass is regulated in direct proportion to the error between the sensed temperature and the ideal, or set-point, temperature of the mass. Such control is accomplished by varying the ratio of ON to OFF time in the control heater's duty cycle. The value of resistance of a temperature-measuring element is converted into the duty cycle appropriate to restoring the temperature of the sensitive mass to the set-point temperature.

The block diagram describing an electronic temperature control circuit is illustrated in Figure 7.1. The error signal output of the bridge is amplified as required, and the appropriate duty cycle ratio, based on the temperature of the sensing element, is selected by the control circuit. The power switching

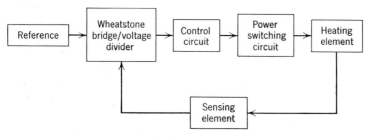

Figure 7.1   Electronic temperature-control circuit.

circuit activates the heating element for the appropriate portion of time during each operating cycle.

The operational characteristics of several elements of the electronic temperature control circuit are treated in this chapter. Solid-state devices that may be used in the control and switching circuits are silicon controlled rectifiers, unijunction transistors, and magnetic amplifiers. These devices characteristically contain no moving parts, can withstand considerable shock and vibration, will operate over a fairly wide range of environmental temperatures, and are stable in their operation with time. Both heating and fluid-circulating elements are discussed at the end of the chapter.

7.2   THE SILICON CONTROLLED RECTIFIER

The silicon controlled rectifier (SCR) is a four-layer-semiconductor, solid-state device which operates as an ON-OFF switch under the control of an

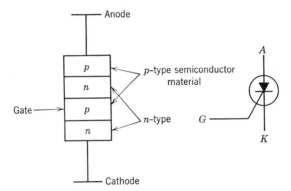

Figure 7.2   SCR schematic representation and symbol.

electrode called a *gate*. The schematic representation of a SCR and the symbol for it are illustrated in Figure 7.2. When no current is applied to the gate the SCR is practically an open circuit. When a relatively small current is applied to it however, the rectifier becomes suddenly conductive in the forward direction from anode to cathode and passes large currents. (The rectifier can also be fired by increasing its forward voltage, with its gate open, above a particular value, called its forward breakover voltage.) Conduction through the SCR cannot be turned off by the control electrode; the current from anode to cathode must be temporarily interrupted to permit the rectifier to return to the nonconducting condition.

The controlled rectifier characteristic is shown in Figure 7.3. In the reverse region it is that of a normal rectifier. A small but relatively constant reverse leakage current flows until the reverse voltage exceeds a particular level above which the device fails. This allowable level, which may be several hundred volts, depends on the process of manufacturing the SCR. In the forward region, with no gate current the device is nonconducting and in the OFF state. The SCR is switched on by the imposition of either sufficient gate current or an excessively large forward voltage. Multiampere currents can flow with a voltage drop of about 1 volt between the anode and the cathode. The rectifier returns to its nonconducting state when the forward current (that between the anode and cathode) is reduced below 1 mil.

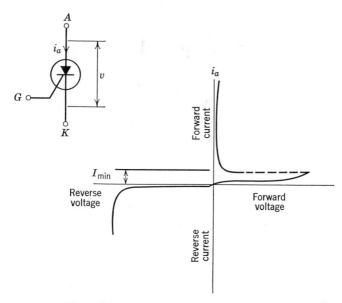

Figure 7.3 Controlled rectifier characteristic.

Controlled rectifiers have a very large power gain. Once they are turned on they stay on, so that, although a certain amount of power is required to turn them on, it can be in the form of a short pulse containing extremely low energy.

The SCR can control large amounts of power by one of four basic methods mentioned in Figure 7.4. In the first method, the device is used simply as an ON-OFF switch (a). By operating on an a-c voltage level between the anode and cathode that is less than the forward breakover voltage, the average current through the device can be controlled by applying a pulse to the gate electrode at specific phase angles of that waveform (b). Also included are techniques that can be used with d-c input power and require an extra circuit to turn the SCR off. This circuit can be varied to turn off the SCR on

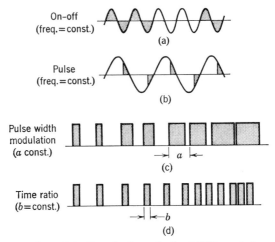

Figure 7.4 Four basic methods of SCR control.

command, as in scheme c; the circuit can automatically turn off the SCR after a certain fixed period, as in scheme d.

7.3 THE UNIJUNCTION TRANSISTOR

The unijunction transistor (UJT), a three-terminal semiconductor device which acts as a voltage sensitive switch, can be used to fire a silicon controlled rectifier. The UJT has a stable firing voltage, a very low firing current, and is capable of operating over a temperature range of -55 to $+140°C$.

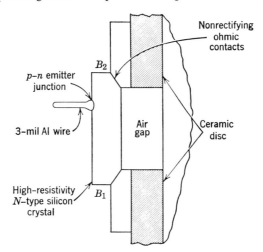

Figure 7.5 Mechanical arrangement of a UJT.

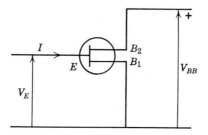

Figure 7.6 Parametric representation of a UJT.

A mechanical arrangement of an UJT is shown in Figure 7.5. An emitter junction is formed at a point part way between the ohmic base contacts which are at the ends of a low-conductivity *n*-type silicon pellet. The emitter junction modulates the conductivity of the silicon crystal.

The UJT is represented parametrically in Figure 7.6. Normally the device is operated with a d-c potential between the two base electrodes. When the voltage between the emitter and base 1 has built up sufficiently and exceeds a proportion of the voltage V_{BB} between base 2 and base 1, the UJT becomes a short circuit. That critical voltage level for a given value of V_{BB} is denoted by the "peak point" of Figure 7.7.

The functioning of the UJT is illustrated schematically in Figure 7.8. The ON condition (the peak-point voltage) having been reached, the conductivity of the device increases rapidly, the resistance, corresponding to R_1, decreases by a larger ratio than the current increases (hence the device is said to have a negative resistance characteristic), and thus the emitter voltage V_E decreases.

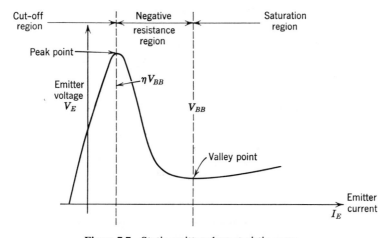

Figure 7.7 Static emitter characteristic curve.

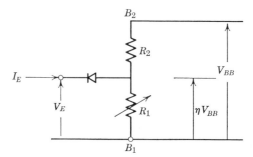

Figure 7.8   Schematic functioning of UJT.

When this voltage falls below the level ηV_{BB}, the *p-n* junction is reverse-biased and little current flows.

The basic UJT trigger circuit used to fire a SCR is the relaxation oscillator shown in Figure 7.9. At the beginning of the operating cycle the UJT is reverse-biased and therefore nonconducting. The capacitor C_1 is charged through the resistor R_1, and the emitter voltage V_E rises exponentially toward the supply voltage V_{BB} until it reaches the peak-point value V_{max}. The UJT then becomes forward-biased (turns on), rapidly discharges C_1, and the emitter voltage drops quickly. When the emitter voltage V_E reaches a value V_{min} equal to the valley-point voltage (of Figure 7.7) plus the valley-point current times the base 1 resistance load, the UJT becomes reverse-biased and ceases to conduct.

In Figure 7.10 voltage V_E across the capacitor C_1 is a sawtooth waveform whose frequency is controlled by the time constant R_1C_1 and the characteristics of the UJT and associated circuitry. The resulting V_3 voltage pulses, similar in shape to current pulses through R_3, are shown together with the sawtooth voltage waveform.

The current pulses through R_3 can be used to fire controlled junction rectifiers. Control over the output of a load connected to a rectifier is

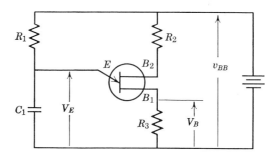

Figure 7.9   Basic UJT trigger circuit.

accomplished by proportionally delaying the firing pulse to the rectifier gate, and thus permitting conduction of current to the load only over a selected portion of the current's cyclic waveform. This typical application is illustrated in the electronic thermostat designed by Ferrie [2]. In the circuit of Figure 7.11, resistor R_T is a thermistor thermally connected to the mass to be controlled. The controlled temperature is determined by the voltage divider formed by resistors R_T and R_1. As the controlled mass's temperature declines, the value of R_T increases, and the UJT emitter voltage increases. When the emitter voltage exceeds the peak-point voltage of the emitter characteristic,

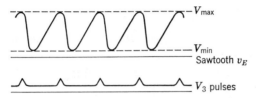

Figure 7.10   Typical waveforms of UJT trigger circuit.

the UJT oscillates and fires the SCR. As the temperature of the controlled mass rises, R_T decreases, the UJT emitter voltage is less than the peak-point value, and oscillations cease. The SCR is no longer fired.

With the resistance of the thermistor $R_T = R_0 \exp [B(1/T - 1/T_0)]$, and for a given SCR and R_T, the value of R_1 required to maintain the temperature T is

$$R_1 = \frac{R_0 \exp [B(1/T - 1/T_0)](E_1 - V_p)}{V_p - I_p R_0 \exp [B(1/T - 1/T_0)]},$$

where R_0 = thermistor resistance at temperature T_0,
   T_0 = reference temperature,
   T = desired temperature,
   B = thermistor constant,
   E_1 = d-c supply voltage,
   V_p = unijunction peak-point voltage,
   I_p = unijunction peak-point current.

7.4   THE MAGNETIC AMPLIFIER

A magnetic amplifier is a combination of a saturable core reactor and rectifying elements. The material used as the core is iron, which is easily magnetized and is characterized by nonlinearity of its magnetic curve (which defines the relationship between magnetizing force H and flux density B) and saturation phenomena. In temperature control applications, these

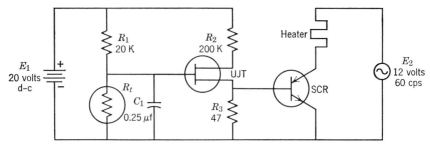

Figure 7.11 Temperature control circuit. (Reprinted from *Electronics*, October 5, 1964; copyrighted by McGraw-Hill.)

properties can be used to provide time-variable impedance in a load circuit controlling a heater or fan.

The functioning of a saturable core reactor, illustrated in Figure 7.12, is now examined. Consider Figure 7.13, the idealized *B-H* loop for a typical core material. When the magnetic reactor is driven by one of the half cycles of the line voltage so that its flux increases along the line *ab*, it presents such a high impedance that substantially all the input voltage is dropped across it. When during that half cycle the core becomes saturated, the magnetizing force increases along the line *bcd*. There, the reactor impedance is negligible and substantially all of the line voltage appears across the reactor output. On the reverse line voltage half cycle the flux is driven out of saturation in a direction opposite to that of the flux change during the previous half cycle

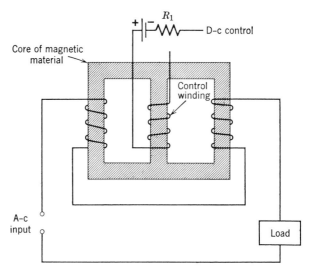

Figure 7.12 Saturable reactor.

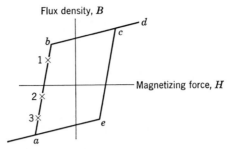

Figure 7.13   Idealized *B-H* curve.

and conduction across the output ceases. The quiescent point on the *B-H* diagram around which the flux density varies as a function of gate current is set by the d-c current in the control winding.

A magnetic amplifier is illustrated in Figure 7.14. Relatively large amounts of power can be controlled across the load by comparatively small amounts of power in the reactor's input windings. In a temperature control application the output power level is regulated by transmitting the signal ultimately derived from a temperature-sensing element to the reactor's control winding. At the start of the positive half cycle of line voltage, the core is at some initial flux density B_0, the value set by the control circuit. The flux density proceeds toward saturation as the line volt-seconds increase. At the firing instant (when saturation has been reached and the core can no longer sustain the load) substantially full line voltage transfers from the core winding to the load. If

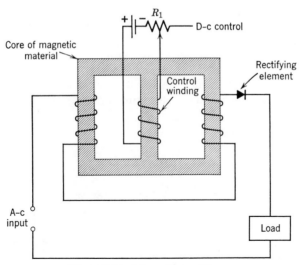

Figure 7.14   Magnetic amplifier.

Figure 7.15   Various waveform outputs from magnetic amplifier.

the control flux corresponds to the abscissa of point b in Figure 7.13 or to that of any point to its right, the reactor core is already saturated and the load voltage waveform is that of the full-wave rectification shown in Figure 7.15a. For any point whose abscissa is to the left of that of point b, such as points 1, 2, and 3, time elapses while the flux builds up the saturation level and effective conduction commences. The effect on the load voltage waveform occasioned by moving increasingly further to the left of the abscissa of point b is illustrated in Figures 7.15b, c, and d. As the temperature of the resistance element used for providing current in the control winding changes, the current flowing through that winding changes also.

In the reactor-rectifier amplifier, no line voltage is applied during the negative half cycle and all the control voltage available is effective in producing flux change. The control circuit must handle only the energy per half cycle necessary to change the flux, and the power gain is much higher than can be obtained with a saturable reactor alone.

Schematic diagrams of magnetic amplifier circuits are illustrated in Figures 7.16 and 7.17. In Figure 7.16 the amplifier is designed to supply both halves of the line voltage waveform to the load. Two windings are used on the saturable core reactor; each is wound around the core in such a direction that the control winding is assisted in saturating that core. The rectifier in series with each winding permits current to flow in only one winding at a time.

7.5   ELECTRICAL RESISTANCE HEATERS

A resistance element heater (in the heating element of which the Joule effect causes power to be generated in direct proportion to the square of the

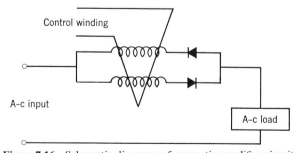

Figure 7.16   Schematic diagrams of magnetic amplifier circuits.

current being passed through it) may be used to increase power dissipation from the vicinity of the controlled mass and to regulate the mass's temperature. (Power may be dissipated at any point on the thermal path connecting the controlled mass to the heat sink, but with decreasing efficiency as the heater is moved away from the mass.) Such heaters are flexible in their size (they can be made rather small) and shape. Two varieties are considered: the cartridge type, which is inserted into a drilled hole, and the blanket type, which is mounted to a surface with a suitable adhesive.

Cartridge heaters are generally cylindrical, as small as $\frac{1}{4}$ in. in diameter and of practically any length. The resistance element in a cartridge heater is

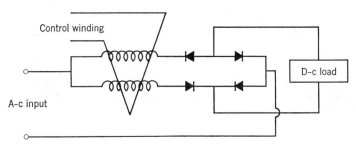

Figure 7.17 Schematic diagrams of magnetic amplifier circuits.

spiraled on a mandrel and is well connected thermally to the device case. Blanket heaters may be less than $\frac{1}{16}$ in. thick and can be made to cover irregularly shaped areas. Typical resistance elements are manufactured by spiraling nickel alloy wires around glass strings; the elements are laminated between two sheets of glass cloth calender-coated with silicone rubber. (Air is purged from the assembly later.)

A heater's *power density* (power divided by area of dissipating surface) is regulated by its allowable operating temperature and the thermal resistance between the heater and heated mass. The life of a heater is determined by its actual operating temperature and by its frequency of cycling.

In the case of a cartridge heater, the magnitude of the heating element's temperature rise above that of the mass in which the device is mounted is determined by the power density of the heater and the thermal resistance between heating element and heated mass. That resistance is a function of the tolerance between the cartridge and the diameter of its mounting hole. Figure 7.18 illustrates the variation in maximum allowable heated mass temperature with watt density for various diametral gaps between heater and mounting hole.

Similarly, in the case of a blanket heater, the thermal resistance between heating element and heated mass multiplied by the power density of the heater

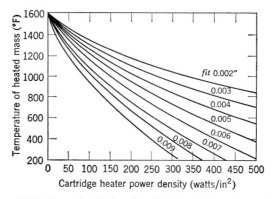

Figure 7.18 Operating limits of typical electrical resistance heaters.

determines the element's operating temperature. The graph of Figure 7.19 shows the variation in maximum allowable heated mass temperature with power density for several heater-mounting arrangements, both for a blanket fixed to a solid surface and for a blanket hanging freely in air.

7.6 BLOWERS AND FANS

The blower (fan) required in a particular thermomechanical situation is defined by the cooling requirements (which may be variable) presented by the situation, by the resistance, in pressure drop, offered by the system through which the coolant is to be piped, by the limitations on blower shaft speed, and by the spatial restrictions of the situation.

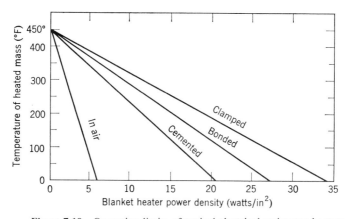

Figure 7.19 Operating limits of typical electrical resistance heaters.

The head (H_L, in feet) developed between the blower inlet and outlet and defined as the shaft work that would be needed per unit weight of fluid, with no friction and no change in elevation between inlet and outlet, is comprised of two components, static pressure $(p_o - p_i)/\rho$ and velocity pressure $(V_o^2 - V_i^2)/2g$. Thus H_L is given by

$$H_L = \frac{p_o - p_i}{\rho} + \frac{V_o^2 - V_i^2}{2g}.$$

Because most of a blower's output is in the form of static pressure, conservative practice dictates that only that portion of the blower's output

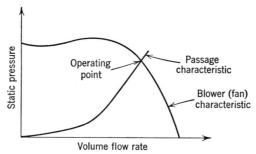

Figure 7.20 Blower-passage characteristics.

be considered. A blower is characterized by plots of air flow versus static pressure for various fixed values of shaft speed. To determine the operating point of a system in which a particular blower, running at a given speed, is forcing air through certain passages, the intersection of the characteristic blower plot and a plot of passage static pressure drop as a function of flow rate is found. Such an operating point is indicated in the plot of Figure 7.20.

The static efficiency η_s of a blower is computed from the product of the weight fluid flow ρQ and static pressure head h_s divided by the input power P. Thus

$$\eta_s = \frac{\rho Q h_s}{33,000P}.$$

Electrical operating power is minimized if the blower is operated at its maximum efficiency, a value at which there will obtain particular related values of flow rate, static pressure, and operating shaft speed.

The specific speed N_s of a blower, defined by the relation

$$N_s = \frac{NQ^{0.5}}{h_s^{0.75}} = \frac{(\text{rpm}) \times (\text{cfm})^{0.5}}{(\text{static pressure})^{0.75}},$$

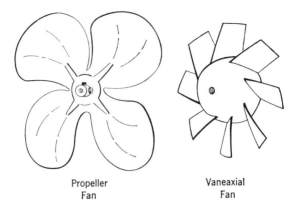

Propeller
Fan

Vaneaxial
Fan

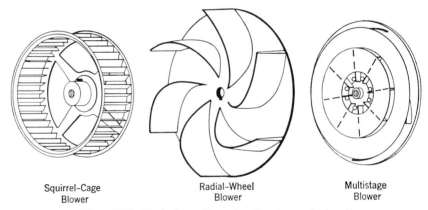

Squirrel-Cage
Blower

Radial-Wheel
Blower

Multistage
Blower

Figure 7.21   Typical impellers of various types of "fans."

serves as the basis of blower-type selection. Ranges of specific speeds for the various blowers and fans shown in Figure 7.21 are given in Table 7.1.

The Fan laws, derived from dimensional analysis of the variables Q, P, d (blower dimension), and N, relate flow rate, static pressure, and power requirements to changes in the value of any one of the parameters—blower size, shaft speed, or coolant density—when the other two are constant.

1. For constant coolant density ρ but at variable blower speed N:
   Q is directly proportional to N,
   h_s is directly proportional to N^2,
   P is directly proportional to N^3.

Table 7.1 Specific Speeds of Typical Fluid Circulators

Type of Fluid Circulator	Specific Speed (RPM)
Propeller fan	100,000–400,000
Vaneaxial fan	50,000–125,000
Radial-wheel blower	4,000–20,000
Multistage blower	900–8,000
Squirrel-cage blower, Forward curved	
Loose scroll	30,000–70,000
Tight scroll	9,000–40,000

2. For variable density and with fan size and speed fixed:
   Q is invariant with ρ,
   h_s is directly proportional to ρ,
   P is directly proportional to ρ.
3. For constant speed N and density ρ but with impeller size variable:
   Q is directly proportional to d^2,
   h_s is invariant with d,
   P is proportional to d^3.

The required altitude to sea-level air weight flow ratios required for a constant rate of cooling of a given surface, for both turbulent and laminar flow conditions, are as follows:

For turbulent flow:

$$\frac{W(\text{altitude})}{W(\text{sea level})} = \frac{\Delta T(\text{sea level})}{\Delta T(\text{altitude})} ;$$

For laminar flow:

$$\frac{W(\text{altitude})}{W(\text{sea level})} = \left(\frac{\Delta T(\text{sea level})}{\Delta T(\text{altitude})}\right)^3 ;$$

where W = air mass flow,
   ΔT = available temperature difference between incoming air and surface temperature.

REFERENCES

[1] Ferretti, A. J., "Fans and Blowers for Cooling Electronic Equipment," *Electromech. Design: System Designer's Handbook*, January, 1965.
[2] Ferrie, R. G., "Thermostat Operates with 0.01°C Differential," *Electronics*, **37**, No. 26, 65–66 (October 5, 1964).
[3] General Electric Co., *SCR Manual* (2nd ed.), 1961.
[4] General Electric Co., *Transistor Manual* (7th ed.), 1964.

[5] Geyger, W. A., *Nonlinear-Magnetic Control Devices*, McGraw-Hill, New York, 1964.

[6] Hill, W. R., *Electronics in Engineering*, McGraw-Hill, New York, 1961.

[7] Osborne, W. C., *Fans*, Pergamon Press, New York, 1966.

[8] RAMA Industrial Heater Co., Brochure (on heaters).

[9] Rotron Manufacturing Co., General Catalogue (on Blowers).

[10] Ruiter, J. H., Jr., and R. G. Murphy, *Basic Industrial Electronic Controls*, Holt Rinehart, and Winston, New York, 1961, 1962.

[11] Shea, R. F., ed., *Amplifier Handbook*, McGraw-Hill, New York, 1966.

[12] Truxal, J. G., ed., *Control Engineers Handbook*, McGraw-Hill, New York, 1958.

[13] WATLOW Electric, *Catalogue* 139 (on heaters).

8

Mechanical Thermostats

8.1 INTRODUCTION

A mechanical thermostat is a device that can be used to control the temperatures of one or more masses contained in a structure. It is generally a component of an ON-OFF temperature control system which also includes the controlled masses, the structure and its environment, regulated heating and cooling components, and heat sources and sinks. The thermostat is usually located on or in close proximity to a controlled mass. It performs the functions of both the feedback element and the reference input of the control system (if thus compares the measured and set-point temperatures) and sends signals (proportional to temperature differences) to heating and cooling components. It is inserted electrically between a current source and the heating or cooling component.

The thermostat operates in the following way. It contains a sensitive element which moves or grows as its temperature changes. This movement (or growth) is used to selectively open or close the heating (or cooling) component circuit. The thermostat performs one switching function at a predetermined temperature, its *set point*, which is fixed in the device by mechanical means. It reverses the switching function at another temperature, displaced from the set point by a certain amount, called the *temperature differential*. In some thermostats it is possible to arrange the element so that it can either open or close on temperature rise; in others, such as the mercury-in-glass type, where bidirectional motion of the element with temperature rise is proscribed, the functioning can be adjusted electronically. The control characteristic of a thermostat which opens on temperature rise is illustrated in Figure 8.1.

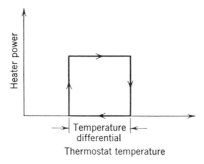

Figure 8.1   Control characteristic of thermostat which opens heater circuit on temperature rise.

Mechanical thermostats suitable for controlling the temperatures of moderate-sized masses have these typical characteristics:

1. They are rather small, generally less than 2 in. long and not more than $\frac{1}{2}$ in. in their next largest dimension.

2. Variations in their construction provide for both surface-mounting and immersion types.

3. Heat is transferred to their sensitive elements by conduction.

4. Their speed of response depends on their size and on the thermal resistance between their sensitive elements and sensed masses.

5. Their control operation is ON-OFF.

6. Their useful life expectancies are heavily dependent on the magnitudes of the electrical loads passed through them.

7. Set-point temperatures of some types are dependent on the electrical load level being switched.

8. Set-point temperatures can be altered.

9. Variations in operating temperature differentials range from several tenths to several degrees Fahrenheit.

10. Set-point temperatures may be set to accuracies varying from several tenths to 1 or 2°F.

8.2   BIMETALLIC ELEMENTS

Two broad classifications of bimetallic elements, creep and snap-action, are covered in the following discussion. The essence of the operation of both types of elements is their propensity for movement upon being heated or cooled. This characteristic is utilized in several ways, usually in mechanical thermostats that open and close electric heater circuits. (Also, bimetallic elements may be used to change thermal resistance values, as described in Section 8.9.) Movement is caused by differential thermal expansion of two metal alloys, of different thermal coefficients of expansion, which are fused together.

Differences in functioning of the two classifications of elements are illustrated in Figure 8.2. The illustrations are based on observations that (*a*) movement of the creep element is directly proportional to sensed temperature (Section 8.3) and (*b*) the nature of the snap-action element is such that it is position-unstable with sufficient temperature change (Section 8.5).

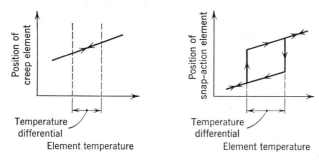

Figure 8.2 Functioning of creep and snap-action bimetallic elements.

The definitive "Analysis of Bi-Metal Thermostats" was published by S. Timoshenko [11] in 1925. In addition to other material, part of his paper is included here, both for convenience and for an indication of the scope of the work.

8.3 BENDING OF BIMETALLIC ELEMENTS

Timoshenko's analysis first treats elements used in creep thermostats (Figure 8.3). They are constructed of two metal strips, of equal length but of different thermal coefficients of expansion, fused together along long edges. The values of coefficients of expansion are invariant with temperature change; the element is considered heated uniformly. As the temperature of the element rises, each component attempts to elongate at a different rate. The less sensitive member restrains the longitudinal elongation of its more expansive mate, so that at the intersurface the unit elongation is equal in each component, and the element bends into a smooth curve with the component of higher thermal coefficient of expansion on the convex side. The internal forces in the less expansive member can be reduced to a tensile force P_1 and a couple M_1; those in the more expansive member, to a compressive force P_2 and a couple M_2.

The analysis proceeds as follows. In a freely supported, uniformly heated bimetallic strip with no external forces acting on it, all internal forces must

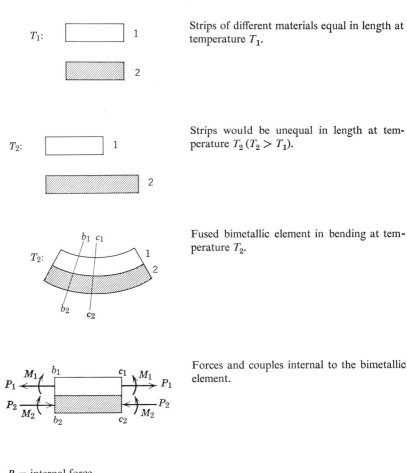

Strips of different materials equal in length at temperature T_1.

Strips would be unequal in length at temperature T_2 ($T_2 > T_1$).

Fused bimetallic element in bending at temperature T_2.

Forces and couples internal to the bimetallic element.

P = internal force,
M = internal moment of force,
α_1, α_2 = thermal coefficients of expansion ($\alpha_2 > \alpha_1$) of materials,
a_1, a_2 = thickness of element's components,
E_1, E_2 = moduli of elasticity of materials,
w = width of bimetallic element ($=$ unity),
t = thickness of element ($= a_1 + a_2$),
ρ = radius of curvature of element caused by temperature rise $T_2 - T_1$,
$m = a_1/a_2$; $n = E_1/E_2$.

Figure 8.3 Analysis of bending of bimetallic strip due to temperature change.

be in equilibrium. Thus

$$P_1 = P_2 = P,$$

and

$$(8.1)$$

$$M_1 + M_2 = \frac{Pt}{2}.$$

The radius of curvature of a beam in bending, ρ, has been shown to be equal to EI/M, and thus, for the bimetallic element,

$$\rho = \frac{E_1 I_1}{M_1} = \frac{E_2 I_2}{M_2}. \tag{8.2}$$

Therefore

$$\frac{Pt}{2} = \frac{E_1 I_1 + E_2 I_2}{\rho}. \tag{8.3}$$

From the condition that at the intersurface the unit elongation of each component must be the same,

$$\alpha_1(T_2 - T_1) + \frac{P_1}{E_1 a_1} + \frac{a_1}{2\rho} = \alpha_2(T_2 - T_1) - \frac{P_2}{E_2 a_2} - \frac{a_2}{2\rho}. \tag{8.4}$$

where the terms $P_n/E_n a_n$ are elongations arising from the longitudinal forces P_n, and the terms $a_n/2\rho$ are elongations (at the farthest distances from the components' neutral axis) resulting from the couples M_n. Rearranging and substituting $P_1 = P_2 = P$, $a_1 + a_2 = t$, and (8.3), we have

$$\frac{1}{\rho} = \frac{(\alpha_2 - \alpha_1)(T_2 - T_1)}{(t/2) + [2(E_1 I_1 + E_2 I_2)/t](1/E_1 a_1) + (1/E_2 a_2)}. \tag{8.5}$$

The component cross sections are rectangular, so $I_1 = a_1^3/12$ and $I_2 = a_2^3/12$. Substituting $E_1/E_2 = n$ and $a_1/a_2 = m$, the following equation is obtained:

$$\frac{1}{\rho} = \frac{6(\alpha_2 - \alpha_1)(T_2 - T_1)(1 + m)^2}{t[3(1 + m)^2 + (1 + mn)(m^2 + 1/mn)]}. \tag{8.6}$$

If the components are of equal thickness, $m = 1$, and

$$\frac{1}{\rho_{m=1}} = \frac{24(\alpha_2 - \alpha_1)(T_2 - T_1)}{t(14 + n + 1/n)}. \tag{8.7}$$

This curvature is a maximum for $n = 1 (E_1 = E_2)$. The curvature $1/\rho_{m=1}$ for any value of n as a percentage of $1/\rho_{m=1}$ for $n = 1$ is

$$\frac{1}{\rho_{m=1}} = \frac{1600}{14 + n + 1/n}. \tag{8.8}$$

If the components are of equal modulus of elasticity, $n = 1$, and

$$\frac{1}{\rho_{n=1}} = \frac{6(\alpha_2 - \alpha_1)(T_2 - T_1)m}{t(1 + m)^2}.$$ (8.9)

This curvature is a maximum for $m = 1$ $(a_1 = a_2)$. The curvature $1/\rho_{n=1}$ for any value of m as a percentage of $1/\rho_{n=1}$ for $m = 1$ is

$$\frac{1}{\rho_{n=1}} = \frac{400m}{(1 + m)^2}.$$ (8.10)

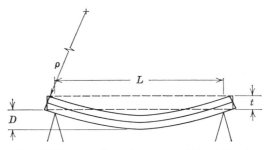

Figure 8.4   Deflection of simply supported bimetallic element.

Finally, the element curvature is a maximum if $a_1/a_2 = (E_2/E_1)^{1/2}$ and the components are not necessarily of equal thickness or equal modulus of elasticity. For $a_1/a_2 = (E_2/E_1)^{1/2} = 1$, however, the curvature is given by

$$\frac{1}{\rho} = \frac{3}{2} \frac{(\alpha_2 - \alpha_1)(T_2 - T_1)}{t}.$$ (8.11)

The thermal deflection of a simply supported bimetallic element whose curvature is given by (8.11) is readily computed. The relationship between the radius of curvature, thermal deflection, and distance between supports is given by

$$\frac{1}{\rho} = \frac{8D}{L^2},$$ (8.12)

where the parameters are found in Figure 8.4.

Combining (8.11) and (8.12) yields the thermal deflection,

$$D = \frac{3}{16} \frac{(\alpha_2 - \alpha_1)(T_2 - T_1)L^2}{t}.$$ (8.13)

For purposes of comparing several shapes of bimetallic strip elements, (8.13) is written so that the thermal deflection is related to the temperature rise, length, and thickness of the element by a deflection constant, K. Thus,

$$D = \frac{K(T_2 - T_1)L^2}{t}. \tag{8.14}$$

The mechanical force required to produce a similar deflection is

$$P = \frac{64EDwt^3}{L^3}. \tag{8.15}$$

The elemental thermal force is defined as that force necessary to return a heated bimetallic strip element to its original position. It is found by substituting the elemental thermal deflection in (8.15) for the mechanical force. Thus the thermal force of a simply supported bimetallic element is

$$P = \frac{64KE(T_2 - T_1)t^2}{L}. \tag{8.16}$$

Table 8.1 is a comparison of the thermal functionings of several shapes of bimetallic strip elements. The deflection constant is equal for all shapes included; the equality indicates that the relative values of thickness, thermal coefficient of expansion, and modulus of elasticity for the element components are equal in all cases.

Both the modulus of elasticity of each component and the thermal deflection constant of each combination of components are determined empirically. The range of values of K is $1 - 8 \times 10^{-5}$; that of EK is $1 - 9 \times 10^2$.

The maximum stress at the intersurface may now be computed. From (8.3) and (8.11),* with $I = \frac{1}{96}t^3$:

$$P = \frac{t}{16}(T_2 - T_1)(\alpha_2 - \alpha_1)E. \tag{8.17}$$

Also,

$$M_1 = M_2 = \frac{3}{2}\frac{(T_2 - T_1)(\alpha_2 - \alpha_1)EI}{t}. \tag{8.18}$$

The maximum intersurface stress is obtained by adding the tensile stress due to the curvature, $1/\rho$, to the tensile stress due to the force P:

$$\sigma_{\max} = \frac{2P}{t} + \frac{tE}{4\rho}.$$

$$= \tfrac{1}{2}(T_2 - T_1)(\alpha_2 - \alpha_1)E. \tag{8.19}$$

* The modulus of elasticity and the thickness of each component are equal.

Table 8.1 Comparison of Thermal Functionings of Several Shapes of Bimetallic Elements

Element	Thermal Deflection	Mechanical Force	Thermal Force
Simply-supported beam	$\dfrac{K(T_2 - T_1)L^2}{t}$	$\dfrac{64EDwt^3}{L^3}$	$\dfrac{64KE(T_2 - T_1)t^2}{L}$
Cantilever	$\dfrac{4K(T_2 - T_1)L^2}{t}$	$\dfrac{4EDwt^3}{L^3}$	$\dfrac{16KE(T_2 - T_1)t^2}{L}$

U-Shape

$$\frac{2K(T_2 - T_1)L^2}{t}$$

$$\frac{16EDwt^3}{L^3}$$

$$\frac{32KE(T_2 - T_1)t^2}{L}$$

8.4 BENDING OF MULTICOMPONENT ELEMENTS

Vasudevan [12] and Johnson have analyzed the use of more than two components in strip thermostat elements. The materials included have different thermal coefficients of expansion but nearly equal moduli of elasticity and equal thicknesses. Multicomponent elements have lower curvatures and intersurface stresses than bicomponent elements if the total thicknesses of both elements are equal and if the greatest difference in the thermal coefficients of expansion in the multicomponent case equals the difference in the thermal coefficients of expansion of the two materials of the bimetallic unit. For a trimetal strip the curvature is given by

$$\frac{1}{\rho} = \Delta T \frac{4}{3t} (\alpha_1 - \alpha_3).$$ (8.20*a*)

For a quadrimetal strip the curvature is given by

$$\frac{1}{\rho} = \Delta T \frac{3}{8t} [3(\alpha_1 - \alpha_4) + (\alpha_2 - \alpha_3)].$$ (8.20*b*)

8.5 SNAP-ACTION ELEMENT OPERATION

The snap-action operation of a bimetallic strip (from which may be inferred the operation of the well-known bimetallic snap-action disk) is as follows. The element is mounted hinged between fixed supports, as shown in Figure 8.5. Two thermostat-metal strips, equal in thickness and nearly equal in modulus of elasticity, are fused so that the composite element is normally (at set-point temperature and below, say) deflected, with the material of higher thermal coefficient of expansion on the concave side. In this position, *ABC*, the element may be supposed to be closing a heating circuit. As the element temperature rises, the more thermally expansive material grows faster than its less active mate, and the element, pushing against the retaining walls, attempts to flatten out. Compressive forces caused by the end constraints are developed. When, at position *ADC*, these forces attain a certain value, the element buckles and snaps to the new position *AEC*, and the heater

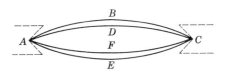

Figure 8.5 Various positions of snap-action bimetallic element.

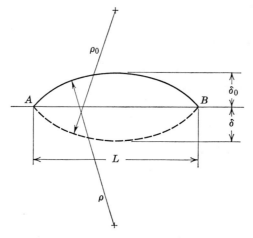

Figure 8.6 Free bending of a bimetallic element.

circuit is broken. As the element cools further it again attempts to flatten out, now in order to accommodate the more active material on the convex side of the curved element. Again compressive forces are developed, and at position AFC the element buckles and snaps to reclose the heating circuit. Element temperature rises, and the cycle is repeated.

Timoshenko's analysis of the functioning of a snap-action bimetallic strip element proceeds from the following computations:

1. The final deflection of a free-bending element that has reversed its curvature with temperature change.

2. The compressive force in an end-restrained element, developed with decrease in the element's deflection.

3. The compressive force in an end-restrained element that will prevent buckling of the element when both the temperature and deflection are given (Figure 8.6).

Nomenclature is as follows:

P = compressive forces on end-restrained bimetallic element,

$\alpha_2 - \alpha_1$ = difference in thermal coefficients of expansion of components of the element,

ρ_0 = initial curvature of element,

ρ = curvature of element at temperature T,

δ = deflection of element in downward direction after heating, for the case of free bending,

δ_0 = initial deflection of element (no compressive forces acting),

δ_1 = deflection of element at which it buckles,

T_0 = initial temperature of the element,
t = thickness of the element,
w = width of the element = unity,
L = distance between ends of the element, when it is either free-bending or held between fixed supports,
T = temperature at which element buckles,
T_2 = temperature when the deflection for the free-bending case is δ_0.

1. The sum of deflections of a free-bending element AB that has reversed its curvature with temperature change can be written after referring to (8.11):

$$\frac{1}{\rho_0} + \frac{1}{\rho} = \frac{3}{2}\frac{(\alpha_2 - \alpha_1)(T - T_0)}{t};$$

$$\delta = \frac{L^2}{8\rho}; \qquad \delta_0 = \frac{L^2}{8\rho_0};$$

$$\delta_0 + \delta = \frac{3L^2}{16t}(\alpha_2 - \alpha_1)(T - T_0). \tag{8.21}$$

2. In order to obtain the increase in compressive force caused by decrease in the element's deflection, it is assumed that the center line of the bent element is a flat curve. The difference λ between the length of the curve and the distance between its end points is

$$\lambda = \int_0^L \left[1 + \left(\frac{dy}{dx}\right)^2\right]^{1/2} dx - \int_0^L dx = \frac{1}{2}\int_0^L \left(\frac{dy}{dx}\right)^2 dx. \tag{8.22}$$

The initial deflection curve is assumed to be a sine wave,

$$y = \delta_0 \sin \frac{\pi x}{L},$$

and therefore

$$y = \frac{(\delta_0 \pi)^2}{4L}. \tag{8.23}$$

In heating to the incipient-buckling deflection, δ_1 (Figure 8.7), compression of the element is, therefore,

$$\frac{\delta_0^2 \pi^2}{4L} - \frac{\delta_1^2 \pi^2}{4L} = \lambda_0 - \lambda_1. \tag{8.24}$$

From Hooke's law and (8.24) the relationship for compressive force at the moment of buckling is

$$P = \left(\frac{\delta_0^2 \pi^2}{4L} - \frac{\delta_1^2 \pi^2}{4L}\right)\frac{EA}{L} = \frac{EA\pi^2 \delta_0^2}{4L^2}\left(1 - \frac{\delta_1^2}{\delta_0^2}\right)$$

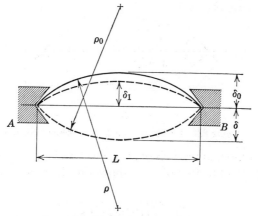

Figure 8.7 Bimetallic element in end-restrained condition.

or

$$\frac{PL^2}{EI\pi^2} = \frac{3\delta_0{}^2}{t^2}\left(1 - \frac{\delta_1{}^2}{\delta_0{}^2}\right). \tag{8.25}$$

3. The compressive force that will prevent buckling of the element is now computed.

Displacement of a point on the snap-action element when buckling between positions ACB and $AC'B$ (in Figure 8.8) occurs is

$$y + \delta \sin\frac{\pi x}{L} .$$

The force necessary to hold the element in position $AC'B$ is related to the aforementioned displacement by use of the differential equation of the deflection curve of a beam in bending, $EI(d^2y/dx^2) = -M$, as follows:

$$EI\frac{d^2}{dx^2}\left(y + \delta \sin\frac{\pi x}{L}\right) = -Py,$$

which is rewritten as

$$\frac{d^2y}{dx^2} + \frac{P}{EI}y = \frac{\delta\pi^2}{L^2}\sin\frac{\pi x}{L}. \tag{8.26}$$

The solution to (8.26) is

$$y = A \sin\left(\frac{P}{EI}\right)^{1/2}x + B\cos\left(\frac{P}{EI}\right)^{1/2}x + \frac{\delta}{(PL^2/EI\pi^2) - 1}\sin\frac{\pi x}{L}. \tag{8.27}$$

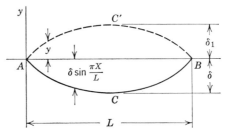

Figure 8.8   Bimetallic element in buckling position.

Boundary conditions at the ends of the element yield $A = B = 0$. Substituting the value of y as a function of x, as shown in Figure 8.8, gives

$$\delta_1 = \frac{\delta}{(PL^2/EI\pi^2) - 1}.$$

Rearranging,

$$\frac{PL^2}{EI\pi^2} = \frac{\delta}{\delta_1} + 1. \tag{8.28}$$

Employing the relationship between δ and δ_0 (element displacements at the initial and at buckling temperatures) (8.21),

$$\frac{PL^2}{EI\pi^2} = \left(\frac{3}{16}\frac{L^2}{t\delta_0}(\alpha_2 - \alpha_1)(T - T_0) - 1\right)\frac{\delta_0}{\delta_1} + 1. \tag{8.29}$$

Given the ratio of initial* and buckled deflections for the snap-action element under discussion, we can find the difference in temperatures corresponding to that ratio by a graphical solution. On the graph of Figure 8.9, with $PL^2/EI\pi^2$ the ordinate and δ_0/δ_1 the abscissa, a plot of $PL^2/EI\pi^2$ versus

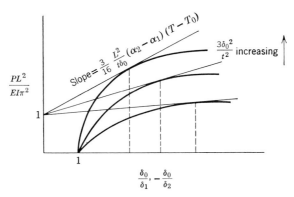

Figure 8.9   Graphical solution for snap-action element.

*Compressive force is zero at the initial deflection.

δ_0/δ_1 in (8.25) yields a curve whose asymptote is $3\delta_0{}^2/t^2$ and whose horizontal axis intercept is 1; a plot of $PL^2/EI\pi^2$ versus δ_0/δ_1 in (8.29) yields a straight line whose slope is given by

$$i = \frac{3}{16}\frac{L^2}{t\delta_0}(\alpha_2 - \alpha_1)(T - T_0) - 1, \tag{8.30}$$

and whose vertical axis intercept is 1. Drawing the straight line representing (8.30) so that it is tangent to the curve representing (8.25) yields a value for the temperature change required to activate the snap-action element. [If the shape of the curve for (8.25) does not permit tangency with a line drawn from (0, 1), the manufactured deflection of the element is not sufficiently large (compared to its thickness) to enable it to perform as a snap-action device.] At the point of tangency of curve and line, when both the deflection and the compressive force are evaluated, buckling is said to commence. The temperature change required for buckling is computed from the tangency condition,

$$T - T_0 = \frac{1 + (2\beta\delta_1{}^3/\delta_0{}^3)}{\frac{3}{16}(L^2/t)(\alpha_2 - \alpha_1)}, \tag{8.31}$$

where $\beta = 3\delta_0{}^2/t^2$.

8.6 DEFLECTIONS IN BIMETALLIC ELEMENT BUCKLING

The deflection to which the element suddenly buckles at temperature T is calculated from the following equations, whose forms have been derived above.

The expression for the abscissa at the point of tangency is

$$\frac{\delta_0}{\delta_1} = \left(\frac{3\beta}{\beta - 1}\right)^{1/2}. \tag{8.32}$$

Substitution yields the following equation:

$$T - T_0 = \frac{1 + (6\delta_0{}^2/h^2)[\frac{1}{3} - \frac{1}{9}(h^2/\delta_0{}^2)]^{3/2}}{\frac{3}{16}(L^2/h\delta_0)(\alpha_2 - \alpha_1)}. \tag{8.33}$$

$$\delta_1 = \frac{\delta}{(PL^2/EI\pi^2) - 1}, \tag{8.28}$$

where δ_1 is the deflection at which element buckling occurs;

$$\delta_2 = \frac{\delta}{1 - (PL^2/EI\pi^2)}, \tag{8.34}$$

where δ_2 is the deflection to which element buckles.

$$\frac{PL^2}{EI\pi^2} = 1 - \left[\frac{3L^2}{16t}(\alpha_1 - \alpha_2)(T - T_0) - 1\right]\frac{\delta_0}{\delta_2} \tag{8.35}$$

replaces (8.29), and

$$\frac{PL^2}{EI\pi^2} = \frac{3\delta_0^2}{t^2}\left(1 - \frac{\delta_2^2}{\delta_0^2}\right) \tag{8.36}$$

replaces (8.25).

The slope,

$$i = \frac{3}{16}\frac{L^2}{t\delta_0}(\alpha_1 - \alpha_2)(T - T_0) - 1,$$

and the vertical-axis intercept, 1, define the line representing (8.35). The abscissa of the intersection of this line with the curve representing (8.36) provides the deflection of the element after sudden buckling.

The complete displacement during sudden buckling, as a function of initial displacement, can now be computed.

8.7 SNAP-ACTION ELEMENT TEMPERATURE DIFFERENTIAL

The temperature at which reverse buckling occurs is computed and the operating temperature differential of the snap-action element is found as follows. After the element has buckled to a new displacement, δ_2, it begins to cool and attempts to flatten out with the component of higher thermal coefficient of expansion on the convex side. At displacement δ_1 sufficient compressive force is attained and the element buckles in the reverse direction. The temperatures corresponding to the displacements at the free-bending and incipient-buckling conditions can be calculated. These temperatures provide the operating temperature differential of the element.

T_2 is defined as the temperature when the element is in the free-bending condition during cooling. T_1 is the temperature at the deflection when reverse buckling occurs. By obvious symmetry,

$$T_2 - T_1 = T - T_0,$$

and

$$T_1 = T_2 - (T - T_0). \tag{8.37}$$

Again by symmetry, and with (8.21),

$$\frac{3}{16}\frac{L^2}{t\delta_0}(\alpha_2 - \alpha_1)(T_2 - T_0) = 2. \tag{8.38}$$

Recalling that

$$i = \frac{3}{16} \frac{L^2}{t\delta_0} (\alpha_2 - \alpha_1)(T - T_0) - 1,$$

$$\left(\frac{i + 1}{T - T_0}\right)(T_2 - T_0) = 2,$$

and

$$T_2 - T_0 = \frac{2}{i + 1} (T - T_0). \tag{8.39}$$

From (8.37) $T_1 - T_0 = T_2 - T_0 - (T - T_0)$ and therefore

$$T_1 - T_0 = \left(\frac{2}{i + 1} - 1\right)(T - T_0).$$

Thus

$$T_1 - T_0 = \left(\frac{1 - i}{1 + i}\right)(T - T_0). \tag{8.40}$$

Thus the operating temperature differential of a snap-action element can be found.

8.8 BIMETALLIC ELEMENT CONSTRUCTION

In 1920 the Nobel prize for physics was awarded to Charles Edouard Guillaume of France, the director of the International Bureau of Weights and Measures, for his discovery of abnormalities of nickel-steel alloys. During a search for inexpensive materials to use as standards of length and mass, he had found that 36% nickel alloy steel was well-nigh invariable in length with temperature change. This material was called Invar because of its property of invariability and was used for hairsprings and balance wheels in watches and chronometers.

Invar is used as the low-expansive component in bimetallic elements. It has an extremely low thermal coefficient of expansion at temperatures up to 400°F. The high-expansion component may be 18–27% nickel steel with 3–5% chromium added. There are four methods of bonding the components: (*a*) hot roll bonding (at temperatures greater than 2000°F and at moderate pressures), in which the material enters the mill in bar form with edges welded; (*b*) *PT* bonding, which is accomplished cold; (*c*) press bonding, similar to hot roll bonding except that pressure is applied statically; (*d*) puddle bonding, in which one alloy is melted and cast onto a second heated but solid alloy.

Bimetallic elements are useful over the temperature range −300°F to 800°F.

8.9   APPLICATIONS OF BIMETALLIC ELEMENTS

Typical applications in commercial thermostats of the two classifications of bimetallic elements, both creep and snap-action, are shown in Figures 8.10 and 8.11. Each application incorporates the following features: (*a*) in the contacts-closed position current from the heater circuit is flowing through the thermostat, while in the contacts-open position this current flow is

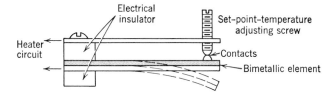

Figure 8.10   Simple creep thermostat.

interrupted; (*b*) opening and closing of the contacts are accomplished by movement of the bimetallic element with temperature change; (*c*) the element components can be arranged so that the contacts either open or close on temperature rise; (*d*) adjusting the position of the stationary contact varies the switching (or set-point) temperature in the creep application, whereas such variation in the snap-action type involves reworking of the element itself.

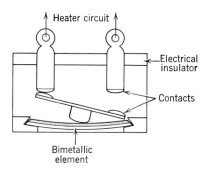

Figure 8.11   Simple snap-action thermostat.

Other uses of bimetallic elements involve the changing of values of thermal resistances, whether the mode of heat transfer is conduction, convection, or radiation. Figure 8.12 illustrates the basic use of bimetallic elements for varying contact thermal resistance. With mass *B* at constant temperature, control of the temperature of mass *A*, with a constant power input *Q*, is desired. The bimetallic element has been installed so that, as temperature T_A rises, the element bends in a downward direction to make contact with surface B and provide a thermal resistance R_{AB} between the contacted surfaces of A and B. (R_{AB} includes the two intersurface resistances and the resistance to heat conduction through the bimetallic element.) Then T_A commences to be lowered toward a value defined by $Q = R_{AB}(T_A - T_B)$; the element bends upward, thereby increasing the thermal resistance between A and B, causing T_A to increase in temperature, and restarting the cycle.

The characteristic movement with temperature change of a bimetallic element can be employed in variably restricting flow in convective heat transfer processes. As a mass of fluid flowing through a port in a barrier

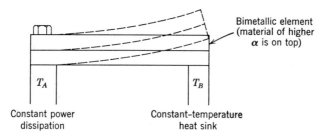

Figure 8.12 Temperature control by variation of contact thermal resistance.

separating a heat source whose temperature is to be controlled from a constant-temperature sink, decreases in temperature, movement of the element will tend to close the port, thus restricting flow and raising the over-all thermal resistance from source to sink. As the fluid temperature rises, the element will tend to reopen the port and lower the temperature again.

The basic application in radiative heat transfer concerns the relative amount of high-emissivity surface which extended elements offer for radiation from a temperature-controlled object dissipating constant power to a constant-temperature surface. (The surface area not covered by the elements has low emissivity.) As the temperature of the controlled object rises, the elements move to decreasing perpendicularity to the surface to which heat is radiated; the mutual radiation view factor between surfaces is thus increased, and thermal resistance between surfaces is decreased. As thermal resistance decreases, the temperature of the controlled object tends to decrease also. With further decrease in temperature, movement of the bimetallic elements reverses to the direction of increasing perpendicularity to the radiation-impinged surface, thus increasing thermal resistance and tending to raise the controlled object's temperature (Figure 8.13).

[The 1831 number of the *Proceedings of the Royal Society* (of London) contains a summary of work accomplished by Andrew Ure, M.D., F.R.S., "On the Thermostat or Heat Governor, a self-acting physical Apparatus for regulating Temperature." Ure constructed bimetallic elements of united zinc

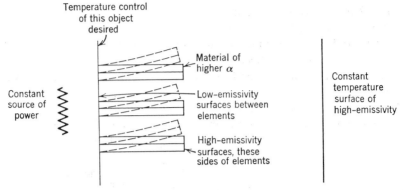

Figure 8.13 Use of bimetallic elements in temperature control for radiative heat transfer.

and steel, and tin and steel, hinged together to regulate the opening of dampers, letting in either cold air or cold water, or closing the draught of a fireplace.]

8.10 COMPARISON OF CREEP AND SNAP-ACTION THERMOSTATS

The choice between the two broad classifications of commercial thermostats (creep and snap-action) involves immediate comparison of their electrical and temperature-differential ratings.

A bimetallic thermostat's electrical rating may be defined as its expected number of cycles of operation for a given value of current passed through it at a particular voltage. The ability of the instrument's electrical contacts to pass the required current and to sharply interrupt or close a circuit at sustained temperature levels describes proper electrical performance. Changes in these performance characteristics are due to erosion of the contact material, the erosion being caused by arcing between the contacts.

[The resistance to current flow increases with reduction of contacts' intersurface area. On sufficient reduction of area the electrical contact resistance level achieved prevents the passage of current altogether.]

Several remarks are in order. The smaller the instantaneous gap between contacts, the smaller the value of current required to create a spark across that gap. The rate of electrical erosion of contact material is increased by arcing-induced local heating of contact material.

If a thermostat's housing is not hermetically sealed, moisture is introduced to the contact surfaces. Oxidation of contact material is initiated and proceeds with increasing rapidity when contact material temperature rises because of arcing-induced heating. Resistance to current flow increases with oxidation.

The reversed-position operation of a snap-action thermostat permits a relatively large gap between contacts while the device maintains an open-circuit posture. Furthermore, the gap is quickly closed when a temperature sufficient to buckle the bimetallic element is reached. Functioning of the multiposition creep thermostat, on the other hand, promotes a gap between contacts that is relatively small at all times. Therefore, for the same life expectancies, the usual amounts of current passed through snap-action thermostats exceed those passed through creep thermostats.

Reliability in contact performance depends on the use of particular materials in certain circumstances. Gold plating, for example, assures reliable circuit making under low-wattage conditions, but it is unacceptable for

Table 8.2 Comparison of Allowable Load Levels for Silver and Gold-Plated Contacts in a Typical Snap-Action Thermostat

Voltages	Silver Contacts Currents (amp)	Gold-Plated Contacts Currents (am)
30 a-c/d-c	3.0–4.0	0.500 and below
125 a-c	1.0–3.0	0.200 and below
250 a-c	0.5–1.5	0.100 and below

heavier loads. Silver contacts, however, are suitable for relatively high currents. A comparison of the allowable limits of current levels for the two materials in a typical snap-action thermostat appears in Table 8.2. The range of current at a particular voltage yields life expectancies of 50,000–200,000 cycles.

Generally, in commercial thermostats, operating-load-level advantages are opposed by disadvantages of large temperature differentials. Thus, for applications where small temperature differentials are desired, creep thermostats are more suitable; the differentials are of the order of half a degree Fahrenheit and higher. Typical temperature differentials for snap-action thermostats are several degrees Fahrenheit and higher.

Temperature response and thermal lag in bimetallic thermostats depend on the thermal path from the surface or volume to or in which the instrument is mounted to its sensitive element. As thermal resistance along the prime thermal path is reduced, response improves. Mechanically linked configurations, in which a material of high thermal coefficient of expansion, such as the device's housing, senses temperature changes directly, are used for such improvements. As shown in Figure 8.14, the high-expanding case causes lowering of the low-expansion internal bridge as the case temperature rises. A further advantage is that the bridge can be normally (at room

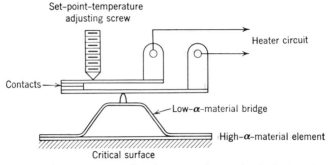

Figure 8.14 Schematic arrangement of surface-mounting mechanically linked thermostat.

temperature) in tension in order to improve constancy of operation in vibration.

8.11 SELF-HEATING OF BIMETALLIC ELEMENTS

Current flowing through bimetallic elements causes resistive heating, thus promoting an increase in temperature independent of temperature changes in the mass to which the thermostat is attached. With the assumption that no heat is transferred away from the element the equation for the temperature rise in the element as a function of the current flowing through it is as follows:

$$i^2R = \rho t w L C_p \frac{\Delta T}{\Delta \theta},$$

where i = current,
R = electrical resistance of element,
ρ = density of element,
t = thickness of element,
w = width of element,
L = length of element,
C_p = specific heat of element,
T = temperature of element,
θ = time.
The electrical resistance of the element is related to its resistivity by

$$r = R \frac{wt}{L}.$$

8.12 MERCURY-IN-GLASS THERMOSTATS

In 1714, Fahrenheit, as a result of his having invented a new method for cleaning mercury so that it would not stick to the walls of tubes, was able to take a crucial step in thermometry by substituting mercury for alcohol.

Triple-distilled mercury is now used in small, necked-down glass tubes* to provide extremely close (small temperature-differential) control of temperatures. These devices are capable of operating for millions of cycles without failure, under certain conditions. Movement of a column of mercury with temperature change defines the thermostatic functioning: on temperature rise the liquid column grows and wets a metal contact of platinum wire protruding into the tube bore, thus completing an electrical circuit; the circuit is broken

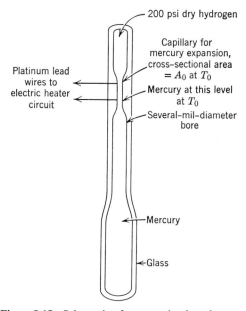

Figure 8.15 Schematic of mercury-in-glass thermostat.

when the liquid column, on temperature decrease, shrinks and no longer wets the contact wire. In order, therefore, to interrupt current to an electric heater on rise of a controlled mass's temperature, means to reverse the action of a mercury thermostat (external to the instrument) must be provided electronically. Also the limitation on current load is rather severe (excessive loads causing fouling of the mercury column), but coordinated use of transistorized amplifiers yields a signal level sufficiently high to drive electric heaters.

Growth of a column of mercury with temperature change is calculated as follows. In the thermostat illustrated in Figure 8.15, the volume of mercury at temperature T_0 is V_0. The volume of mercury overfilling the new bore volume at temperature $T_0 + \Delta T$ can be calculated from the differential rates of expansion of the mercury and the glass tube, where β_M is the cubical

* Obtainable, not necked down, from the Corning Glass Works, priced by the pound.

thermal coefficient of expansion of mercury and β_G is the relevant coefficient of glass:

$$V_{\text{mercury}} = V_0[1 + \beta_M(T_0 + \Delta T)],$$

$$V_{\text{glass}} = V_0[1 + \beta_G(T_0 + \Delta T)], \tag{8.41}$$

$$(V_{\text{mercury}} - V_{\text{glass}})_{T_0+\Delta T} - (V_{\text{mercury}} - V_{\text{glass}})_{T_0} = V_0 \Delta T(\beta_M - \beta_G).$$

The cross-sectional area of the capillary used for the expansion of the mercury is

$$A = A_0(1 + 2\alpha_G \Delta T), \tag{8.42}$$

where α_G is the linear thermal coefficient of expansion of glass. The term $2\alpha_G \Delta T$ is small compared to 1 and may be neglected. Then LA_0 is the overfill expansion of mercury:

$$LA_0 = V_0 \Delta T(\beta_M - \beta_G),$$
$$L = \frac{V_0}{A_0} \Delta T(\beta_M - \beta_G). \tag{8.43}$$

The height of mercury in the capillary is thus directly proportional to the liquid's change in temperature.

The value of β_M is 0.182×10^{-3} ($^\circ C^{-1}$) and that of β_G is 12–27 $\times$ 10^{-6} ($^\circ C^{-1}$).

It is possible, in the small (under 2 in. long) handmade, mercury-in-glass thermostats manufactured at several plants in and near Philadelphia [7, 8] (Figure 8.16), to obtain temperature differentials of as little as several hundredths of a degree Fahrenheit. Three-mil-diameter platinum wire is used for the contacts; wires are inserted in the glass tube where its bore is necked down to 3–5 mils (for increased sensitivity). Machine-made thermostats, however, are incapable of attaining such small temperature differentials. Ability to obtain predetermined set points (temperature levels at which the mercury contacts the upper platinum lead wire) is greater in handmade

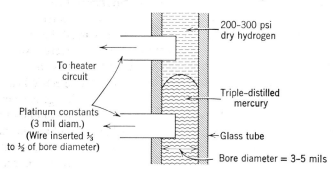

Figure 8.16   Section of part of a mercury-in-glass thermostat.

(settings can be within several tenths of a degree Fahrenheit) than in machine-made varieties. The costs of the latter are generally less than those of the former, however.

Values of current which can be passed through the thermostat without fouling the mercury are increased by the use of 200–300 psi of arc-suppressing dry hydrogen.* The gas also serves to reduce the tendency of the mercury column to separate under shock and vibration and to change the thermostat's set point. Allowable electrical loads are, however, far below those suitable for bimetallic thermostats. But if the specified loads are not exceeded the life expectancy of a mercury-in-glass thermostat far outdistances that of a bimetallic-element type.

REFERENCES

[1] "Thermometer Tubing Price List," Corning Glass Works.

[2] Eskin, S. G., and J. R. Fritze, "Thermostatic Bimetals," *Trans. ASME*, **62**, No. 7 (July, 1940).

[3] "How to Get Better Temperature Control," Fenwal, Inc., 1961.

[4] "Electric Controls," Chapter 7, *Machine Design*, December 31, 1964.

[5] "Designers' Guide to TRUFLEX Thermostat Metals," *Brochure* TRU-IA, Metals and Controls, Inc., 1963.

[6] "Precision Controls," *Brochure* CP-2, Metals and Controls, Inc., 1965.

[7] *Bulletin* T, The Philadelphia Thermometer Co.

[8] *Bulletin* T-20, Precision Thermometer & Instrument Co., 1965.

[9] Salerno, P. G., "Mercury-in-Glass Controller," *Instr. Control Systems*, **37**, No. 6, 123–125 (June, 1964).

[10] Sears, R., "Fundamentals of Thermostat Metals," *Mater. Res. Std.*, **III** (December, 1963).

[11] Timishenko, S., "Analysis of Bi-metal Thermostats," *J. Opt. Soc.*, 233–255 (September, 1925).

[12] Vasudevan, M., and W. Johnson, "On Multi-metal Thermostats," *Appl. Sci. Res.*, Sec. B, **9**, 420–430 (1961–1963).

* Fouling of mercury produces solid particles floating on the column surface; these particles can effect premature circuit-making.

9

Thermoelectric Devices

9.1 INTRODUCTION

Thermoelectric devices, the principles of which are described in this chapter, can control the temperatures of a given mass, or complex of thermally connected masses, by selectively effecting cooling and heating. The use of such devices, then, can be appropriate to situations in which the temperature of the given mass's ambient is either above or below that of the mass. Operation of thermoelectric components can be either proportional or ON-OFF. Other advantages of thermoelectric components are inherent in their basic construction. There are no moving parts; fabrication in an infinite variety of sizes and shapes is possible, and miniaturization is feasible.

In 1821 Seebeck discovered that there is an electromotive force in a closed circuit of two dissimilar metals whose junctions are at different temperatures. About a dozen years later, Peltier, a French watchmaker and amateur scientist, observed temperature anomalies at the junction of two dissimilar conductors when a current was passed through them. Properly formulated, the Peltier phenomenon is the generation or absorption (which one depends on the direction of current flow) of heat at the junction of two different conductors when a current flows through them. The Peltier heating effect is not the same as the Joule resistance heating effect.

According to Ioffe's account [5], neither Seebeck nor Peltier accepted the meaning of his experimental results. Seebeck claimed (in the Reports of the Prussian Academy of Sciences) that his experiments showed that temperature differences produce magnetic polarization of metals and ores; he attempted to relate the earth's magnetism to the temperature difference between the equator or a range of southern volcanoes and the polar ice cap. He was not

168

interested in finding a new source of electric current. Ioffe describes Seebeck's fight against those who explained his results by thermoelectric current theory.

Peltier sought confirmation of his preconceived notion that Joule heat could be generated only by strong currents. He believed that the bulk properties of metals (hardness or electrical conductivity, for example) affected heat generation in the case of the weak currents produced by a thermocouple. He overlooked the temperature anomalies at the couples' junctions and refused to believe his measurements when the facts did not confirm his expectations. In 1838, however, Lenz, the St. Petersburg academician, demonstrated the nature of the Peltier phenomenon when he alternately froze and melted a droplet of water at the junction of bismuth and antimony rods by reversing the direction of current flow.

The Seebeck and Peltier phenomena are expressed by the equations

$$V = \alpha_{12} \Delta T, \tag{9.1}$$

$$q = \pi_{12} I, \tag{9.2}$$

respectively, where, referring to Figure 9.1, ΔT is the temperature difference established between the junctions, C and D, of conductors 1 and 2, V is the open-circuit electromotive force developed between A and B, and α_{12} is the thermoelectric power, or differential Seebeck coefficient between the conductors of materials 1 and 2; also, with $\Delta T = 0$, and I a current caused to flow around the circuit by connecting a battery between A and B, q is the rate of heating or cooling at the junctions (which one, at each junction, depends on the direction of current flow), and π_{12} is the differential Peltier coefficient.

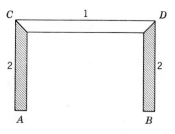

Figure 9.1 Circuit for defining the thermoelectric coefficients.

In 1855, William Thomson demonstrated by thermodynamic analysis both the relationship between the Seebeck and Peltier effects and the existence of a third thermoelectric phenomenon, namely, the generation or absorption of heat q by the passage of current I through a conductor in which there is a temperature gradient. The equation describing the Thomson effect is

$$q = \tau I \frac{\partial T}{\partial X}, \tag{9.3}$$

where τ is the Thomson coefficient. The Kelvin relations developed by Thomson are

$$\pi_{12} = \alpha_{12} T \tag{9.4}$$

and

$$\tau_1 - \tau_2 = T\frac{\partial \alpha_{12}}{\partial T} .\tag{9.5}$$

By using (9.4) the rate of Peltier cooling can be found with the Seebeck coefficient, whose determination is accomplished more easily than that of the Peltier coefficient.

The Thomson coefficients are for single conductors, and the Seebeck and Peltier coefficients refer to junctions between two conductors. If the latter differential coefficients could be conveniently replaced by the differences between coefficients relating to single conductors, the existence of a standard metal whose absolute coefficients are zero would be implied [2]. It is an accepted assumption, then, that with the values of π_{12} and α_{12} equal to zero at $0°K$, the absolute values of Peltier coefficient and thermoelectric power for all individual conductors are zero at $0°K$. With the standard metal defined as having a zero value of τ at all temperatures,

$$\tau = T\frac{d\alpha}{dT}\tag{9.6}$$

and

$$\pi = \alpha T\tag{9.7}$$

for a single conductor.

9.2 BASIC STEADY-STATE EQUATIONS AND PERFORMANCE OF THERMOELECTRIC REFRIGERATORS

Consider the thermocouple, used for cooling, shown in Figure 9.2. The elements are joined by a strap of zero electrical resistance at the heat source and a current I at the heat sink. The temperatures at source and sink are T_C

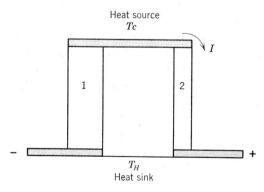

Figure 9.2 Thermocouple used for cooling.

and T_H, respectively. The cross-sectional area of each element A_i is constant along its length; the lengths of the elements are identically l. For an element α_i is the Seebeck coefficient; σ_i, its electrical conductivity; k_i, its thermal conductivity.

Zero heat is transferred anywhere except at the source or sink. Also, the Thomson effect is ignored without peril [2].

At a distance X from the heat source, the equation for the energy balance in an incremental portion of a thermoelement is

$$\frac{I^2}{\sigma_i A_i} + k_i A_i \frac{\partial^2 T}{\partial X^2} = 0. \tag{9.8}$$

By use of the boundary conditions $T = T_C$ at $X = 0$ and $T = T_H$ at $X = l$, (9.8) is solved.

Integrating once,

$$\frac{I^2}{\sigma_i A_i} X + k_i A_i \frac{\partial T}{\partial X} + C_1 = 0. \tag{9.9}$$

Integrating again,

$$\frac{I^2}{2\sigma_i A_i} X^2 + k_i A_i T + C_1 X + C_2 = 0. \tag{9.10}$$

By substituting the aforementioned boundary conditions, C_1 and C_2 are found:

$$C_2 = -k_i A_i T_C;$$

$$C_1 = -\frac{I^2 l}{2\sigma_i A_i} - \frac{k_i A_i}{l}(T_H - T_C). \tag{9.11}$$

Substituting and rearranging, we obtain

$$\frac{k_i A_i}{X}(T - T_C) + \frac{I^2}{2\sigma_i A_i}(X - l) - \frac{k_i A_i}{l}(T_H - T_C) = 0 \tag{9.12}$$

The rate of heat flow in one of the thermoelements at the distance X from the heat source is

$$q_i = \pm \alpha_i IT - k_i A_i \frac{\partial T}{\partial X}, \tag{9.13}$$

where $\alpha_i IT$ is the Peltier heat flow.

Combining (9.12) and (9.13), we have

$$q_i = \pm \alpha_i IT + \frac{I^2}{2\sigma_i A_i}(X - l) - \frac{k_i A_i}{l}(T_H - T_C). \tag{9.14}$$

The total heat absorbed at the cold junction $X = 0$ is the sum of the heat flows of the individual conductors at that point:

$$q_c = q_1 + q_2 = (\alpha_2 - \alpha_1)IT_C - \frac{I^2R}{2} - K(T_H - T_C), \qquad (9.15)$$

where

$$R = \frac{l}{2}\left(\frac{1}{\sigma_1 A_1} + \frac{1}{\sigma_2 A_2}\right) \qquad (9.16)$$

and

$$K = \frac{1}{l}(k_1 A_1 + k_2 A_2). \qquad (9.17)$$

The electrical energy expended in one thermoelement is given by

$$q_{w_i} = \pm \int_{T_c}^{T_H} \alpha_i I l T + \int_0^l \frac{I^2}{\sigma_i A_i} l X \qquad (9.18)$$

$$q_{w_i} = \pm \alpha_i I(T_H - T_C) + \frac{I^2 l}{\sigma_i A_i}. \qquad (9.19)$$

For the couple, then, the expended electrical energy is

$$q_w = (\alpha_2 - \alpha_1)I(T_H - T_C) + I^2R \qquad (9.20)$$

The coefficient of performance of a thermocouple used for cooling is the ratio of the power absorbed at the cold junction to the total electrical power expended:

$$\eta = \frac{q_c}{q_w} = \frac{IT_c - I^2R/2 - K(T_H - T_C)}{\alpha_{21}I(T_H - T_C) + I^2R} \qquad (9.21)$$

The value of current corresponding to maximum thermocouple coefficient of performance is of interest. That value is found by first differentiating η with respect to I and setting the differential equal to zero. Equating the parts of the numerator and removing like terms, we obtain

$$0 = I^2 R \alpha_{12}\left(\frac{\Delta T}{2} + T_C\right) - 2RKI\,\Delta T - K\alpha(\Delta T)^2, \qquad (9.22)$$

where $\Delta T = T_H - T_C$.

Solving the quadratic for I and simplifying,

$$I_\eta = \frac{K\,\Delta T\{1 + [1 + (\alpha^2/RK)(\Delta T/2 + T_C)]^{\frac{1}{2}}\}}{\alpha(\Delta T/2 + T_C)}. \qquad (9.23)$$

(The sign before the bracket must be positive to prohibit the possibility of negative current and to ensure cooling.)

The quantity α^2/RK is the couple's figure of merit, denoted commonly by Z.

Using the mean element temperature $T_m = (T_H + T_C)/2$, we multiply numerator and denominator by

$$Ra(\sqrt{1 + ZT_m} - 1),$$

and by rearranging we have the maximum-coefficient-of-performance current in more convenient form:

$$I_\eta = \frac{K\,\Delta TR\alpha}{R\alpha^2}\left(\frac{(1 + \sqrt{1 + ZT_m})(\sqrt{1 + ZT_m} - 1)}{T_m(\sqrt{1 + ZT_m} - 1)}\right), \tag{9.24}$$

$$I_\eta = \frac{K\,\Delta TR\alpha}{R\alpha^2}\left(\frac{ZT_m}{T_m(\sqrt{1 + ZT_m} - 1)}\right). \tag{9.25}$$

Since $\alpha^2/KR = Z$, furthermore,

$$I_\eta = \frac{\alpha\,\Delta T}{R}\left(\frac{1}{\sqrt{1 + ZT_m} - 1}\right). \tag{9.26}$$

The maximum coefficient of performance of a thermocouple may be computed by first substituting (9.26) into the expression for coefficient of performance, (9.21) and rearranging:

$$\eta_{\max} = \frac{\alpha^2 T_C(\sqrt{1 + ZT_m} - 1) - (\alpha^2/2)\,\Delta T - KR(\sqrt{1 + ZT_m} - 1)^2}{\alpha^2\,\Delta T\sqrt{1 + ZT_m}}. \tag{9.27}$$

Letting $B = \sqrt{1 + ZT_m}$,

$$\eta_{\max} = \frac{T_C(B - 1) - \frac{1}{2}\Delta T - (1/Z)(B - 1)^2}{\Delta TB}. \tag{9.28}$$

From $B^2 = 1 + ZT_m$, and therefore

$$\frac{B^2 - 1}{T_m} = Z = \frac{(B + 1)(B - 1)}{T_m},$$

it follows that

$$\eta_{\max} = \frac{T_C(B - 1) - \frac{1}{2}\Delta T - T_m(B - 1)/(B + 1)}{\Delta TB}. \tag{9.29}$$

After much rearranging,

$$\eta_{\max} = \frac{T_C}{T_H - T_C}\left(\frac{\sqrt{1 + ZT_m} - T_H/T_C}{\sqrt{1 + ZT_m} - 1}\right). \tag{9.30}$$

The value of current corresponding to maximum thermocouple cooling power is found by differentiating (9.15) with respect to current I and equating the result to zero:

$$\frac{dq_c}{dI} = 0 = -IR + \alpha T_C. \tag{9.31}$$

Therefore

$$Iq_c = \frac{T_c}{R}. \qquad (9.32)$$

The corresponding coefficient of performance is computed by substituting $Iq_c = T_c/R$ into (9.21) and rearranging:

$$\eta_{q_c} = \frac{T_c^2/z - (1/Z)\,\Delta T}{T_C T_H}. \qquad (9.33)$$

The temperature difference relevant to the maximum thermocouple cooling power is computed by substituting the current defined by (9.32) into (9.15). Thus

$$\Delta T_{\max\,q_c} = \tfrac{1}{2}Z T_c^2 - \frac{q_c}{K}. \qquad (9.34)$$

The thermocouple hot-junction temperature is considered regulated by the heat sink temperature; only the cold-junction temperature, therefore, varies with the level of current applied to the device.

Equation 9.15 is rewritten to include the hot-junction temperature and the temperature difference between junctions:

$$q_c = \alpha I(T_H - \Delta T) - \tfrac{1}{2}I^2 R - K\,\Delta T. \qquad (9.35)$$

The hot-to-cold junction temperature difference is

$$\Delta T = \frac{\alpha I T_H - \tfrac{1}{2}I^2 R - q_c}{\alpha I + K}. \qquad (9.36)$$

If q_c is zero, the current at which the above temperature difference is a maximum is found by differentiation with respect to current and equating the result to zero. Thus

$$I_{\Delta T} = \frac{K}{\alpha}(\sqrt{1 + 2ZT_H} - 1). \qquad (9.37)$$

The maximum temperature difference is found by substitution.

$$\Delta T_{\max} = \frac{T_H(\sqrt{1 + 2ZT_H} - 1) - (1/2Z)(\sqrt{1 + 2ZT_H} - 1)^2}{\sqrt{1 + 2ZT_H}}. \qquad (9.38)$$

Normalized to T_H, (9.38) is

$$\frac{\Delta T_{\max}}{T_H} = \frac{2ZT_H(\sqrt{1 + 2ZT_H} - 1) - (\sqrt{1 + 2ZT_H} - 1)^2}{2ZT_H\sqrt{1 + 2ZT_H}}. \qquad (9.39)$$

Equation 9.39 is now rewritten with respect to a normalized current variable $I/I_{\Delta T}$ and to cognizance of the appearance of that variable in (9.40):

$$\frac{\Delta T_{\max}}{T_H} = \frac{2ZT_H(\sqrt{1 + 2ZT_H} - 1)(I/I_{\Delta T}) - (\sqrt{1 + 2ZT_H} - 1)^2(I/I_{\Delta T})^2}{2ZT_H[1 + (\sqrt{1 + 2ZT_H} - 1)(I/I_{\Delta T})]}.$$

(9.40)

Equation 9.40, the behavior of the unloaded temperature difference as a function of applied current, is illustrated in Figure 9.3 for several values of $Z_0 T_H$.

With a current passing through a thermocouple the maximum possible temperature decrease is achieved when zero power is absorbed at the cold junction, and the efficiency is zero:

$$\Delta T = \tfrac{1}{2}ZT_C^2.$$

(9.41)

The importance of the figure of merit is now more fully realized. Its value is maximum when the product RK is minimum. That product is given, $L_1 = L_2$, by

$$KR = (A_1 k_1 + A_2 k_2)\left(\frac{1}{A_1 \sigma_1} + \frac{1}{A_2 \sigma_2}\right)$$

$$= \frac{k_1}{\sigma_1} + \frac{k_2}{\sigma_2} + \frac{A_1 k_1}{A_2 \sigma_2} + \frac{A_2 k_2}{A_1 \sigma_1}.$$

(9.42)

The optimum ratio of element areas is found to be

$$\left(\frac{A_1}{A_2}\right)_{\text{opt}} = \left(\frac{k_2 \sigma_2}{k_1 \sigma_1}\right)^{1/2}.$$

(9.43)

Therefore

$$(KR)_{\text{opt}} = \frac{k_1}{\sigma_1} + \frac{k_2}{\sigma_2} + 2\left(\frac{k_1 k_2}{\sigma_1 \sigma_2}\right)^{1/2} = \left[\left(\frac{k_1}{\sigma_1}\right)^{1/2} + \left(\frac{k_2}{\sigma_2}\right)^{1/2}\right]^2$$

(9.44)

and

$$(\Delta T_{\max})_{\text{opt}} = \frac{1}{2} \frac{\alpha^2 T_c^2}{\left[\left(\frac{k_1}{\sigma_1}\right)^{1/2} + \left(\frac{k_2}{\sigma_2}\right)^{1/2}\right]^2}.$$

(9.45)

The equations for thermoelectric heating differ from those for cooling in that the Joule heat $\tfrac{1}{2}IR^2$ is additive rather than subtractive in the expression for total heat flowing to the heat-generating junction.

9.3 COOLING CAPABILITIES OF THERMOELECTRIC COUPLES

Seebeck, in his effort to disprove the electric origin of thermoelectric currents, compiled a thermoelectric series whose best couple, its first and last terms, would have yielded an efficiency of about 3%, which was as much

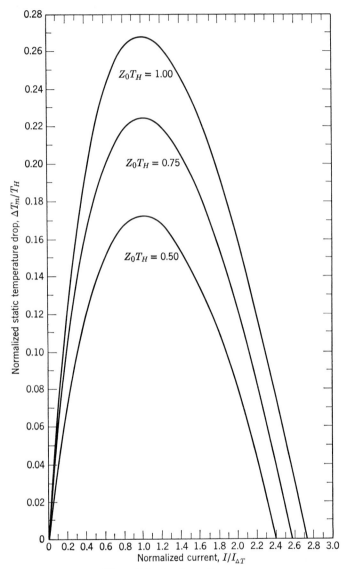

Figure 9.3 Static cooling curves.

as that of the top steam engines of his time. (In 1947, Maria Telkes [10] reported in America on the thermoelectric nature of the same couple, lead sulphide and zinc antimony.) By the early part of the twentieth century, however, when metals were, technically, the only conductors known, the efficiencies of thermoelectric generators were no higher than 0.6%. Altenkirch, a German scientist, considered (in 1911) employing the Peltier effect for refrigeration but lacked materials that would yield reasonable efficiencies. Hence interest in thermoelectric refrigerators and generators was slight until the late forties, when semiconductor materials were introduced; their Seebeck coefficients exceed by far those of metals.

In 1954 Goldsmid and Douglas [5] used bismuth telluride as the positive, and bismuth as the negative, branch of a thermocouple. (Positive and negative semiconductor elements differ in their excesses or deficiencies of electrons; they are called *p*-type and *n*-type elements, respectively.) In 1956 Ioffe et al. proposed the use of alloys of semiconductors as thermoelements. The best and now most widely used thermoelements are alloys of bismuth telluride (Bi_2Te_3): Bi_2Te_3 with antimony telluride for the *p*-type element and with bismuth selenide for the *n*-type element.

Goldsmid [2] has definite ideas (other workers in thermoelectrics agree with him, according to several conversations with the author) about thermoelectric refrigerating capabilities. Until the figure of merit of thermoelements is improved, thermoelectric refrigeration is preferred to the conventional compressor type when the level of cooling power is about 10 watts or less. Furthermore, Goldsmid summarizes his estimation of the upper limit of ZT, the dimensionless figure of merit, as follows:

"1. Present trends indicate that ZT cannot be much more than unity.

2. It seems unlikely that ZT will exceed 2.

3. Values of ZT greater than 4 seem out of the question."

9.4 CONSTRUCTION OF THERMOELECTRIC COOLING MODULES

The following comments pertain to the regulation of structural and electrical parameters in thermoelectric cooling units, such as those shown in Figures 9.4 and 9.5. The couples are connected electrically in series, in order to reduce the current requirements and increase the voltage levels when the amount of power to be pumped is of significant magnitude, and thermally in parallel. The individual thermoelements are connected by copper straps. The straps must be flat, parallel, and suitably thick to ensure proper mechanical and thermal contact between cooling unit and heat source and sink. Goldsmid provides a description of the preparation of semiconductor thermoelements and the construction of cooling units by various techniques.

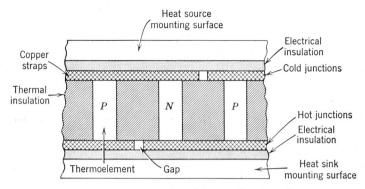

Figure 9.4 Cross section of thermoelectric cooler.

In an ideal unit, in which there is no electrical resistance between the thermoelements, operating characteristics are unchanged with changing values of l and A but constant l/A ratio. Within the limits imposed by the desired temperature difference between junctions and cooling capacity, both the length and cross-sectional area of the elements can be kept to a minimum.

Optimum current $I_{\Delta T}$ depends only on the parameter l/A. As that ratio increases or decreases, the value of $I_{\Delta T}$ for a given thermoelectric material increases or decreases proportionally. Merritts and Taylor [7] have provided values of optimum current for typical values of l/A employed in actual modules (Table 9.1).

As the module volume decreases, the electrical contact resistance between the thermoelements in series becomes a significant fraction of the total electrical resistance, and thus the module's coefficient of performance decreases. Electrical contact resistance at the cold junction causes heating there, reducing the module cooling capability; electrical resistance at the hot junction increases the amount of cooling power necessary to effect a certain cold-junction temperature.

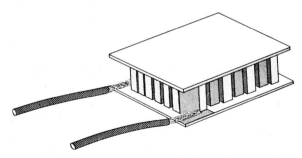

Figure 9.5 A thermoelectric cooling module.

Table 9.1 Effects of Typical Thermocouple Length/Area Values on Optimum Current

Length (cm)	Area (cm^2)	$\dfrac{l}{A}$	Optimum Current (amp, d-c)
0.3175	0.403	0.788	60.0
0.635	0.403	1.576	30.0
0.635	0.1008	6.300	7.5
1.270	0.1008	12.600	3.75

Coefficient of performance changes monotonically with length and area [see (9.21)], so that modules cannot be sized for optimum performance. For the same cooling capacity per unit volume of material, however, relatively longer elements can be shown to provide larger coefficients of performance. Furthermore, because of the thermal resistance of the layer of electrical insulation which separates by a necessary amount the thermoelement straps from a solid and electrically conductive heat source or heat sink, the elements are spread out so that the cross-sectional areas of the insulator and the module are increased; the insulator's thermal resistance is thus decreased. Insulation must be used in the volume between thermoelements to inhibit Fourier heat transfer between the hot and the cold junction. The optimum spacing between elements (providing optimum coefficient of performance) has been compiled for various thermoelement lengths. For elements 3–5 mm long, for example, insulation should occupy about three-fourths of the total module cross section.

9.5 THERMOELECTRIC MODULES IN CASCADE

Spatial and cooling requirements may be such that the thermoelectric modules must be arranged in cascades. A two-stage cooler is shown schematically in Figure 9.6. p_1 is the electrical power expended to pump the heat load q_1 up to the temperature $T_{C2} - T_{C1}$. The efficiency of the first-stage cooler is, then,

$$\eta_1 = \frac{q_1}{p_1}. \tag{9.46}$$

The power pumped by the second-stage cooler is, then,

$$q_2 = q_1 + p_1, \tag{9.47}$$

and the pumping power of the second stage is p_2. That stage's efficiency is

$$\eta_2 = \frac{q_2}{p_2} = \frac{q_1 + p_1}{p_2}. \tag{9.48}$$

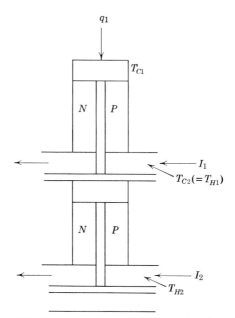

Figure 9.6   Schematic of two-state thermoelectric cooler.

The over-all efficiency of the cascade is given by

$$\eta = \frac{q_1}{p_1 + p_2}.$$ (9.49)

By substitution and rearrangement, the over-all efficiency may be found in terms of the efficiencies of the individual stages:

$$\eta = \frac{\eta_1 \eta_2}{\eta_1 + \eta_2 + 1}.$$ (9.50)

By extension, the over-all efficiency of a cascade of n stages in terms of the efficiencies of the individual stages can now be found: the efficiency of the ith stage is the ratio of the power pumped by that stage to the electrical power expended for that pumping. Thus

$$\eta_i = \frac{q_i}{p_i}.$$ (9.51)

The power pumped by the ith stage q_i is the sum of the power pumped, q_{i-1}, by the $(i-1)$th stage and the electrical energy expended, p_{i-1}, by this stage. Thus

$$q_i = q_{i-1} + p_{i-1}$$ (9.52)

and

$$q_i = q_{i-1}\left(1 + \frac{1}{\eta_{i-1}}\right). \tag{9.53}$$

Then, for the $(i-1)$th stage,

$$q_{i-1} = q_{i-2} + p_{i-2} \tag{9.54}$$

and

$$q_{i-1} = q_{i-2}\left(1 + \frac{1}{\eta_{i-2}}\right). \tag{9.55}$$

Therefore,

$$q_i = q_{i-2}\left(1 + \frac{1}{\eta_{i-1}}\right)\left(1 + \frac{1}{\eta_{i-2}}\right). \tag{9.56}$$

Finally,

$$q_n = q_1\left(1 + \frac{1}{\eta_1}\right)\left(1 + \frac{1}{\eta_2}\right)\cdots\left(1 + \frac{1}{\eta_{n-1}}\right). \tag{9.57}$$

The power pumped by the nth stage is also given by

$$q_n = q_1 + \sum_{i=1}^{i=n-1} p_i.$$

Then

$$q_n = q_1\left(1 + \frac{\sum_{1}^{i=n-1} p_i}{q_1}\right) = q_1\left(1 + \frac{1}{\eta_{n-1}}\right). \tag{9.58}$$

By comparison with rearrangement of (9.50)

$$1 + \frac{1}{\eta} = \left(1 + \frac{1}{\eta_{n-1}}\right)\left(1 + \frac{1}{\eta_n}\right). \tag{9.59}$$

Substituting (9.58) and (9.59) into (9.57), we reach the relationship between over-all cascade efficiency and the efficiency of the individual stages:

$$1 + \frac{1}{\eta} = \left(1 + \frac{1}{\eta_1}\right)\left(1 + \frac{1}{\eta_2}\right)\cdots\left(1 + \frac{1}{\eta_{n-1}}\right)\left(1 + \frac{1}{\eta_n}\right). \tag{9.60}$$

Rearranging,

$$\eta = \left[\prod_{i=1}^{n}\left(1 + \frac{1}{\eta_i}\right) - 1\right]^{-1}. \tag{9.61}$$

9.6 TEMPERATURE CONTROL WITH AND DYNAMIC RESPONSE OF THERMOELECTRIC MODULES

Temperature control with a thermoelectric heat pump is accomplished either by selective reversal of the direction of the flow of current applied to the device, thus using it for both heating and cooling, or by the appropriate continuous adjustment of the level of the current.

In the selective reversal ON-OFF temperature control scheme the commanding element of the control circuit is a mechanical thermostat and the direction of input current to the thermoelectric modules is switched by a relay. The thermostat is in series with the relay coil and either permits or prohibits power to be supplied to the coil, thus regulating the switching of the relay contacts and supplying full power to the modules for heating or cooling.

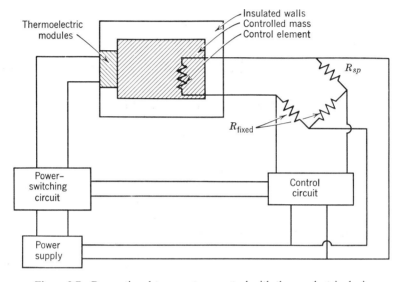

Figure 9.7   Proportional temperature control with thermoelectric device.

In the continuous adjustment proportional temperature control scheme, as shown in Figure 9.7, an electrical signal proportional to the difference between the actual temperature of a mass being controlled and a set-point temperature level determined by the resistance R_{sp} either augments or diminishes the current applied to the heat pump, thus causing variation in its cold-junction temperature. The commanding element of the control system is a resistance element operating in a Wheatstone bridge, and the control and switching circuits are composed of elements such as those described in Chapter 7.

Any additions to the average value of input current to the thermoelectric device produces Joule heating but not heat-pumping power, and thus diminishes pump efficiency. (The temperature difference between hot and cold junctions is decreased.) The level of input current ripple that is tolerated is 10%. (The temperature difference between junctions is about 4% less than the greatest theoretical value.)

The dynamic behavior of thermoelectric heat pumps is of interest in temperature control applications. Calculations and measurements have been made by Gray [3] to predict heat pump response to small changes in applied current, in heat source load, or in heat sink temperature, for the case of the thermal capacities of pump and heat source being of equivalent orders of magnitude. The assumptions and restrictions pertaining to Gray's work are as follows:

1. The connecting metal straps are neglected.
2. The thermoelements are perfectly insulated; heat and current flow along one axis only.
3. The thermoelements are homogeneous materials, and their physical parameters (thermal conductivity, etc.) are invariant with temperature.
4. The Thomson effect is neglected.
5. The heat rate at the cold junction can be related to its temperature by a linear homogeneous differential equation.
6. The variable associated with the heat-pumping process can be expressed as the sum of a quiescent or steady-state term and a small-signal dynamic or incremental term that is small compared with the quiescent term. For example, the cold-junction temperature can be expressed by

$$T_c(t) = T_{c_{ss}} + \phi_c(t),$$

where $T_{c_{ss}}$ is the quiescent term and ϕ_c is the dynamic term.

Gray [3] derives transfer functions for the small-signal behavior of a heat pump from the small-signal equations, which are themselves derived from substitution of the expressions for the variables into the basic thermoelectric-heat-pump equations and separation of the equations into steady-state and dynamic components. He illustrates the response of a heat pump to a unit-step change in current, for various normalized values of current (see Figure 9.3), for example, as in Figure 9.8.

After noting that the pump cannot be operated at $\gamma^* = 1$ (the hot- to cold-junction temperature difference is a maximum there and *any* change in current will diminish this difference), the following observations can be made concerning the values of current more suitable for dynamic behavior of the device. For currents in the $\gamma > 1$ region of the curve of Figure 9.3, the response of the thermocouple system to a unit-step change in current shows a reversal in sign, whereas for currents in the $\gamma < 1$ region there is no reversal.† It is more difficult to achieve stable operation of a closed-loop

---

* $\gamma = I/I_{\Delta T}$

† The reason for this reversal is that the Peltier cooling effect is felt at the cold junction immediately, whereas the Joule heating effect at that junction increases with time.

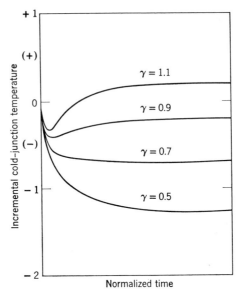

Figure 9.8 Response of a heat pump to a unit-step change in current.

temperature control system in the $\gamma > 1$ region, therefore. Also, for some value of $\gamma < 1$, the bandwidth of the control system is a maximum. Furthermore, the steady-state coefficient of performance, for the same temperature difference, diminishes as the current increases.

9.7 THERMOCOUPLES FOR MEASUREMENT AND CONTROL OF TEMPERATURE

Thermoelectric couples of thin, flexible, insulated wires can be used to measure and control temperatures of portions of masses. The temperature difference between the junctions of a thermocouple is roughly proportional to the electromotive force (emf) produced in, and the current caused to flow around, the thermocouple circuit. The magnitude of the emf depends on the materials in the couple, on the temperature difference between junctions, and on the actual junction temperatures. Thus, if the temperature at the cold junction is known and is either controlled or allowed to change in the presence of a device compensating for any such change (by adjusting resistance in the circuit), the temperature at the hot junction can be measured or controlled electrically and continuously.

Extensive tables have been published giving the thermoelectric emf (in volts) for junction temperature differences in small increments and over a wide range with the cold-junction temperature at 32°F and for several pairs of materials. To find the emf corresponding to a junction temperature difference with the cold junction at a temperature other than 32°F, the procedure is as follows: find the emf corresponding to the cold-junction temperature minus 32°F, and subtract that total from the emf corresponding to the hot-junction temperature minus 32°F.

For cases in which the controller is somewhat remote from the hot junction (Figure 9.9) the question of lead wires must be considered.

Let E_{AB} be the thermoelectric emf for metals A and B for the temperature difference $T_1 - T_i$ of the junctions; let E_{CD} be that for the metals C and D

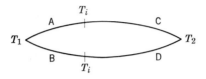

Figure 9.9

and for the temperature difference $T_i - T_2$. The circuit's over-all emf E_{ABCD} is

$$E_{ABCD} = E_{AB} + E_{CD}.$$

Let α_{AB} be the average thermoelectric power for the couple A, B over the temperature range T_1 to T_i and α_{CD} be that for the couple C, D over the range T_i to T_2.

Therefore

$$E_{ABCD} = \alpha_{AB}(T_1 - T_2) - \alpha_{AB}(T_i - T_2) + \alpha_{CD}(T_i - T_2)$$

$$= \alpha_{AB}(T_1 - T_2) - (\alpha_{AB} - \alpha_{CD})(T_i - T_2).$$

If C and D are of the same material, α_{CD} is zero and the intermediate location at temperature T_i is effectively the cold junction. That location, therefore, must be temperature controlled. If, however, α_{AB} is approximately equal to α_{CD}, $E_{ABCD} = E_{AB}$ and the maintenance of the intermediate location at T_i is not required.

Materials commonly used for thermocouples are mentioned and discussed in Table 9.2. For use at temperatures up to 1300°F thermocouple junctions may be made by twisting together exposed lengths of wires and applying silver solder; however, fusion welding is preferable and is required for temperatures exceeding 1300°F. The intrusion of stray emf's in the thermocouple circuit (generally resulting from electrical leakage through moisture) results in error and is a major problem. The usual rules of good thermal contact between sensor and controlled mass and the traditional preference for small sensor size are to be heeded in order to provide quick thermocouple thermal response. Furthermore, minimum cross-sectional area and thermal conductivity of the metallic portion of the external leads are desirable

Table 9.2   Thermocouples for Measurement and Control of Temperatures

Couple Materials	Operating Temperature Limits (°F)	Comments
Copper-constantan (60% Cu with 40% Ni)	−300 to 650	Widely used at subfreezing temperatures; withstand corrosion well, but copper oxidizes at temperatures above 650°F; thermoelectric power high, 23.8 $\mu v/°F$ in the range 32–212°F, for example; inexpensive; copper highly thermally conductive.
Iron-constantan	0 to 1600	Should be protected against oxidation at temperatures exceeding 1000°F; thermoelectric power high, 30 $\mu v/°F$ in the range 32–212°F, for example; inexpensive.
Chromel (90% Ni and 10% Cr) versus Alumel (95% Ni with Al, Si, and Mn comprising the remainder)	0 to 2000	In heavy-gage sizes and with suitable protection against corrosion, superior to iron-constantan in the 1000–1800°F range; thermoelectric power 22.4 $\mu v/°F$ in the working range 900–2000°F.
Platinum-platinum rhodium (90% Pt with 10% Rh, or 87% Pt with 13% Rh)	0 to 2700–3100, depending on the atmosphere	Should always be provided with a high-temperature ceramic protection tube; very stable and reproducible in output; thermoelectric power low, 6.6 $\mu v/°F$ in the working range 200–2900°F.

features. As the size of a thermocouple decreases, however, so does its ruggedness, and difficulties in handling it are increased.

REFERENCES

[1] Baker, H. D., E. A. Ryder, and N. H. Baker, *Temperature Measurement in Engineering*, Vol. I, Wiley, New York, 1953.

[2] Goldsmid, H. J., *Thermoelectric Refrigeration*, Plenum Press, New York, 1964.

[3] Gray, P. E., *The Dynamic Behaviour of Thermoelectric Devices*, Wiley, New York, 1960.

[4] Hartz, R. A., "Temperature Transducers," *Machine Design*, Sept. 15, 1966.

[5] Ioffe, A. F., *Physics of Semiconductors*, Academic Press, New York, 1960.

[6] Kraus, A. D., *Cooling Electronic Equipment*, Prentice-Hall, Englewood Cliffs, N.J., 1965.

[7] Merritts, T. D., and J. C. Taylor, "Thermoelectric Temperature Control," *The Westinghouse Engr.*, July, 1963.

[8] Rittner, E. S., "On the Theory of the Peltier Heat Pump," *J. Appl. Phys.*, **30**, 702 (1959).

[9] Snyder, N. W., ed., *Energy Conversion for Space Power*, Academic Press, New York, 1961.

[10] Telkes, M., "The Efficiency of Thermoelectric Generators," *J. Appl. Phys.*, **18**, 1116–1127 (1947).

10

Control of Spacecraft Temperatures

10.1 INTRODUCTION

The purposes of this chapter are to mention the basic theory and equations used to calculate surface and internal temperatures of vehicles in orbit around the earth, and to illustrate, by examination of methods of selection and alteration of values of various parameters in these equations, the approaches to the control of satellite temperatures.

The basic theory used to predict the temperature of an external element of an earth-orbiting object is predicated on two observations: (*a*) that space, which is the absence of matter, has no internal energy and, therefore, no temperature; and (*b*) that the temperature of the aforementioned surface element is defined by the difference between the various amounts of heat that are transferred into (and absorbed by) the element by radiation from the earth-sun system and by radiation and conduction from other portions of the satellite and the amount that is transferred away from the element by radiation to deep space. Direct radiation from the sun, radiation from the sun that is reflected by the earth and its atmosphere (this reflected sunlight is called albedo), and radiation from the sun that is absorbed by the earth and then reradiated (this flux is called earth thermal emission), are the energy fluxes from the earth-sun system transferred to the surface element. The temperature of the element depends on the balance struck by its orientation-dependent abilities to dissipate or accept the solar-driven heat fluxes, by its thermal connections to other parts of the satellite and to other sources of power within the satellite, and by its thermal capacity.

Thus, the temperature of a satellite is controlled by means of its internal thermal connections and the orientation and conditioning of its external surfaces. Of interest, then, are the thermal effectivities of various surface finishes and coatings, of different schemes for automatically altering the view, to the earth-sun system or to deep space, of the several portions of the satellite's surface, and of a surface having the ability to act as either a heat generator or a heat sink (thus removing the direct thermal connection between the satellite interior and the universe).

10.2   TERMS IN THE ENERGY BALANCE EQUATION

The energy balance relevant to an isothermal space vehicle in orbit around the earth is given by the equation

$$q_S + q_R + q_E + q_I = \sigma A_v \int_0^\infty \epsilon_\lambda T_v^4 \, d\lambda + (MC)_v \frac{dT_v}{d\theta}, \qquad (10.1)$$

where q_S = the absorbed insolation,
  q_R = the absorbed earth albedo radiation (solar radiation reflected and scattered by the earth and its atmosphere),
  q_E = the absorbed earth emission,
  q_I = the energy generated within the vehicle,
$\sigma A_v \int_0^\infty \epsilon_\lambda T_v^4 \, d\lambda$ = radiation emitted from the vehicle to deep space,
  $(MC)_v$ = the thermal capacity of the vehicle,
  T_v = the vehicle mean temperature.
Each term for absorbed environmental radiation is of the form

$$q = \int_0^\infty \alpha_\lambda E_\lambda A_p F \, d\lambda, \qquad (10.2)$$

where A_p = the vehicular surface projected to the irradiation,
  α_λ = the emissivity or absorptivity of that surface,
  E_λ = the absorbed energy level,
  F = the radiation view factor.
A space vehicle is traversing the sunlit part of its earth orbit. Consider an element of the vehicle surface area, dA. The amount of insolation is

$$q_S = \int_0^\infty \alpha_{\lambda S} S_\lambda F_{sv} \, dA \, d\lambda, \qquad (10.3)$$

where $\alpha_{\lambda S}$ = the surface's solar-wavelength absorptivity,
  S_λ = the intensity of solar irradiation at wavelength λ on a surface normal to the earth-sun line at the earth's mean distance from the sun,
  F_{sv} = the cosine of the angle between a vector normal to the surface and a vector directed at the sun from the surface.

The amount of earth albedo radiation is

$$q_R = \int_0^\infty \alpha_{\lambda S} a S_\lambda F_{Rv} \, dA, \tag{10.4}$$

where a is the earth's albedo (the fraction of solar radiation incident on the earth which is reflected), and F_{Rv} is a view factor dependent on the height of the vehicle above the earth, the angle between a vector normal to the surface and earth vertical, the angle between the earth-sun line and earth

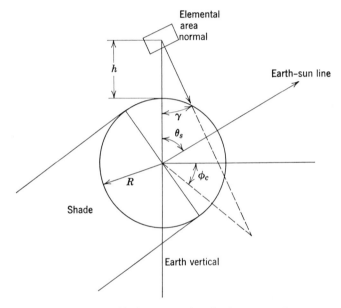

Figure 10.1   Orbital geometry for albedo computation.

vertical, and the angle between the plane defined by earth vertical and the normal to the surface and the plane defined by earth vertical and the earth-sun line (Figure 10.1) ($\phi_c = 0$ when the elemental surface normal lies in the latter plane).

Stevenson and Grafton [23] have provided tables for values of the reflected solar radiation view factor for flat plates, spheres, hemispheres, and cylinders in orbit. Previously, Camack and Edwards [5] showed [in curves useful for preliminary computations (Figures 10.2 and 10.3)] that for elemental surfaces facing the earth with the entire horizon visible and illuminated

$$F_r = AS_z + BS_y, \tag{10.5}$$

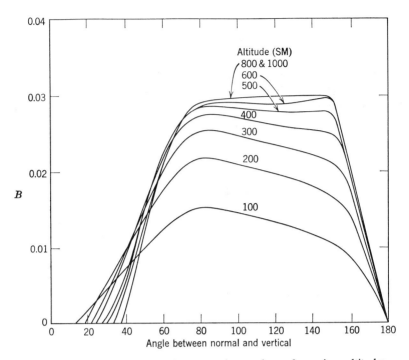

Figure 10.2 Earth reflection to an elemental area for various altitudes.

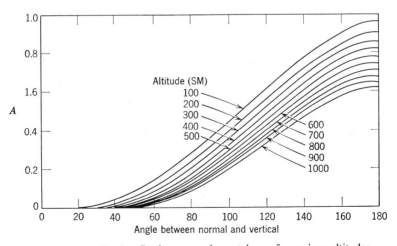

Figure 10.3 Earth reflection to an elemental area for various altitudes.

where A and B are plotted for various heights as functions of the angle between the surface normal and earth vertical, and $S_z{}^*$ and $S_y{}^*$ are components of the insolation dependent on the spatial geometry of the elemental area.

The amount of earth emission is

$$q_E = \int_0^\infty \alpha_{\lambda E} E_{\lambda T} F_{Ev} \, dA \, d\lambda, \tag{10.6}$$

where $\alpha_{\lambda E}$ is the surface absorptivity for earth emission, equal (because the satellite has approximately the same temperature as the earth) to the surface emissivity, ϵ, and F_{Ev} is a function of the vehicle's altitude above the earth and the angle between earth vertical and the normal to the surface.

The total earth emission, E_T, is computed as follows. The thermal energy balance for the earth is

$$4\pi R^2 E_T = \pi R^2 (1 - a)S, \tag{10.7}$$

where $(1 - a)S$ is the amount of insolation the planet absorbs.

$$E_T = \frac{1 - a}{4} S \tag{10.8}$$

is the thermal emission of the earth.

Values of F_{Ev} for several shapes at various heights and orientations have been tabulated by Stevenson and Grafton [23]. Camack and Edwards [5] demonstrated the view factor's dependence on an altitude parameter,

$$n = \frac{R}{R + h}, \tag{10.9}$$

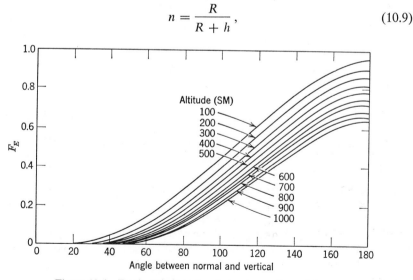

Figure 10.4 Earth emission view factor to an elemental area.

* $S_y = j \cdot s$, where j is a unit vector orthogonal to both earth vertical and a tangent to the element, $S_z = k \cdot s$, where k is a unit vector in the earth-vertical direction.

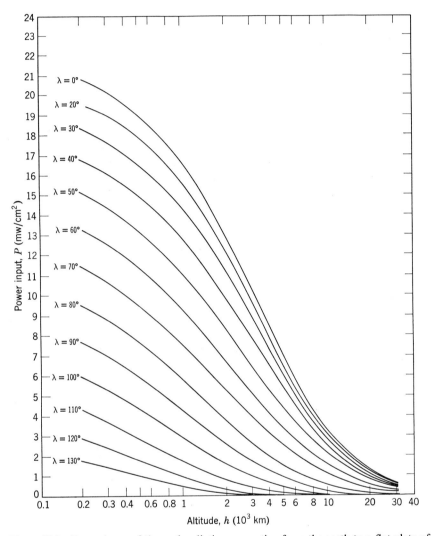

Figure 10.5 Power input of thermal radiation emanating from the earth to a flat plate of absorptivity 1 for the altitude range $200 \le H \le 32{,}000$ km.

where R is the planet radius and h is the altitude of the vehicle above the planet, and on the angle between the surface normal and the zenith direction, $\cos^{-1} N_z$. For surfaces so oriented that the entire horizon is visible, $N_z < -n$, the view factor F_{Ev} is

$$F_{Ev} = -n^2 N_z, \tag{10.10}$$

shown in Figure 10.4.

Cunningham [6] shows (in Figure 10.5) several curves describing the amount of difference in thermal radiation emanating from the earth (at 250°K) to a flat plate of absorptivity 1 at various altitudes (200–32,000 km above the earth) and with its normal vector at various orientations with respect to earth vertical. (λ is the angle between the normal to the plate surface and earth vertical.)

10.3 PARAMETERS OF THE ENERGY BALANCE EQUATION

The emissive power of the sun is equivalent to that of a black body at 10,400°R, which has a peak intensity at 0.47 μ (Figure 10.7). The value of the solar radiation, S, varies inversely as the square of the distance from the

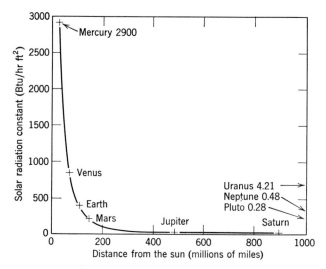

Figure 10.6 Solar radiation in the solar system. Earth albedo (reflected sunlight) varies widely with terrain and cloud cover, angle of incidence of direct solar radiation, and other factors. (By permission of Academic Press.)

sun, as shown in Figure 10.6. Its value at the earth's mean distance is 1.99 ± 0.02 cal cm^{-2} min^{-1} (or 442 Btu/hr ft^2), and its rays are considered collimated.

The emissive power of the earth is equivalent to that of a black body at 450°R, which has a peak intensity at 11.6 μ. Reflection varies from 0.80–0.90 for clouds and snow to 0.10 or less for water and certain terrain features. Mean values range from 0.34 to 0.50. Values of 0.35, 0.40, and 0.43 have been suggested for calculations.

The integrated average of absorptivity due to either direct or reflected solar radiation is used in the following analysis and is denoted by α_S; for

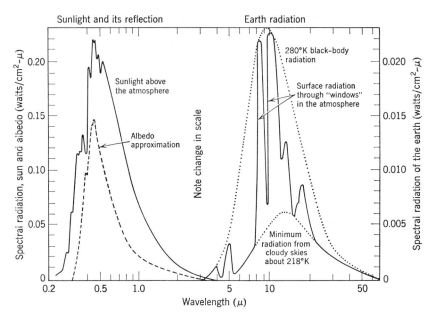

Figure 10.7   The spectral distribution of solar radiation as compared to albedo and earth radiation.

engineering purposes the integrated average of absorptivity due to earth emission is taken equal to the integrated average of space vehicle surface emissivity and is denoted by ϵ.

10.4   SOLUTION TO THE ENERGY BALANCE EQUATION

The solution for the temperature distribution within an earth satellite proceeds in two sections. First, the thermal inputs to the various satellite surfaces from the earth-sun system and for a particular orbit are computed at various orbital positions. Such a calculation must account for radiation interchange between surfaces of an irregularly shaped satellite in view of one another. Second, a thermal analogue describing the satellite is written. The analogue includes the various heat inputs to, and heat dissipations within, the satellite, and the thermal capacities of, and the thermal resistances between, the parts of the satellite. Computation will provide the temperature histories of these parts.

Consider the simple example of finding the temperature of a portion of an earth satellite's surface. For travel in sunlight, the thermal energy balance of an element of vehicular surface area dA is

$$\left(\alpha_S SF_{sv} + \alpha_S a SF_{Rv} + \epsilon \frac{1-a}{4} SF_{Ev}\right) dA + q_i$$

$$= \sigma\epsilon T_{dA}{}^4 dA + (MC)_{dA} \frac{dT_{dA}}{d\theta}, \quad (10.11)$$

where q_i is the heat generated within the element plus the heat transferred to it from the interior of the vehicle or from other vehicle surfaces.

At steady state $dT_{dA}/d\theta$, of course, is zero, and the temperature of the element is

$$T_S = \left\{\frac{1}{\sigma}\left[\frac{\alpha_S}{\epsilon}(\overline{SF_{sv}} + a\overline{SF_{Rv}}) + \frac{1-a}{4}\overline{SF_{Ev}} + \frac{q_i}{dA}\right]\right\}^{0.25} {}^{*}. \quad (10.12)$$

For travel in shade the thermal energy balance is

$$\epsilon \frac{1-a}{4} SF_{Ev} dA + q_i = \sigma\epsilon T_{dA}{}^4 dA + (MC)_{dA} \frac{dT_{dA}}{d\theta}. \quad (10.13)$$

Equilibrium temperature is

$$T_{SH} = \left\{\frac{1}{\sigma}\left[\left(\frac{1-a}{4}\right)\overline{SF_{Ev}} + \frac{q_i}{dA}\right]\right\}^{0.25}. \quad (10.14)$$

Simplified forms of solutions for satellite surface temperatures based on (10.11) through (10.14)—the satellite circular orbit including, therefore, periods of sunlight and shade—are as follows:

Sun: $T = T_S + (T_1 - T_S)e^{-\theta/\tau_S}$,

Shade: $T = T_{SH} + (T_2 - T_{SH})^{-\theta/\tau_{SH}}$, $\quad (10.15)$

where T_S = sunlight equilibrium temperature,

T_{SH} = shade equilibrium temperature,
T_1 = temperature at the end of the shade period,
T_2 = temperature at the end of the sunlight period,
$\tau_S = MC/4\epsilon(dA)\sigma T_S{}^3$,
$\tau_{SH} = MC/4\epsilon(dA)\sigma T_{SH}{}^3$.

The fraction of the circular orbit spent in sunlight is

$$\psi = \frac{1}{2} + \frac{1}{\pi}\cos^{-1}\left(\frac{(1-n^2)^{1/2}}{\sin\beta}\right), \quad n \geq \cos\beta, \quad (10.16)$$

$$\psi = 1, \qquad\qquad n \leq \cos\beta,$$

* The bars indicate orbital average values.

where β is the angle of the sun's rays to the orbit normal and $n = R/(R + h)$ (10.9).

10.5   METHODS OF SPACECRAFT TEMPERATURE CONTROL

Control of the various external heat fluxes contributing to the spacecraft energy balance can be accomplished as follows:

1. Selection of spacecraft launching data and the characteristics of the vehicle's orbit.*
2. Vehicle attitude control (thus regulating the values of the various absorptivity–view factor parameters for each element of surface area; the effect of spin-stabilizing a vehicle is to tend to equalize temperatures on any plane perpendicular to the spin axis).
3. Prelaunch control of the several absorptivities and emissivities of external surfaces (which change with time in space).
4. Control of effective absorptances and emittances in flight, as described in Section 10.6.

If a vehicle is not spin-stabilized and it is desired to reduce temperature gradients on its skin, a circulating fluid system may be considered. The attendant weight, sealing, freezing, and pumping-power problems are severe. A heat pump operating off temperature gradients may also be studied. Sandorff and Prigge [19] note that the isothermality of the skin of a non-rotating spherical satellite is dependent on a kt/R^2 parameter, where k is the thermal conductivity of the skin, t is the skin thickness, and R is the satellite radius. For $R^2/t < 100$, the skin conductivity is dominant; for $R^2/t \sim 10^4$, conduction and radiation play equal parts; for $R^2/t > 10^6$ or $R^2/kt > 10^8$, radiation is dominant. Thus, as R^2/t increases, the potential isothermality of the satellite skin decreases.

In large, manned vehicles, because of considerable power dissipations and high thermal resistances between equipment packages and vehicle skins, an environmental cooling system and space-radiating heat exchangers are employed. Such systems are discussed in References 8 and 15.

Electric heater and variable-resistance schemes are discussed in general terms elsewhere. Active temperature control systems for varying external thermal parameters are treated in Section 10.8. The relationships alluded to there may be used in other applications, the sizes and shapes of enclosures permitting.

---

* The characteristics of a vehicle's orbit change with time; thermal control of long-life satellites must be developed for worst-case thermal orbital conditions.

10.6 PASSIVE CONTROL

The ratio of the short-wavelength solar absorptance to the long-wavelength emittance of a satellite's surface has great influence on the equilibrium temperature of the surface. [Cf. (10.2) and Figure 10.7.] For a given ratio of α_S/ϵ, furthermore, surface temperature fluctuations are reduced when ϵ is low. [Cf. (10.11) and (10.13).]

Metallic coatings, ceramic or metal oxide coatings, and organic coatings are the three types generally used to provide particular values of the ratio α_S/ϵ or of the individual parameters α_S and ϵ.

Metallic coatings provide a ratio α_S/ϵ invariably greater and frequently much greater than 1. The highest values of α_S/ϵ are obtainable with electrically conductive coatings (gold and aluminum are examples) because their long-wavelength emissivities are low. The value of α_S/ϵ for a particular metallic surface can be reduced, however, by roughening the surface excessively, as by sand-blasting.

Ceramic coatings provide low α_S/ϵ ratios when applied to surfaces as white enamels or as flame-sprayed white coatings. Ceramic and metal oxide coatings tend to have high long-wavelength emissivities unless they are extremely thin. These coatings provide values of α_S/ϵ ranging from 0.25 up to that for an uncoated metal substrate, the value increasing as the coating film thickness decreases. The value of α_S can be increased by adding a short-wavelength radiation-absorbing oxide to the film.

Organic coatings are similar to ceramic and metal oxide coatings. Those pigmented with leafing aluminum provide values of α_S/ϵ of approximately 1 with α_S in the range 0.3–0.4. Aluminum pigments also reduce the long-wavelength emissivity of black organic coatings. White paints with metal oxide pigments provide rather low values of α_S/ϵ. The addition of a short-wavelength radiation-absorbing pigment to a white reflective coating increases the value of α_S while maintaining the value of ϵ constant.

Table 10.1 is a tabulation of approximate values of short-wavelength solar absorptance and long-wavelength emittance for various surfaces and coatings. The data [1, 18] should be used with caution. Radiation properties of metallic surfaces, for example, vary with surface smoothness, material crystal structure, and degree of oxidation of the material. Radiation properties of coatings depend on type, preparation, and condition of substrate surfaces. The requirements for preparing substrate surfaces and curing coatings at elevated temperatures should be investigated before a particular coating is selected.

A number of materials which change their optical properties with variations in temperature have been mentioned in various articles [20]. Silicon monoxide and similar coatings experience increases in thermal emissivity with temperature rise, but emissivity is too weak a function of temperature to allow

Table 10.1 Solar Absorptances and Emittances of Various Spacecraft Materials

Material	Mean Solar Absorptance	Mean Emittance (at room temp.)	Mean $\dfrac{\alpha_S}{\epsilon}$
6061 aluminum, chemically cleaned	0.16	0.07	2.7
Polished aluminum (2024)	0.19	0.05	3.8
Sand-blasted aluminum	0.42	0.21	2.0
Gold plate			
Polished	0.215	0.043	5.0
Unpolished	0.215	0.041	5.3
Sand-blasted stainless steel AI SI 410	0.75	0.85	0.88
Anodized aluminum	0.53	0.77	0.69
Reynolds wrap foil			
Smooth dull side	0.20	0.04	5.0
Shiny side	0.19	0.03	6.3
Oxide, flame sprayed (Rokide E, 85% CR_2O_3)	0.90	0.85	1.06
Rokide A (aluminum oxide)	0.75	0.27	0.36
White acrylic paint	0.28	0.89	0.33
White epoxy paint	0.22	0.91	0.24
White silicone paint	0.14	0.88	0.16
Aluminum silicone paint	0.25	0.28	0.89
Aluminum acrylic paint	0.41	0.48	0.85
Silicone paint	0.22	0.24	0.92
Black acrylic paint	0.93	0.88	1.06
Black silicone paint	0.89	0.88	1.01

successful exploitation of such materials for temperature control. Thermochromic materials reversibly change color and therefore α_S as a sharp function of temperature, but they generally must be encapsulated.

The thermal expansion properties of mercury have been considered for shutter applications, again with attendant problems of encapsulation.

10.7 STABILITY OF COATINGS IN SPACE

The major causes of the degradation of the thermal properties of spacecraft materials are

> handling,
> solar ultraviolet radiation,
> particulate radiation,
> outgassing in a hard vacuum,
> extreme temperatures,
> micrometeoroid erosion.

Coatings with low α_S/ϵ ratios, for example, unfortunately tend to increase in solar absorptivity with exposure to solar ultraviolet radiation (with long-wavelength emittance substantially unaffected). Figure 10.8, based on simulated exposures in ultraviolet radiation from an AH-6 lamp at six times the intensity of solar radiation in vacuum of 10^{-7} torr, indicates the extent of increase in α_S for several coatings. Olson et al. [12] note that such an increase depends on the total energy absorbed, with acceleration at increased temperature. Steel and Beveridge [12] indicate a large increase in α_S and a

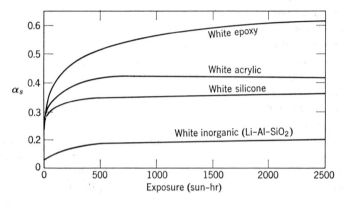

Figure 10.8 Changes in solar absorptivity in simulated ultraviolet radiation. (From [8].)

small decrease in ϵ for coatings with various silicone-based binders in ultraviolet radiation. Coatings with relatively high values of solar absorptance, however, are largely unaffected by such radiation.

10.8 ACTIVE CONTROL OF EFFECTIVE EMISSIVITY/ABSORPTIVITY

Thermostatic control of space vehicle temperatures with zero control power expenditure is accomplished by the selective exposure of surfaces with various α_S/ϵ ratios. When the absorption of heat or the retention of internally generated heat is desired, the surfaces of high α_S/ϵ ratio are exposed; when no absorption or no retention is wanted, surfaces of low ratio are bared. In one example, a portion of a vehicle's shell is painted in stripes of alternating α_S/ϵ ratio; a hood, whose position is controlled by a bimetallic element, exposes different stripes depending on the element's temperature. In another example, an array of louvers, whose outside surfaces are of low α_S/ϵ ratio, are position-controlled by a bimetallic element; the surface of the vehicle's shell is of high α_S/ϵ ratio, so the angular position (with respect to the shell's surface) of the louvers regulates the amounts of heat externally absorbed and dissipated.

The terms in the equation describing the thermal balance of the satellite housing of the first example above are appropriately modified by factors of the form

$$\epsilon_1 A_1 k + \epsilon_2 A_2 (1 - k) + \epsilon_3 A_3 + \epsilon_4 A_4,$$

where ϵ_1 = the emissivity (or solar absorptivity in some terms) of one variety of stripe,

ϵ_2 = the emissivity (or solar absorptivity) of the other variety of stripe,

ϵ_3 = the emissivity of the hood,

ϵ_4 = the emissivity of the unhooded portion of the vehicle,

A_1 = the total area of stripes of emissivity ϵ_1,

A_2 = the total area of stripes of emissivity ϵ_2,

A_3 = the area of the hood,

A_4 = the unhooded area,

k = a coefficient (whose value is between 0 and 1) dependent on the bimetallic element's temperature.

The coefficient $k(T)$ is dependent on the location of the bimetallic element, the various possible vehicular orbits or excursions, and solutions to the standard equations for thermal balance in spacecraft.

Operation of a louvered control system is dependent on the louver width, the spacing between louvers, the radiative characteristics of the inside and outside louver surfaces, and the characteristics of the vehicle shell's surface, among other quantities. Plamondon [17] presents a number of simultaneous equations whose solution (on a computer) yields instantaneous values of effective vehicular external emissivities for various angles of blade opening. Several of his results are shown in Figures 10.9 through 10.11. The effective emissivities of the abscissae operate directly on the relevant terms of radiant interchange.

Figure 10.9 indicates that the value of effective emissivity with the blades closed and the blade width equal to the blade spacing is nearly independent of the value of skin emissivity. Within the first 20 degrees of blade opening, the values of effective emissivity change by an order of magnitude. Plamondon notes that the blades must be completely closed in order to limit effectively heat dissipation by radiation. *Furthermore, the louver system is capable of effecting large changes in thermal resistance with small changes in temperature (blade opening).*

Figure 10.10 indicates that large changes in the emissivity of the back sides of the blades have decreasing effect with increasing blade angle.

In Figure 10.11 the effects of changes in the ratio of blade width to blade spacing may be observed. Overlapping blades ($b/L > 1$) increase the insulating

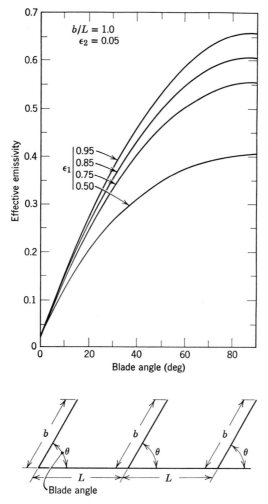

Figure 10.9 Effective emissivity for blade-opening angle for various values of ϵ. (By permission of American Institute of Aeronautics and Astronautics.)

abilities of incompletely closed blades and coincidentally reduce effective emissivity at any blade-opening angle.

Plamondon [17] and Ollendorf [16] advise that, in addition to maximizing the emissivity of the shell's outside surface, the louver-blade back surfaces be made of specularly reflecting material (usually the reflectance characteristic of low-emissivity material in the infrared regime). This quality would minimize the amount of energy reflected to the shell, but to a decreasing extent as the blades closed.

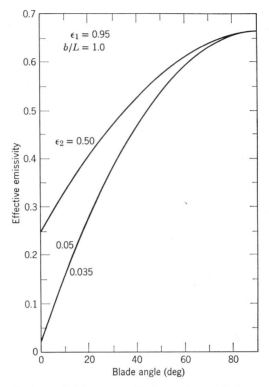

Figure 10.10 Effective emissivity versus blade-opening angle for various values of ϵ_2. (By permission of American Institute for Aeronautics and Astronautics.)

10.9 ACTIVE CONTROL WITH PHASE-CHANGE MATERIALS

Materials which can be caused to change phase reversibly at desired temperatures (generally in the range of 50–100°F) and in the process dissipate or absorb large amounts of heat per unit mass* may be considered for satellite thermal control. In such an application the chosen material is sandwiched between the outside wall of the satellite and an inside wall thermally connected to the temperature-controlled equipment. When the thermal-controlling portion of the satellite is facing the sun, the phase-change material absorbs heat and melts, remaining at a constant temperature; when that part of the satellite is in shadow, the phase-change material solidifies and dissipates heat, remaining at the same temperature. Thus, the satellite's temperature-controlled equipment is thermally connected to a constant-temperature heat sink operated without any requirement for externally driven power.

---

* Termed *heat of fusion*.

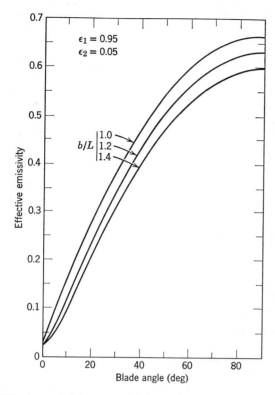

Figure 10.11   Effective emissivity versus blade-opening angle for various values of b/L. (By permission of the American Institute of Aeronautics and Astronautics.)

Other criteria for materials to be used in the above scheme are a low coefficient of volumetric expansion in both solid and liquid phases; high density; small density difference, $\rho_S - \rho_L$; high thermal conductivity and specific heat in both phases; low vapor pressure at fusion temperature T_f; and high compatibility with satellite materials, environment, and user. Examples of such materials are polyethylene glycol (Carbowax 600), technical eicosane, and various compounds marketed by Cryo-Therm, Inc. Properties of phase-change materials tested by Fixler [7] for satellite thermal control are given in Table 10.2.

The phase-change material used in the given satellite thermal control scheme absorbs insolation, dissipates heat to deep space, and absorbs heat from the equipment to which it is thermally connected. A temperature distribution for that material, in which as freezing occurs the latent heat of fusion is released at a moving solid-liquid interface, can be found with a many-node thermal analogue in which conduction is the only mode of heat

Table 10.2 Properties of Typical Phase-Change Materials

Property	Material	
	Polyethylene Glycol (Carbowax 600)	Technical Eicosane
Chemical formula	...	$C_{20}H_{42}$
Molecular weight	570–630	282.54
Density at 20°C/lb/ft³	70	46.8 @ 176°F
Melting point (°F)	68–77	94.64
Viscosity (centistokes)	10.5	...
Specific heat (Btu/lb°F)	0.54	0.528 (sol.)
		0.481 (liq.)
Heat of fusion (Btu/lb)	63	71.21
Solubility in water at 20°C, (%)	100	100
Vapor pressure at 100°C (torr × 10⁶)	5.2	...
Flash point (°F)	475	...
Surface tension at 25°C (dynes/cm)	44.5	...
Boiling point (°C)	...	205
Volumetric coefficient of expansion at 55°C (°C)	0.0075	0.0003 (liq.)
Thermal conductivity at 50°C (Btu/hr ft °F)	0.0924	0.133

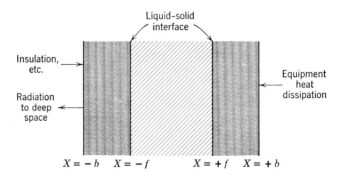

Figure 10.12 Schematic operation of phase-change material used for spacecraft temperature control.

transfer. That temperature distribution is the distribution in space where convection is absent because of the lack of gravity. [Fixler has observed that in the presence of gravity convection currents in the liquid-phase material should be dealt with.] The inner and outer walls are considered single nodes in the analogue since their thermal conductivities are much higher than that of the phase-change material. The walls are held apart by spacers of low thermal conductivity in order to prevent thermal short-circuiting between them.

The solid-liquid interfaces may move at different speeds, and one motion may start later than the other. Bounding conditions relevant to the thermal situation of Figure 10.12 are

at $X = f$, $T_{\text{solid}} = T_{\text{liquid}} = T_{\text{fusion}}$,

at $X = b$, $k \dfrac{\partial T}{\partial X}\bigg|_{X=b} = Q_i(\theta)$ (the energy balance at that surface),

at $X = -b$, $k \dfrac{\partial T}{\partial X}\bigg|_{X=-b} = \alpha_s S \cos \phi - \sigma \epsilon T_0^4$

(the energy balance at that surface).

where k = the thermal conductivity of the phase-change material,

$Q_i(\theta)$ = the heat dissipation transferred from the temperature-controlled equipment to the phase-change material,

α_s = the outer surface solar absorptivity,

S = the insolation,

ϕ = the angle between the sun-satellite vector and the normal to the satellite surface,

σ = Boltzmann's constant,

ϵ = the outer surface emissivity,

T_0 = the outer surface temperature.

The equations describing the over-all thermal performance of the phase-change-material control system are, for the time that the control surface is facing the sun,

$$\alpha_s S + Q_i - \sigma \epsilon T_0^4 = \frac{\overline{W} Q_f}{\theta_S}, \tag{10.17}$$

and for the time that the surface is in shade,

$$Q_i - \sigma \epsilon T_0^4 = -\frac{\overline{W} Q_f}{\theta_{SH}}, \tag{10.18}$$

where $\overline{W}$ = the weight of the phase-change material per square foot of cross section,

Q_f = the material's latent heat of fusion,

θ_S = the time in sunshine,

θ_{SH} = the time in shade.

For given values of α_s and Q_i, the magnitudes of ϵ and $\overline{W}$ required for thermal control and computed from (10.17) and (10.18) are

$$\frac{\alpha_s S}{Q_f}\left(\frac{1}{\theta_S} + \frac{1}{\theta_{SH}}\right)^{-1} = \overline{W};$$ (10.19)

$$\frac{Q_i(1 + \theta_{SH}/\theta_S) + \alpha_s S}{\sigma T_0^4(1 + \theta_{SH}/\theta_S)} = \epsilon.$$ (10.20)

A figure of merit for a phase-change-material thermal control system can be defined as follows:

$$\text{figure of merit} = \left(\frac{\Delta T_{\text{pcm}}}{\Delta T_{\text{npcm}}} \times \frac{\overline{W}}{\alpha_s Q_s \theta_{\text{sun}}}\right)^{-1},$$ (10.21)

where ΔT_{pcm} = equipment temperature change with a phase-change-material control system,

ΔT_{npcm} = equipment temperature change without such a system,

αQ_s = solar heat rate.

REFERENCES

[1] Adams, J. L., *Space Technology*, Vol. II, NASA SP-66, 1965.

[2] Allen, C. W., *Astrophysical Quantities*, University of London, Athlone Press, 1955.

[3] Andeson, J. W., E. A. La Blanc, and H. Cohan, "Experimental and Analytical Assessment of Space Thermal and Vacuum Environment Simulation Requirements," *J. Spacecraft and Rockets*, **3**, No. 7 (July, 1966).

[4] Bobco, R. P., and T. Ishimoto, "A Suggested Solar-Simulation Standard for Thermal Testing," *ASME Paper* 64-WA/HT-17.

[5] Camack, W. G., and D. K. Edwards, in "Effect of Surface Thermal-Radiation Characteristics on the Thermal-Control Problem in Satellites," in *Surface Effects on Spacecraft Materials*, F. J. Clauss, ed., Wiley, New York, 1960.

[6] Cunningham, F. G., "Power Input to a Small Flat Plate from a diffusely Radiating Sphere, with Application to Earth Satellites," *NASA Tech. Note* D-710.

[7] Fixler, S. Z., "Satellite Thermal Control Using Phase-Change Materials," *J. Spacecraft and Rockets*, **3**, No. 9 (September, 1966).

[8] "Radiator Design for Space Vehicles," *Publ.* MS-AP 0069, The Garrett Corp., 1963.

[9] Hanel, R. A., "Thermostatic Control of Satellites and Space Vehicles," *Am. Rocket Soc. J.*, **29**, 358–361 (May, 1959).

[10] Heller, G. B., "Thermal Control of Explorer Satellites," *Am. Rocket Soc. J.*, **30**, 344–352 (April, 1960).

[11] Heller, G. B., "A First for Thermophysics," *Astronautics and Aeronautics*, January, 1966; also, "Thermophysics and Temperature Control of Spacecraft and Entry Vehicles," in *Progress in Astronautics and Aeronautics*, Vol. 18, Academic Press, New York, 1966.

[12] Katzoff, S., ed., *Proceedings of the 1964 Symposium on Thermal Radiation of Solids*, NASA SP-55, 1965.

[13] Kreith, F., *Radiation Heat Transfer for Spacecraft*, International Textbook, Scranton, Pa., 1962.

[14] Liphis, R, P., "Temperature Control of Spacecraft," in *Materials for Missiles and Spacecraft*, E. R. Parker, ed., McGraw-Hill, New York, 1963.

[15] Mackay, D. B., *Design of Space Powerplants*, Prentice-Hall, Englewood Cliffs, N.J. 1963.

[16] Ollendorf, S., "Effective Emittance of an Insulated Louver System," *J. Spacecraft and Rockets*, **III**, No. 6.

[17] Plamondon, J. A., "Analysis of Movable Louvers for Temperature Control," *J. Spacecraft and Rockets*, **I**, No. 5.

[18] Rittenhouse, J. B., and J. B. Singletary, *Supplement to Second Edition of Space Materials Handbook*, NASA SP-3025; ML-TDR-64-40, Suppl. 1.

[19] Sandorff, P. E., and J. S. Prigge, Jr., "Thermal Control in a Space Vehicle," *J. Astronautics*, **III**, No. 1 (Spring, 1956).

[20] Schach, M., and R. Kidwell, "Thermal Control of Spacecraft," *Space/Aeronautics*, July, 1965.

[21] Stambler, I., "Surface Effects in Space," *Space/Aeronautics*, February, 1966.

[22] Steinberg, S., and V. D. Landon, "Satellites Systems" in *System Engineering Handbook*, R. E. Machol, ed., McGraw-Hill, New York, 1965.

[23] Stevenson, J. A., and J. C. Grafton, "Radiation Heat-Transfer Analysis for Space Vehicles," ASD61-119, December, 1961.

[24] Ordway, F. I., III, ed., *Advances in Space Science and Technology*, Academic Press, New York, 1961.

[25] Bonneville, J. M., "Techniques for Computing the Thermal Radiation Incident on Vehicles in Space," *NASA Rept.* 63270-04-05, June, 1962.

[26] Van Vliet, R. M., *Passive Temperature Control in the Space Environment*, Macmillan, New York, 1965.

[27] *NASA Contributions to the Technology of Inorganic Coatings*, NASA SP-5014.

Index